D1196855

REBUILDING AMERICA'S INFRASTRUCTURE

Books of related interest

Duke Press Policy Studies in cooperation with The Council of State Planning Agencies

Financing State and Local Economic Development
Edited by Michael Barker

State Taxation Policy
Edited by Michael Barker

State Employment Policy in Hard Times
Edited by Michael Barker

Duke Press Policy Studies

What Role for Government?
Lessons from Policy Research
Edited by Richard J. Zeckhauser *and* Derek Leebaert

Being Governor
The View from the Office
Edited by Thad Beyle *and* Lynn Muchmore

Published in cooperation with
The Council of State Planning Agencies

REBUILDING AMERICA'S INFRASTRUCTURE

AN AGENDA FOR THE 1980s

Edited by

Michael Barker

Foreword by

Robert N. Wise

Duke Press Policy Studies

Duke University Press   Durham, N.C.   1984

Printed in the United States of America on acid-free paper

Library of Congress Cataloging in Publication Data
Main entry under title:

Rebuilding America's Infrastructure.

(Duke Press policy studies)
"Published in cooperation with the Council of State
Planning Agencies."
Reprint (1st work). Originally published: America in
ruins / Pat Choate and Susan Walter.—Washington, D.C.:
Council of State Planning Agencies, 1981.
Reprint (2d work). Originally published: Financing
public works in the 1980s / Roger J. Vaughan.—Washington,
D.C.: Council of State Planning Agencies, c1983. (Rebuild-
ing America; v. 2)
Bibliography: p.
Includes index.
1. United States—Public works. 2. Infrastructure
(Economics)—United States. I. Barker, Michael, 1951–
II. Choate, Pat. America in ruins. 1983. III. Vaughan,
Roger J. Financing public works in the 1980s. 1983.
IV. Council of State Planning Agencies. V. Series.
HD3887.R42 1984   364'.0973   83-16614
ISBN 0-8223-0568-2

Publisher's Note

Rebuilding America's Infrastructure is part of a series published in cooperation with The Council of State Planning Agencies, which previously published, in paperback editions only, the two books that make up the substance of this volume. In the interest of making these analyses available promptly and at the lowest possible cost to institutions and individuals requiring a hardcover edition, Duke University Press has reprinted these two works in the page formats in which they originally appeared. We hope that the timely availability of these two important works in this form will compensate for any inconvenience caused by the resulting variations in type, design, and page size.

CONTENTS

I. America in Ruins: The Decaying Infrastructure
Pat Choate and Susan Walter

II. Rebuilding America: Financing Public Works in the 1980s   Roger J. Vaughan

TABLES AND FIGURES

Part I. Tables

Part I. Figures

Part II. Tables

Part II. Figures

FOREWORD

President Reagan's proposal to "return to the states" the responsibility for a wide spectrum of domestic policy matters has drawn a decidedly mixed reaction—not only from Congressional committee barons unwilling to relinquish their patronage powers, but also from activist groups and others who see greater state involvement in domestic policy as tantamount to a retreat from the social contract of the American welfare state and as a positive attack on the poor, on minorities, on the quality of the environment, and on the safety of the workplace. Conservative and New Right activists, by contrast, have tended to view the Reagan "New Federalism" proposal as a happy means of minimizing the public sector's meddling with the American economy and of reducing the governmental role in societal and community life—apparently hoping that many states will "localize" their treatment of this or that national malady in a prescription for benign neglect. Somewhere between these two extremes are the majority of state officials, who are desperately eager to control the allocation of federal program dollars but quite unwilling to assume the political risks associated with raising those dollars through local tax sources.

For all these reasons and more, Reagan's New Federalism, in and of itself, seems unlikely to have many far reaching effects on federal-state relations.

Nevertheless, there are a growing number of people who believe that state and local governments have a larger role to play in our public life, and that this role can only grow through a diminished federal presence in certain domestic affairs. They are people who hold with Justice Brandeis the belief that state governments have always provided the nation with a margin for innovation and experiment in its public life.

The studies that are republished in this volume grew out of the efforts of the Council of State Planning Agencies to explore this "margin for innovation." They were the most tangible product of a four-year economic development project directed by Michael Barker, who was then the Council's Director of Policy Studies. He commissioned the studies and shaped the final reports, of which more than thirty-six were issued over the years 1978–81. At the same time, he assembled a small group of economic policy consultants, including many of the authors whose work Duke University Press is now republishing, to provide detailed assistance to state officials on the implementation of the recommendations contained in the Council's published research. Much of the current interest in small business development, the investment of public pension funds, the decay of the nation's infrastructure, and national industrial policy grew out of the formal and informal work of this select group.

Robert N. Wise
Executive Director
The Council of State Planning Agencies

INTRODUCTION

Michael Barker

The "infrastructure crisis" is upon us. One of the two studies contained in this volume, "America in Ruins," helped to precipitate it by drawing the attention of the press to the creaky state of the nation's public works; the other, "Rebuilding America," describes many of the actions that will be necessary to alleviate it.

Until quite recently, the general public paid scant attention to public works. What was being built, or why, or by whom was either ignored or taken for granted. Public facilities were expected to be there, like the weather. Apart from the relatively small number of projects with particularly volatile political implications, the man in the street was quite content to leave the matter to government, so long as the government provided the street.

All that is now changed. The accelerating decay of America's public works has succeeded in capturing the fancy of the press and the attention of the public. The newsstands groan with evidence of the nation's creeping decrepitude. As a result, people are suddenly concerned that the country is about to crumble beneath them. What were once merely potholes are now jarring reminders that the nation seems to be coming apart at the seams.[1]

Unfortunately, the collapse of the country's infrastructure is more than fancy. Sewer systems are overloaded. Water systems are operating at or near capacity. Streets and bridges are being declared unsafe in increasing numbers. Port facilities are suddenly inadequate to the demands of today's economy. Jails are so crowded that violence—even riots—is becoming commonplace.

Just how serious is the problem? It is hard to say. Most public facilities are the property of state and local governments, but few governments keep any useful record of the condition of their public works. Estimates on how much must be spent to reverse the current rate of deterioration range from a doubling of current annual spending to a quadrupling of yearly expenditures. By the most cautious estimate, we need to increase total spending on public works by at least $75 billion annually, an amount equal to roughly 10 percent of the FY1984 federal budget.[2]

There is another reason why it is so difficult to be precise about the magnitude of current investment needs: who is to say what genuine needs are? The only thing that really defines them is the public's desire for a certain level and quality of services, together with its willingness to accept the price these services pose. This desire differs not only from community to community, but it fluctuates substantially over time. What is affordable this year may seem a crushing burden in the future. What we deem essential now was only recently an unimaginable luxury. And then, too, from time to time the concept of what is properly a "public good" undergoes substantial change. Roads and bridges, for example, were once the almost exclusive province of private corporations; today they are exclusively public. Garbage disposal, on the other hand, is still a privately provided service in many communities.[3]

Nevertheless, there is substantial agreement about the broad outlines of the problem:

■ *Highways.* Although highway spending by all levels of government increased in the 1970s, so did the rate of inflation. As a result, the real dollar value of public investments in highways has been systematically eroded. The interstate highway system alone will need $33 billion in repairs over the next decade. On the much larger network of primary and secondary roads, conditions are even worse: just to maintain these roads in their current, inadequate condition will cost more than $500 billion over the next ten years (or more than was spent on all public works by all levels of government in all of the 1970s).

■ *Bridges.* Forty-five percent of the nation's bridges are either structurally deficient or functionally obsolete. Repairing them—all 248,537 of them —could cost as much as $47.6 billion. In the past ten years Washington has financed the rehabilitation or replacement of some 8,659 bridges—an impressive total until it is remembered that at that rate it will take 247 years to replace just those bridges with existing deficiencies. And there is additional cause for alarm: most bridges are designed to last no more than fifty years, yet more than 200,000 of the nation's bridges were built prior to 1940.

■ *Water and sewer systems.* Age is catching up with our cities. Just to maintain their existing water systems, the nation's 750 largest urban areas will need to spend more than $75 billion over the next twenty years. Even if water rates are doubled, about 20 percent of these communities will be unable to finance needed expenditures. Moreover, nearly half the nation's communities have wastewater treatment facilities operating at or near full capacity. Unless this capacity is expanded, most of these communities will be unable to support further economic growth.

■ *Pollution controls.* Meeting federal and state pollution control standards will cost $25 billion over the next four years.

And then there is the cost of repairing *city streets* (less than one-third of the nation's major roads and streets are rated "good" by the Federal Highway Administration); *mass transit systems* ($36.5 billion over the next ten years for modernization of fixed rail systems, planned rail extensions, the completion of new systems, and improvements in bus facilities);

railroads ($90 billion over the next ten years to repair and upgrade existing facilities); *dams* (8,794 of them—or 13 percent of the nation's total—are classified as a "high hazard" to life and property); *port facilities and waterways* (just replacing the aging system of locks in Pittsburgh alone will cost more than $2.5 billion, while dredging deep water ports to facilitate competitive coal exports will cost another $3.5 billion, and according to the Corps of Engineers a total of $12.3 billion will be needed for channel improvements, locks, dams, and other inland waterway improvements over the next thirty years); and *public buildings* (including schools, hospitals, police stations, firehouses, courthouses, jails and prisons, public housing, and libraries).

The list is formidable. And it is made more daunting when it is remembered that deteriorating public facilities impose a real cost on our economy. By creating inefficiencies in the operation of private firms, decaying public works can greatly increase the cost of doing business, consuming capital that would otherwise be available for new investment in plant and equipment. (It is more expensive for a truck to travel on a poor road than a good one—36 percent by one estimate.) Public works are also an important component of national income growth. Fully 20 percent of the growth that occurred in our national income in the 1950s and 1960s was attributable to increases in the public capital stock. While the overall rate of growth slackened during the 1970s, public capital expenditures continued to provide a significant share of the overall growth rate.

Without a major effort to rebuild America's public works, we jeopardize our ability to sustain an economic recovery, we weaken government's capacity to deliver essential public services, we seriously threaten the quality of the environment, and we pose a major threat to public health and safety. Thus, a crucial first step in rebuilding America's public works is forging a public consensus that infrastructure is as essential to economic recovery as private investments in plant and equipment.[4]

A Short History of Decay

How did we get into this mess? There are a wide variety of reasons, each of which contributes something to the magnitude of the crisis as a whole. Public works have a natural life span, after which they must be replaced or abandoned. For a bridge the usual period is fifty years. For an interstate highway the period seems to be much shorter. A number of different types of public works—all built during the 1930s, 1940s, and 1950s—are starting to wear out simultaneously. In addition, the combination of suburbanization, the energy crisis, and the sharp recession of 1974–75 forced sudden, rapid adjustments in the spending patterns of local governments across the nation. Belt tightening became the order of the day. Needed maintenance activities were deferred, or canceled altogether. New investments were shelved as cities struggled to keep their existing facilities in operation. New York and Cleveland had widely publicized brushes with bankruptcy, and other cities—Chicago, Boston, Newark, Los Angeles—were not far behind.

Another contributing factor has been the emphasis our public policies have always placed on accommodating the expansion and relocation of population. By stressing capital over operating expenditures, the federal government has ensured that many local governments, which commonly fail to consider full operating costs of projects financed by Washington, would build facilities that they could maintain only with difficulty. Federal grant programs—ranging from the railroad land grants of the nineteenth century to rural electrification in the Depression and waste-water treatment plants today—have always shown a strong bias for the new and have ignored the maintenance needs of those facilities already in place. The effects of these programs have been reinforced by state capital investment programs, virtually all of which discriminate against existing urban areas and effectively subsidize the outmigration of urban populations from cities to suburbs and beyond.

Congress has supported this local behavior. Every time a new domestic "crisis" is discovered, Washington produces yet another set of categorical grant programs. State and local governments have grown accustomed to the idea of the federal government as the provider of last resort. In 1980, for example, 40 percent of state and local capital spending was paid for by scores of federal categorical programs. Today, with federal deficits at unprecedented levels, the tide appears to have turned. But the legacy of the past twenty-five years remains in the extraordinarily confused allocation of responsibility for building and maintaining public facilities among the various levels of government. More than 100 separate federal agencies, 50 state governments, 3,042 counties, 35,000 local governments, and 15,000 local school districts—all are engaged in the planning, construction, and maintenance of public works projects.

The impact of these grant programs is further reinforced by the extremely short time horizons imposed on public investment decisions. It is an unfortunate fact of life that most public facilities have useful lives far in excess of the political lives of most elected officials. Thus, there is always a powerful incentive to defer needed and often expensive repairs, particularly if the work is not going to be immediately visible to the public. As George Peterson of the Urban Institute has noted, "The consequences of deferred maintenance . . . may not show up for four or six years, which is a political lifetime. Therefore, if public officials have to choose between trimming maintenance or trimming current services, or between cutting back capital expenditures or laying-off public employees, there is a built-in bias against capital preservation."[5] Thus, the rusting pipes and mains beneath the surface are ignored—at least until they rupture.

Federal grant programs have subsidized these bad habits by implicitly discouraging state and local officials from developing effective maintenance procedures for federally financed facilities. For example, federal grants for highway construction pay 90 percent of the cost of interstate highways; 75 percent of the cost of primary, secondary, and urban roads; and 80 percent of the cost of bridge replacements. As a result, many states choose to let their roads, bridges, and highways deteriorate until they become eligible for "total rehabilitation" funds from Washington. A recent survey of state and local governments by the American Public Works Association found that 90 percent of the respondents freely admitted that the availability of federal capital funds causes them to place a low priority on maintenance and repair activities. To some extent the need to go to such extremes is offset by the fact that the states themselves are usually permitted to perform the inspections that are a prerequisite to federal funding—they can simply exaggerate the extent of a facility's deficiencies without actually letting it teeter on the verge of ruin. But not all states are so ingenious. It is at least arguable, however, that increased federal capital expenditures would only make the existing situation worse.

Another problem results from the increasingly hostile environment provided by the bond market, through which state and local governments finance roughly half their total capital expenditures. The advantages of tax-exempt financing have been substantially eroded as the interest differential between taxable and nontaxable bond rates has narrowed from more than 30 percent to only 17 percent at the beginning of 1983. The bond market has been squeezed by two distinct forces: (1) a declining demand for municipal bonds—the result of changes in federal tax policy; and (2) a dramatic increase in the volume of state and local offerings. In 1981 less than half the revenues realized through the sale of long-term tax exempts were used for traditional public works projects. The rest—with the help of the increasingly notorious industrial revenue bond—went to finance a wide variety of corporate, profit-making projects, a far cry from what was intended when Congress exempted state and local bond issues from taxation.

Who pays?   Where can we hope to find the tremendous sums of public capital that will be needed to rebuild the nation's public works? First (and we needn't shrink from saying it), money can come from a reduction in the defense budget. Holding the real rate of growth of military spending to 3 percent annually would free up tens of billions of dollars during the next decade for productive investments in infrastructure without jeopardizing the nation's security. Middle-class entitlements, such as the deductibility of mortgage interest, should also be reexamined, as should the excessively low rate of taxation on capital gains. The recent increase in the gasoline tax should be regarded as only an interim measure—to be followed by further increases in the mid-1980s.

Most of the money, however, that will be needed to build and repair our public facilities will have to come from state and local governments. Yet the ability of states and cities to finance capital expenditures has been drastically curbed by (1) changes in the market for tax-exempt bonds that have made these securities much less attractive to both institutional investors and households, and (2) such ill-conceived (and politically motivated) experiments as the All-Savers Certificate, which present needless competitors to municipal securities. Their problems have been made worse by record federal deficits and the Federal Reserve's tight money policy, which together have driven real interest rates to extraordinarily high levels. One very useful step would be for Congress to improve the ability of states and localities to finance needed projects by enacting legislation that allows the issue of taxable bonds underwritten by a 35 percent interest subsidy from the Treasury. An interest subsidy of this sort would not increase the federal deficit at all—it would be paid for by the tax revenues from the holders of the bonds. (Since the marginal tax rate of the bond purchasers is at least 35 percent, the tax revenues collected by the Internal Revenue Service would roughly equal the subsidy.) The cost of borrowing would be dramatically reduced. If, for example, the long-term taxable bond rate were 13 percent, the post-subsidy cost to a locality would be 8.45 percent, or nearly 200 basis points below what was prevailing at the beginning of 1983. Federal payments would provide, in effect, a partial guarantee to bondholders, further reducing the rates. It would also allow local governments to sell their issues in a much broader market. The taxable bond option should be allowed only for public infrastructure projects and should explicitly exclude industrial development bonds, mortgage revenue bonds, and the myriad of other private purpose/public subsidy bonds. (To encourage a rapid increase in state and local capital spending, an additional 10 percent interest subsidy could be offered for all bonds issued to finance projects that "break ground" in the year following enactment.) A federal deficit reduced by military spending cuts would easily allow room in the taxable bond market for an additional $10–20 billion in state and local borrowing. And it would provide a costless and effective way to start the rebuilding of America's infrastructure.

Another useful step would be to reduce the abuses that now plague the state and local tax-exempt bond market. As mentioned earlier, less than half the revenues from the sale of long-term tax exempts are for public purposes—the rest are used to finance private industrial projects, home mortgages, and not-for-profit health facilities. By eliminating these subsidies, and by restricting the use of the states' tax-exempt privileges to truly public purposes, the amount of state and local public construction spending could be doubled. Indeed, after the overly generous tax incentives provided by Congress in 1981, further subsidies to private development are both unnecessary and unwise.

For their own part, state and local governments will have to develop new mechanisms to finance increases in public capital spending. Many water systems, for example, could be entirely self-financed through user fees. This would avoid inequitable subsidies to large users, encourage conservation, and reduce the need to expand system capacity. Another useful step would be to create "bond banks" that permit counties and local jurisdictions to use the state's superior credit rating and access to the bond market to reduce local borrowing costs. (Five states—Alaska, Maine, New Hampshire, North Dakota, and Vermont—have already created such banks and are effectively reducing local borrowing costs by as much as two percentage points.) An interesting variant on the traditional bond bank idea is provided by New Jersey's qualified local bond program, which permits local governments to earmark future state local-aid allotments as a guarantee to bondholders of future repayment. By improving the creditworthiness of local issues in this way, the program has enabled several New Jersey cities to upgrade their credit ratings from "BAA" to "A," thereby saving as much as 200 basis points per issue.

Inevitably, some state and local taxes will have to be raised. More than thirty states have raised gas taxes and other fees in the past few years. Many are considering the establishment of toll roads. This is a useful beginning, but it is only that. Additional revenue sources are sorely needed. A good place to start would be with the elimination of the tax "incentives" and abatements used by state and local governments to lure businesses from one location to another. By most estimates the cumulative cost of these programs is more than $1 billion annually. Yet there is increasing evidence that they are almost always ineffective in stimulating new investment.[6] State and local governments should wake up to this fact and start applying their scarce fiscal resources to more productive ends. However difficult that may seem in purely political terms, it is surely more palatable than presiding over the destruction of the nation's infrastructure. State and local officials must realize that Washington is simply not going to help so long as it faces the prospect of gargantuan deficits of its own.

Planning   But money, by itself, will not solve the problem. Some measure of the current rate of decay is the result of too much money being hurriedly and thoughtlessly spent. Projects were built before any consideration was given to their long-term operating costs. Indeed, there is seldom a serious effort to project the ultimate costs of a public facility to the community that must support it or to monitor the condition of public works over time. What "planning" is performed by public agencies is usually so modest in scale that any other result would be impossible.

One reason for this problem is that our public planning lacks continuity. Every time an administration changes, on either the state or federal level, the government's resident planners are sacked and replaced with a new crew. This may be fun for those charged with dispensing patronage, and comforting to those grim souls who think that technical analysis is at bottom an expression of ideology, but it also wreaks havoc with the capacity of government to sustain a coherent analytic framework over time. And some degree of continuity is crucial to avoiding mismanagement. Roger Vaughan has suggested an analogy. When a ship sets sail, its crew has more constant obligations than guiding the ship out of harbor and pointing it in the right direction. Constant adjustments will be necessary to keep the ship on course, and a host of adaptations must be made reflecting the characteristics and demands of the captain, the crew, and the ship itself. If an emergency arises, there is never time to contemplate what needs doing. And even without an emergency, the ship's position and performance must be carefully and continuously monitored. The problems confronting public officials, particularly on the state and local level, are rarely as immediate or violent as those that can befall a ship at sea (governors and mayors are, from time to time, removed from office, but they are seldom drowned). But the monitoring function of government—the planning function—needs to be just as continuous as for a ship.

"Planning" is one of those words that nobody likes. In the minds of many Americans it conjures up images of an Orwellian state, coldly imposing dicta on the hapless multitudes, arrogating liberties and choices that were previously the province of all (or at least believed to be). Thus, many politicians find it a convenient subject for the most shameless demagoguery. (When President Reagan proposed abolishing the Economic Development Administration, he claimed that its billions had supported only "grantsmen, planners, and middlemen.")

But it is certainly true that most publicly conducted planning activities have generated very little in the way of useful products. Most development planning has been little more than a paper chase conducted by local governments at the behest of federal agencies seeking "products" to justify their own grant programs. Thus, reams of information, most of it useless, moves silently from typewriter to file cabinet, read by no one other than those responsible for seeing that it vaguely corresponds to the requirements of the federal "planning grant." It has been a harmless, if occasionally expensive, activity. This partially explains why the "comprehensive land use plans" prepared by states and cities for the U.S. Department of Housing and Urban Development were always so dreadful. These regularly prepared plans should have set out a program for systematic infrastructure renewal, state by state, city by city. Indeed, it was one of their principal objectives. But the federal government was unwilling to support them with its own capital investments, and no one above the level of GS-12 ever read them.

Unless there are policies and programs for plans to drive, unless plans have force, they will never be done well. Nor will state and local governments devote adequate human and fiscal resources to the task of preparing them. As things now stand, most state and local governments are ill-equipped to devise policies based on more than the most simplistic perceptions of public needs. Their planning staffs are poorly trained and are usually unable to present their findings to elected officials in a digestible manner. Yet the support of these officials is crucial to the success of any planning activity (just as strategic planning in the private sector requires the close involvement of the chief executive officer and his immediate staff). Many who oppose the concept of an "elite" group of public servants preparing governmental planning documents have advocated the development of "planning" that proceeds from the "bottom-up"—devising policies, setting priorities, on the basis of broad democratic participation. Such "grass-roots" exercises invariably fail. Those in authority are seldom willing to commit their power to anyone else's goals and objectives, for they believe that to do so would reduce their ability to maneuver politically and, thereby, to survive politically.[7] This explains, in part, why planning staffs are so often purged during changes in administration. The chief executive wants to have people around him whom he can trust, people whose judgment and priorities are consistent with his own. Most planning operations are bureaucratically isolated, and those that are not isolated often are perceived as harboring political operatives of the chief elected official.

There is no simple solution to the current inadequacies of the planning profession. To be taken seriously, planning needs to be directed more toward the immediate needs of those with elected authority. At the same time it needs to be more technically sophisticated, more adept at transforming raw information and frequently questionable forecasting techniques into useful policy choices. The conflict between these two needs is more apparent than real. Budgeting is already professionalized in this way (although the number of state and local "budgeters" with more than a superficial grasp of economics is appallingly small). Budget staffs—who are bureaucratic survivors of the first order—are well accustomed to imposing the priorities of elected officials in the annual preparation of the budget. Planners should pause to ask themselves why it is that so many in their profession view budgeting as the antithesis of planning.

In the case of public works the most useful planning device is the capital budget, which not only separates capital from operating expenditures but also provides a means of integrating a long-term capital investment plan with annual budget priorities. As recently noted by the U.S. General Accounting Office, relatively few states project the impact of current public works projects on future operating budgets, compare the net present value of all future costs with the future benefits of alternative projects, properly account for the costs and benefits associated with capital expenditures, evaluate alternative means of financing capital projects, or include their public works projects in an overall capital investment plan that considers the consequences of not making each investment.

Capital budgets would go a long way toward solving these problems. When we pass by a public construction project we commonly see a large sign advertising the project's merits. In letters only slightly smaller than those spelling out the name of some local politician, we see a claim made for the number of jobs the project will create and the amount of tax revenues it will generate. What we do not see is any mention of the debt service costs of the project to the community, or of the fact that any operating deficits it develops will have to be paid out of general revenues. It is not surprising. Even if these figures were readily available, many local officials would be unlikely to advertise them. But they should at least be aware of what the numbers are. The fact is that few states or cities even consider such issues when undertaking new projects. The purpose of a capital budget is to see that they do.

By separating capital and operating expenditures for each budgeting year, by analyzing the impact of proposed projects on the operating expenditures of future years, and by evaluating the merits of alternative methods of financing public construction projects, capital budgets can substantially reduce the confusion and haphazard spending that now characterize state and local construction activity. They also can provide a means of selecting projects based on need rather than the temporary availabilty of construction funding.

Public Works and Jobs

It's bandwagon time. If the Republicans don't climb on board, it may well be that the only make-work, dead-end jobs will be those of Republican congressmen.

—An aide to House Speaker Thomas P. O'Neill, Jr., commenting on the imminent passage of the 1983 public works "jobs program."

It would be difficult to find a better example of projects built with little regard to their long-term consequences than those financed under the last three federal countercyclical public works programs. Recessions bring out the worst in our political system. We seem compelled to transform every economic issue before the Congress into a "jobs bill." Thus, the long-run problem of how to increase investment in public infrastructure is confused with the short-run issue of how to provide jobs for the unemployed.

Again, it is not surprising. Because so much attention has been given to the deterioration of roads, bridges, water systems, schoolhouses, and prisons, and because about one in four construction workers is now idle, many in Congress and elsewhere have proposed resurrecting some version of the Works Progress Administration, thereby solving both problems simultaneously. *Newsweek* has called the idea "irresistible." The editors of *Harper's* and *The Washington Monthly* have presented the idea as if it were their own. With the advent of a new presidential election season, a permanent public works program for the unemployed seems certain to work itself into the platform of at least one of our political parties. If nothing else, this outburst of nostalgia for past policies suggests that Gresham's Law applies as inexorably to public policy as it does to currency—the bad expels the good from circulation.

As is so often true of simple solutions to complex problems, a new WPA would not work. It would neither build what needs building nor employ those who most need employment. Rehabilitating public works is not so simple as passing out overalls and paint to people in line for unemployment benefits and pointing them toward a crumbling bridge. For one thing, the federal government keeps no records on the condition of public facilities; thus, it is in a poor position to know where a new WPA army should march. Moreover, with the exception of the interstate highway system, the decaying infrastructure around us is largely the property of state and local governments. But few state or local governments now have the type of construction projects on the shelf that would enable them to spend a sudden infusion of federal funds either quickly or wisely. (Of course, there is never any shortage of projects that provide photo opportunities at ribbon cuttings for politicians. But that, presumably, would not be the central object of the program.) In fact, while they waited to see which of their local projects would be underwritten by the new WPA, states and cities would be likely to cut back drastically on their own capital spending, just as they did in the fall of 1976 when Congress passed the Local Public Works Program (LPW), and as they now appear to be doing as a result of the "jobs bill" passed in early 1983. (By one estimate, state and local governments postponed some $22 billion in construction spending in anticipation of LPW, and thereby lowered the GNP by as much as $30 billion.) Inventing allocation procedures that satisfy key congressmen and interest groups, evaluating proposed projects, and letting construction contracts for them all take time. In the case of the 1976 LPW program this meant that tens of millions of dollars were still unused more than four years after the program was begun.

The ostensible purpose of a countercyclical program is to spend money at an appropriate moment in the recessionary trough, stimulate demand, and thereby induce an economic recovery. But because countercyclical public works programs take so long to get going, their dollars are rarely put to work until long after a recovery is well under way. Thus, the jobs they produce come too late to help those who are the putative object of congressional concern. Indeed, in many parts of the country they simply bid up the already high price of construction labor. Thus, when federal funds are finally drawn down and spent, it is rarely the case that the jobs created are "new" jobs at all—federal funds simply replace local funds, providing local officials with an opportunity to knock a few dollars off the tax rate until the next election is over, but adding nothing to the overall amount of local construction spending. Attempts to get around this problem by funding "quick" projects invariably lead to waste, such as the resurfacing of roads that require a thorough reconstruction or building tennis courts and golf courses (favorites during the 1976 LPW program).

What few jobs might be created by a new WPA would be of little help to most of the unemployed. Less than one person in ten has skills even remotely applicable to a modern construction site. Nor can these skills be assimilated during a two-hour site orientation. Plumbing, carpentry, electrical work, the operation of heavy equipment—these are skills that take years to learn. As a result, few of those who lost their jobs in the 1974–75 recession were even eligible for LPW employment. Those who grow misty-eyed at the prospect of the unemployed being put to work "digging ditches" should acquaint themselves with the backhoe, which has made ditch diggers as obsolete as blacksmiths and lamplighters. Construction today is a very different activity than it was fifty years ago. Many proponents of the WPA would circumvent these "minor obstacles" by abolishing Davis-Bacon, paying minimum wages, destroying craft unions, and financing only labor-intensive projects. Federal work gangs, taking home scarcely more than they would receive on welfare, would acquire preindustrial skills useless in a postindustrial economy. The WPA army would march on, but the nation's infrastructure would continue to erode, economic recovery would be delayed, the vast majority of the unemployed would remain jobless, and the congressional bandwagon would roll merrily along.[8]

AMERICA IN RUINS: THE DECAYING INFRASTRUCTURE

"America in Ruins" was not the first study of the economic impact of public works projects, nor was it the most elaborate. But by making its points succinctly (and somewhat dramatically), and by offering specific recommendations for reform, it managed to catch the attention of those who set fashion in public policy, and that was all that mattered.

"America in Ruins" was first published in 1981 by The Council of State Planning Agencies. Its principal author, Pat Choate, was then a senior fellow at the Academy for Contemporary Problems, a not-for-profit research group supported by a consortium of local and state lobbying organizations. Choate had earlier written a monograph entitled *As*

Time Goes By: The Costs and Consequences of Delay, which examined the impact of various contracting procedures and construction methods on the overall cost of public capital facilities, and he thought it might be useful to expand that work to include a survey of the current condition of the nation's public capital stock as a whole. So he set about documenting the current condition of the nation's public facilities: its roads and bridges, highways and sewers, ports and water systems. When that was in hand, it seemed useful to say a few words about why all these things seemed to be falling apart, and what might be done about it. When the Academy concluded that the topic was too esoteric to warrant general publication, The Council of State Planning Agencies worked with Choate to refine and publish a limited edition of the text.

A curious thing then happened. Almost overnight the press took it up with a vengeance. (One national business magazine was so eager to tell the story of America's "decaying infrastructure" that whole paragraphs from "America in Ruins" started turning up verbatim in its news pages.) Today, more than two years later, it is still difficult to pick up a magazine or newspaper without reading something about the deplorable condition of the nation's "infrastructure." Even the stately *New Yorker* magazine has taken note: one of its cartoons depicts an open manhole into which several hardhats are descending; a big sign warns oncoming traffic, "Infrastructuralists at Work."

This publishing history is important for two reasons. First, it shows how quickly a seemingly obscure and certainly dreary topic (the condition of public works) can become a central focus of public policy debate—how quickly fashion can seize hold of the popular mind. Second, it serves as an important reminder that the current interest in infrastructure is just that, a fashion, and is just as likely to be cast aside as any of the many previous passions of politics and the press. Remember the urban crisis? Or the energy crisis? Or the social perils posed by minority youth unemployment? The problems held up to public attention by these manufactured crises were real then, just as they are real today. The only difference is that those who make fashion in public policy, always restless and easily bored, have turned away—just as they will turn away in time from the topic of "infrastructure." The question is whether public opinion, in its brief focus on "the infrastructure issue," can react intelligently—and usefully—before it is turned away to something new.

The principal recommendation of "America in Ruins" is for the creation of a national capital budget. As the authors note, it is no accident that the federal government does not have one. There is undoubtedly an unacknowledged fear that it would be difficult to ram through special projects—such as the Tennessee-Tombigbee Waterway or, more recently, the $33 million highway project hidden in the 1983 jobs bill by House Appropriations Committee Chairman Jamie Whitten—if capital expenditures were subjected to detailed cost-benefit analysis and weighed against competing domestic spending priorities. Certainly this is a more basic objection to the use of a capital budget than those cited, perhaps disingenuously, by the Office of Management and Budget (see Choate and Walter's chapter 6).

But the idea has merit. The annual budget's Special Analyses section now contains a detailed summary of federal loan programs, permitting close analysis of the magnitude and character of federal intervention in the credit market. It does not evaluate the performance of these programs as a portfolio manager might, nor gauge their full impact on private lending activity. (Indeed, the disastrous performance of federal loan programs, including default rates ranging as high as 90 percent, is one of the most closely kept secrets of the executive branch.) But it does show the numbers as nothing else in the budget does. A similar section on capital facilities would be useful. As the authors point out, it would have to consist of at least three elements: current and projected capital needs and expenditures, current and projected operation and maintenance needs and expenditures, and sources of financing. Both direct federal facility investments and state and local projects employing federal grant-in-aid funds would have to be incorporated for the analysis to be meaningful.

A more substantial hurdle lies in getting both Congress and the executive branch to use it. No one really doubts that the gnomes at the Office of Management and Budget could sharpen their pencils and assemble the numbers. That is not the issue. The essence of capital budgeting is to make obvious what is hidden, and to provide a means of making difficult choices. That is precisely what both the Congress and the Executive will resist. Making choices is unpleasant. (Congressional politics thrives on the trading of favors, most of which bear a price tag. Take away the ability to submerge the substantial differences that exist between competing interest groups in a rising tide of discretionary pork and things would grow awkward very quickly.) Moreover, keeping the ultimate costs of capital projects hidden is essential to securing the initial round of funding. (Who wants to see a public project abandoned half-built? As Robert Moses used to say, once the stakes are planted, the appropriations battle is over.) Not making difficult choices may be expensive in a fiscal sense (the current and projected deficits would seem to provide some evidence to that effect), but making them could be more painful still.

The rigorous implementation of a national capital budget would require a significant reduction in the amount of pure pork dished out to powerful members of Congress. Since any sane person knows how implausible that is, how are we to account for the great enthusiasm shown for the idea in both houses of Congress by members of both parties? The answer is plain. By separating capital expenditures from the remainder of the budget, by moving them "off budget," one can make them appear relatively small. The smaller they appear in aggregate, the easier it will be for individual members to add their own special projects to the list. The recommendations made concerning the merits of individual projects will be ignored, as are most recommendations made by professional bodies (such as the Congressional Budget Office, the General Accounting Office, and the Congressional Research Service). By enlarging the size of the barrel, the capital budget permits Congress to greatly increase the amount of pork available to its members. Of course, another result is "more money for public works." But it is hard to believe that it will be money spent on the country's most urgent capital needs. As pointed out earlier and throughout both books that follow, the way in which Washington makes its public facility investments is as much to blame for the current state of the country's infrastructure as the actual amount of money it expends. A simple increase in federal spending would create jobs for construction workers and provide a mild stimulus to the scissors and ribbon industries. But it would be unlikely to do anything more. Thus, one must seriously question whether a substantial increase in federal spending, particularly now when deficits are draining credit from the private economy, is all that desirable.

REBUILDING AMERICA: FINANCING PUBLIC WORKS IN THE 1980S

Where "America in Ruins" is principally concerned with documenting the extent of the nation's public works investment needs and with recommending changes in federal policy, "Rebuilding America" attempts to show how new facilities can be more easily financed and more effectively managed, particularly on the state and local levels. As Roger J. Vaughan points out, there are no easy solutions to the "infrastructure crisis": both state and federal agencies will have to adopt more efficient planning methods, including capital budgeting. They will have to impose or increase a wide variety of user fees and design a host of new financing mechanisms. They will have to require the private sector to assume the responsibility for financing those "public" facilities that provide largely private benefits. And they will have to raise taxes by a significant degree.

Vaughan suggests four basic principles to guide an evolving partnership among federal, state, and local agencies. First, wherever possible, those who benefit from a particular facility should be required to pay for its construction and maintenance. Road users should pay for roads; water users should pay for water. Second, the capital costs of public facilities should be amortized over the expected life of that facility. Maintenance costs should never be deferred. Third, the costs of a public facility should be absorbed by the jurisdiction enjoying its benefits. While some allowances must be made for differing fiscal capacities among localities, this requirement is an essential first step to reducing the use of public works monies for pork barrel boondoggles. And, fourth, where user fees (or other charges) have the effect of denying access to a facility or service to the poor, special provisions should be made for low-income households.

Vaughan also argues for the development of a national capital investment strategy—a strategy built on eight elements:

■ *Developing cost-effective maintenance, replacement, and design standards for public works projects.* Present engineering standards have a tendency to inflate estimates of facility investment needs and are too often used, inappropriately, to assign investment priorities.

■ *Reducing the use of public funds to subsidize private sector investments, terminating public sector service programs that could be provided by private firms, and transferring ownership of facilities that would be better managed in public hands.* Scarce public funds should be used only for those projects needed to fulfill truly public obligations.

■ *Improving planning, budgeting, and management procedures for capital investments.* Costly construction delays, inappropriate investment priorities, and the sloppy management of existing facilities inflate the costs and accelerate the deterioration of our public works. Vaughan suggests that state and local governments adopt a capital budget. On the federal level Vaughan recommends extensive involvement in state and local planning and budgeting procedures to avoid incompatible data, duplication of resources, and other inefficiencies which now disrupt the administration of many programs.

■ *Relying more on user fees—charges and dedicated tax revenues—to pay for both the construction and operating costs of public facilities.* Well-designed user fees can establish public prices for public goods and services, encourage the wiser use of public facilities, reduce capital investment needs, and produce better public investment decisions.

■ *Improving bond financing mechanisms to avoid the proliferation of small issues and the consequent increase in financing costs.* Bond banks, state loans to local governments, and state guarantee programs all provide mechanisms for reducing costs. Vaughan also advocates the creation and use of the taxable bond option discussed earlier.

■ *Shifting a larger share of the costs of public infrastructure onto private corporations, especially the cost of facilities associated with large-scale projects.*

■ *Rationalizing the allocation of capital financing responsibilities among federal, state, and local government agencies to avoid needless duplication and to ensure that all jurisdictions have adequate resources to make needed investments.* Vaughan advocates decentralizing responsibility for public capital investments from Washington to the states, along with federal assumption of income maintenance program costs.

■ *Raising taxes in order to increase overall spending on public works by a substantial margin.*

As Vaughan points out, none of these steps is particularly easy. The remainder of his book provides guidelines for financing public capital facilities, weighs alternative capital financing mechanisms, and discusses how the allocation of financing responsibilities among the various levels of government could be improved. In Vaughan's view the greatest increase in fiscal and administrative responsibility for public capital investments will have to be assumed by state governments. Not only will they have to change their own practices and levels of effort, they will also have to provide increased fiscal, technical, and regulatory assistance to local governments. All of these actions will invariably be opposed by those individuals and interest groups that have benefited from implicit and explicit public subsidies in the past and who face higher taxes or user fees in the future. Thus, genuine political leadership, always a rare commodity, will be needed to secure passage of enabling legislation and budgetary obligations.

NOTES

I thank my colleague at The Gallatin Institute, Roger Vaughan, for contributions to this Introduction.

1. In this introduction we use the word "infrastructure" to refer to highways, streets, bridges, water supply and wastewater treatment systems, waterways and ports, railroads, and mass transit facilities—all that part of the nation's capital stock which is public in nature. Others have used this term to also include a wide variety of traditional public services—public health, education, fire safety, criminal justice, housing assistance, and other service-oriented programs. We do not feel that these two categories of public spending have much in common. That they are being joined in public debate is only a tribute to the indefatigable efforts of service program advocates to use each and every fashion in public policy to promote additional spending. While this may not be a bad thing, it deserves to be seen for what it is.

2. "America in Ruins" suggests a quadrupling of such spending. This seems excessive. After all, in the absence of a major increase in federal spending, unlikely so long as federal deficits approach Brobdingnagian proportions, it would mean a 50 percent increase in all state and local taxes. As Roger Vaughan has suggested, the prospect of a tax increase that large would drive the beleaguered taxpayer to something less democratic than a tax referendum. On the other hand, innovative financing mechanisms are unlikely to increase the current level of public capital investment by more than 20 percent—far less than what is needed to meet even the most immediate investment needs.

3. Two particularly mischievous articles have suggested that there is, in fact, no problem with the nation's public works; that concern for their rehabilitation is little more than an elaborate "scam" devised by current and former federal bureaucrats to promote their own dark—and presumably expensive—ends. The more amusing of these articles appeared in *Fortune* (December 13, 1982), long known for its interest in public policies that might reduce the profit margins of the nation's largest corporations. While the burden of the author's argument was sound—federal public works projects are a notoriously poor way to create jobs for the structurally or cyclically unemployed—he went on to suggest that because there are no absolutely reliable numbers on the magnitude of the nation's public works investment needs (i.e., sources of data prepared by people who are not involved in one way or another in the "public works industry"), the problem cannot be too serious. By trivializing the issue in this

way, *Fortune* apparently hoped to derail the growing interest in public works investments among Republican senators, who were at that time joining with their Democratic colleagues to support a variety of new public works initiatives, including the creation of a national capital budget, one of the proposals made in "America in Ruins." The other article appeared in the libertarian *Inquiry* (February 1983). It recycled most of the *Fortune* analysis and suggested that "the entire infrastructure debate is a fraud, a well-managed PR campaign designed to provide a smokescreen for an old-fashioned shakedown of the American taxpayer." The author went on to argue that virtually all public facilities should be turned over to the private sector, where they could be managed—and maintained—at a profit. Those facilities that could not generate a sufficient market demand to support their continuing operations would be abandoned ("Must a road, once constructed, remain in place forever?"). There are two problems with this analysis. First, it is seldom the case that market demand for a public facility drops off all at once. The process is gradual and entails a great deal of fluctuation. Nor is a community's capacity to pay always a fair measure of the economic benefits provided by its public facilities. As the population of our older cities is reduced by migration and suburbanization, the remaining taxpayers (often old, poor, and/or ill-educated) are left with public facilities that are inappropriately sized for the diminished local market they have to serve—at precisely the moment when the diminished local tax base makes the continued maintenance of these facilities difficult or impossible. Because these facilities can seldom be operated as economically as those more recently constructed in affluent, developing areas, the governments of our older cities are placed at a double disadvantage: they must pay the cost of maintaining more facilities than they actually need just when their ability to pay anything at all has been substantially reduced. Second, public facilities frequently offer substantial benefits to nonresidents who contribute little or nothing to their upkeep. The most obvious example is provided by the suburban and bedroom communities that ring the older cities of the Northeastern and Midwestern states. The residents of these communities, usually more affluent than city residents, enjoy the benefits of the public facilities of the city—its roads, bridges, police and fire protection—while largely escaping the responsibility for contributing to their operation and maintenance. As Albert Gallatin noted in his 1808 report to the U.S. Senate, the most substantial benefits of a public work are frequently enjoyed not by those in whose community or state the facility is located, but by those others, residing at quite distant points, whose commerce and trade is supported and promoted by the facility.

4. Many opponents of increased federal and state spending on public works have argued that any increase in taxes to finance public works would slow economic recovery. That may or may not be true; it is surely irrelevant. Without adequate financing of public works today, a sustained economic recovery will be impossible.

5. George Peterson's painstaking research on urban public works provides much of the empirical foundation for the two studies contained in this volume. Without Peterson's work, neither study would have been possible.

6. See Michael Kieschnick, "Taxes and Growth: Business Incentives and Economic Development," in Michael Barker, ed., *State Taxation Policy*, (Durham: Duke University Press, 1983).

7. Continuity also requires that information flows be well managed. Planners must have all the necessary data on prevailing social and economic conditions as well as the capacity to apply appropriate analytic techniques. They must have the ability to continually revise and update both the raw data and the techniques applied to their analysis. And they must also be as good about communicating information as they are at gathering it in the first place; not only the general public but also those who provide the data must receive constant information about governmental policy objectives and the issues currently under analysis. Otherwise the planners themselves are likely to be deprived of information that is vital to their operations. And finally, public planners must have the whole-hearted support and cooperation of their chief executives. If these executives become accustomed to making decisions that disregard the results of the planning process, planning invariably breaks down. (See Vaughan and Pollard, chapter 5.)

8. See Roger Vaughan, "Inflation and Unemployment," in Michael Barker, ed., *State Employment Policy in Hard Times* (Durham: Duke University Press, 1983). See also Michael Barker, ed., "Mr. Gresham and the Democrats: Part One," *Politics & Markets* (November 24, 1982). The perverse fixation of liberals and left economists on public works programs is difficult to explain, particularly in the face of so much evidence that public works are almost universally ineffective in providing employment to those in need. But it has always been thus. When, in 1932, Al Smith advocated a large public works program to produce "immediate productive employment for millions of people," Walter Lippmann wrote a series of columns about the idea and concluded, somewhat regretfully, that "there is no ground for believing that a public works program as such can really absorb or even substantially alleviate the present volume of unemployment." (See Walter Lippmann, *Interpretations: 1931–1932* [New York: Macmillan, 1932], pp. 78–91.) And Lippmann was right. The WPA exerted a trivial impact on the nation's unemployment rate and did nothing to stimulate an overall recovery. It did, of course, build thousands of public facilities, some of which were needed and many of which survive in use today. And it did give many the feeling that the federal government was not indifferent to the plight of the unemployed. But that was not the purpose for which the program was advocated (although it may explain why Congress was so willing to create it). Nor is that why others advocate it today.

FOR FURTHER INFORMATION

Associated General Contractors. *Our Fractured Framework: Why America Must Rebuild.* Washington, DC.: November 1982.

Barker, Michael, ed. *Financing State and Local Economic Development.* Durham: Duke University Press, 1983.

———. "Mr. Gresham and the Democrats: Part One," *Politics & Markets.* Washington, D.C.: The Gallatin Institute, November 24, 1983.

———. *State Employment Policy in Hard Times.* Durham: Duke University Press, 1983.

———. *State Taxation Policy.* Durham: Duke University Press, 1983.

Break, George F. "The Role of Government: Taxes, Transfers, and Spending." In Martin Feldstein, ed., *The American Economy in Transition.* Chicago: The University of Chicago Press, 1980. Pp. 617–56.

Denison, Edward F. "The Contribution of Capital to Economic Growth." *American Economic Review* 70, 2 (May 1980): 220–31.

Feldstein, Martin. "Inflation and the American Economy." *The Public Interest* 67 (Spring 1982): 63–76.

Gallatin, Albert. *Report of the Secretary of the Treasury on the Subject of Public Roads and Canals.* Submitted to the United States Senate, April 4, 1808.

Highway Users Federation. *The Highway Book.* Washington, D.C.: HUF, 1982.

Rivlin, Alice M. "Statement Before the Committee on Environment and Public Works, United States Senate." Washington, D.C.: Congressional Budget Office, December 1, 1982.

Vaughan, Roger J., and Robert Pollard. *Planning and Managing Public Works in the 1980s.* Washington, D.C.: Council of State Planning Agencies, 1983.

Part I

AMERICA IN RUINS
THE DECAYING INFRASTRUCTURE

Pat Choate and Susan Walter

1

DETERIORATING FACILITIES/ DECLINING INVESTMENTS

America's public facilities are wearing out faster than they are being replaced. The deteriorated condition of the basic public facilities that underpin the economy presents a major structural barrier to the renewal of our national economy. In hundreds of communities, deteriorated public facilities threaten the continuation of basic community services such as fire protection, public transportation, water supplies, secure prisons and flood protection.

The United States is seriously underinvesting in public infrastructure. Because of tight budgets and inflation, the maintenance of a growing number of national and local public facilities has been deferred. Replacement and rehabilitation of obsolescent public works have been postponed. New construction has been cancelled, delayed or "stretched out."

Because the Congress has tended to dominate national public works policy, the Executive Branch of the federal government has failed to produce a capital budget to guide federal public works expenditures. The attention of Congress to public works is fragmented among numerous committees. In turn, the disorder in federal policies and administrative procedures creates major obstacles to effective state and local public works policy-making and management.

Despite a number of recent analyses, the precise condition of the nation's public works inventory—and the future investments we face—remains unknown. While comprehensive and reliable information is still lacking, the partial information that is available paints a disturbing picture:

■   The nation's 42,500-mile Interstate Highway System, only now approaching completion, is deteriorating at a rate requiring reconstruction of 2,000 miles of road per year. Because adequate funding for rehabilitation and reconstruction was not forthcoming in the late 1970s, over 8,000 miles of this system and 13 percent of its bridges are now beyond their designed service life and must be rebuilt.[1] Although the system constitutes less than one percent of the nation's highways, it handles over 20 percent of all highway traffic. Its further decline will adversely affect the national economy and the well-being of thousands of communities and individual firms.

■   The costs of rehabilitation and new construction necessary to maintain existing levels of service on non-urban highways will exceed $700 billion during the 1980s.[2] Even excluding the estimated $75

1

billion required to complete the unconstructed final 1,500 miles of the Interstate System, the balance required for rehabilitation and reconstruction is still greater than *all* the public works investments made by *all* units of government in the 1970s. Since inflation in highway construction has averaged 12.5 percent since 1973 (doubling costs each six years), continuation of present investment levels will permit less than one-third of needs to be met in this decade.[3]

■ One of every five bridges in the United States requires either major rehabilitation or reconstruction. The Department of Transportation has estimated the costs of this task to be as high as $33 billion. Yet in Fiscal Year 1981 Federal Highway Authorizations, only $1.3 billion was allocated to repair bridge deficiencies.[4]

■ Estimates of the amounts required to rebuild the deteriorating road beds and rolling stock of the railroads of the Northeast and Midwest are not available. While economic necessity may compel reductions in CONRAIL trackage by as much as half, or total reorganization of the system itself, this will not obviate the need for rail modernization. Railroads will play a critical role in national efforts to reduce transportation energy consumption and ship more coal to power plants to replace imported oil. This is a national issue of major importance. A viable eastern rail system is essential to the economic health of the western and southern systems since these regional rail systems can thrive only as part of a national network linking all markets and centers of production.

■ No reliable estimates exist of the investments required to modernize our ports, but numerous instances exist of harbor facilities unable to service efficiently world shipping coming to American docks. Vessels in some ports must wait for as long as a month to pick up their cargo.

■ The nation's municipal water supply needs will make heavy demands upon capital markets in the 1980s. The 756 urban areas with populations of over 50,000 will require between $75 billion and $110 billion to maintain their urban water systems over the next 20 years. Approximately one-fifth of these communities will face investment shortfalls, even if present water rates are doubled to produce capital for new investment. At least an additional $10-$13 billion beyond that generated by existing user charges will be required.[5]

■ Over $25 billion in government funds will be required during the next five years to meet existing water pollution control standards.[6]

■ Over $40 billion must be invested in New York City alone over the next nine years to repair, service, and rebuild basic public works facilities that include: 1,000 bridges, two aquaducts, one large water tunnel, several reservoirs, 6,200 miles of paved streets, 6,000 miles of sewers, 6,000 miles of water lines, 6,700 subway cars, 4,500 buses, 25,000 acres of parks, 17 hospitals, 19 city university campuses, 950 schools, 200 libraries, and hundreds of fire houses and police stations.

Because of its fiscal condition, New York City will be able to invest only $1.4 billion per year to repair, service, and rebuild these facilities.[7]

■ At least $1 billion will be required to rebuild Cleveland's basic public works—$250 to $500 million is needed to replace and renovate the publicly-owned water system; over $150 million is required for major repairs of city bridges; and over $340 million must be spent for flood control facilities. In addition to these expenditures, Cleveland must find additional funds to rebuild or resurface 30 percent of its streets, now in a state of advanced deterioration, and to reconstruct the city's sewer collection system, which frequently floods commercial and residential buildings.[8]

■ Even fiscally healthy cities face large public works investment requirements. For example, Dallas must raise almost $700 million for investment in water and sewerage treatment systems in the next nine years. More than $109 million must be generated to repair deteriorating city streets.[9]

■ Over one-half of the nation's 3,500 jails are over 30 years old. At least 1,300 and perhaps as many as 3,000 of these facilities must be either totally rebuilt or substantially rehabilitated in the 1980s.[10] This construction, in most cases, is court ordered. Thus, it often takes legal precedence over most, if not all, other public capital expenditures.

■ Rural facility needs, as yet unknown, are the subject of a major survey by the U.S. Department of Agriculture currently underway.

■ Water resource development will require major investments in *all* regions of the nation in the 1980s. The agricultural base in the old "Dustbowl" will be in jeopardy toward the end of the decade unless new water sources can be developed. After the Second World War, vast underground water resources close to the surface were tapped for irrigation. Today, this area in the Texas and Oklahoma panhandles and surrounding states has over 10 million acres under irrigation (23 percent of the nation's total irrigated farmland). This irrigated production produces over 40 percent of the nation's processed beef and major portions of wheat, sorghums, and other crops that supply much of America's agricultural exports. The region's water source is being depleted. At present rates it will be gone by the year 2000. The reversion of the region's agricultural production back to low-yield dryland farming would have a devastating effect on the economics of six states. It would seriously harm the nation's balance of payments and ultimately reduce the value of the dollar in international markets.[11] If this production is to be retained, major public works to bring surplus water from adjacent regions are required.

Even such water "surplus" areas as New England, Pennsylvania, New Jersey, and New York are in water crises, in part, because of the inadequacies of their water supply, storage, treatment, and distribution systems that become apparent in times in drought.

■ A large number of the nation's 43,500 dams require investment to reduce hazardous deficiencies. The Corps of Engineers has already inspected 9,000 of these facilities and found many of them in need of safety improvements. The funds to inspect even the balance of these dams have not been available. A majority of the dams that are potentially hazardous are privately owned and the dam owners lack the financial resources, willingness, or understanding to take remedial measures. Nor do the states have the legislative authority, funds, or trained personnel to conduct their own inspection and remedial efforts.[12]

These are not isolated or extreme examples. They represent broad trends of decline in both the quantity and quality of virtually every type of public works facility in the nation. Unless these trends are reversed—and soon—the number of public facilities in usable condition will fall to even more dangerous levels.

DECLINING INVESTMENT IN PUBLIC WORKS

Since the 1960s, the value of the nation's stock of public works has not been growing. The net value (investment minus straight-line depreciation) of federal public works investments actually declined during eight of the nine years between 1969 and 1977. While the value of state and local investments in public facilities increased during the same period, it was at a declining rate (Table 1).

Traditional investment depreciation techniques are not always an accurate means of accounting for the value of public works. For example, some facilities (such as cast iron water mains) can satisfactorily perform their functions for 100 years or more—and are doing so in many cities. Even when these investments are devalued to zero, they still present a valuable national and community asset.

A more satisfactory means for assessing the condition of our public works is to evaluate the actual quality of services provided by such facilities and their actual condition. Such assessments during the past several years strongly suggest that many public facilities are deteriorating or are inadequate to meet the needs of the coming decade. For example, George Peterson, of the Urban Institute, has assessed the condition of selected public works in nine cities (Baltimore, Dallas, Des Moines, Hartford, New Orleans, Pittsburgh, St. Louis, Seattle, and Newark). Using a 12-level rating system for evaluating the condition of water systems, sewer systems, streets, bridges and mass transit in these cities, (Table 2), this study found some facilities in good condition in each of the cities, but widespread deterioration in most facilities. For example:

1. The mass transit system in each city, with the exception of St. Louis, was found in poor condition.

Table 1
Total (residential and non-residential) PWI, Gross and Net, and Depreciation
(millions of constant 1972 dollars)

Year	Federal				State and Local				Total Government			
	Gross Invest-ment[1]	Depreci-ation	Depreciation As Percent of Gross Investment	Net Invest-ment	Gross Invest-ment[1]	Depreci-ation	Depreciation As Percent of Gross Investment	Net Invest-ment	Gross Invest-ment[1]	Depreci-ation	Depreciation As Percent of Gross Investment	Net Invest-ment
1957	3,571	5,395	151.1	-1,824	20,374	8,325	40.86	12,049	23,945	13,720	57.30	10,225
1958	4,364	5,039	115.5	-675	21,663	8,752	40.40	12,911	26,027	13,791	52.99	12,236
1959	3,783	4,679	123.7	-896	22,081	9,128	41.34	12,953	25,864	13,807	53.38	12,057
1960	3,787	4,335	114.5	-548	22,300	9,523	42.70	12,777	26,087	13,858	53.12	12,229
1961	4,424	4,058	91.7	366	23,988	9,929	41.39	14,059	28,412	13,987	49.23	14,425
1962	4,981	3,865	77.6	1,116	24,660	10,342	41.94	14,318	29,641	14,207	47.93	15,434
1963	5,784	3,963	68.5	1,821	26,799	10,780	40.23	16,019	32,583	14,743	45.25	17,840
1964	6,602	3,756	56.9	2,846	28,652	11,259	39.30	17,393	35,254	15,015	42.59	20,239
1965	6,872	3,829	55.7	3,043	30,281	11,775	38.89	18,506	37,153	15,604	42.00	21,549
1966	7,040	3,949	56.1	3,091	32,422	12,327	38.02	20,095	39,462	16,276	41.24	23,186
1967	5,911	4,056	68.6	1,855	35,041	12,933	36.91	22,108	40,952	16,989	41.49	23,963
1968	4,401	4,132	93.9	269	36,944	13,608	36.83	23,336	41,345	17,740	42.91	23,605
1969	3,684	4,170	113.2	-486	34,749	14,277	41.09	20,472	38,433	18,447	48.00	19,986
1970	3,716	4,189	112.7	-473	32,741	14,902	45.51	17,839	36,457	19,091	52.37	17,376
1971	3,931	4,185	106.5	-254	31,882	15,510	48.65	16,372	35,813	19,695	54.99	15,538
1972	4,010	4,164	103.8	-154	31,125	16,111	51.76	15,014	35,135	20,275	57.71	14,860
1973	4,128	4,138	100.2	-10	31,135	16,712	53.68	14,423	35,263	20,850	59.13	14,413
1974	3,845	4,094	106.5	-249	32,147	17,335	53.92	14,812	35,992	21,429	59.54	14,563
1975	3,482	4,026	115.6	-544	30,680	17,997	58.66	12,683	34,162	22,023	64.47	12,139
1976	3,765	3,954	105.0	-189	27,510	18,571	67.51	8,939	31,275	22,525	72.02	8,750
1977	4,122	3,893	94.4	229	25,826	19,076	73.86	6,750	30,037	22,969	76.47	7,068

1. Estimates differ from those in Exhibit 3.1 due to the use of different data sources.

Source: J.C. Musgrave, BEA, special tabulation.

Source: United States Department of Commerce, *A Study of Public Works Investment in the United States*, Washington, D.C., 1980 p. 1-63.

Table 2

Comparative Public Facilities Condition Rating for Each Functional Area by City, January-February 1979

Condition Rating	Functional Category				
	Water System	Sewer System	Streets	Bridges	Mass Transit[1]
Poor and Deteriorating Rapidly				N, P	
Poor		N (collection)			SL
Poor-Fair, But Worsening			H, NO	H	
Poor-Fair			B, N, P, SL	B, NO, SL	
Poor-Fair, But Worsening		N (treatment)			NO
Fair, But Worsening	SL				
Fair	N (city)	SL	S	S	D
Fair, But Improving					DM, H, S
Fair-Good	B, NO, N (regional)	B, P (collection)	D		P
Good	D, H, P, S	D, DM, H, NO, S (treatment), S (collection)	DM	D	B
Good-Very Good					
Very Good	DM	P (treatment)		DM	

Note: B – Baltimore; D – Dallas; DM – Des Moines; H – Hartford; N – Newark; NO – New Orleans; P – Pittsburgh; SL – St. Louis; and S – Seattle.

1. Data on Newark's privately owned bus system were unavailable. Its condition rating is therefore omitted.

Source: Consad Corporation, *A Study of Public Works in the United States*, U.S. Department of Commerce, Washington, D.C., 1980.

2. The condition of streets in each of the surveyed cities (including fast-growing Dallas) was found to be poor.

3. The bridges in Pittsburgh and Newark were found to be deteriorating badly, and those of Baltimore, Hartford, New Orleans, and St. Louis to be in need of major repair.

Despite unmistakable evidence of such deterioration, the nation's public works investments, measured in constant dollars, fell from $38.6 billion in 1965 to less than $31 billion in 1977—a 21 percent decline. On a per capita basis, public works investments in constant dollars dropped from $198 per person in 1965 to $140 in 1977—a 29 percent decline. When measured against the value of the nation's Gross National Product, public works investments declined from 4.1 percent in 1965 to 2.3 percent in 1977—a 44 percent decline (Table 3). Each of these measures reflects that, although government expenditures have significantly increased during this same period, federal investments in public facilities have been declining both relatively and absolutely.

Part of the decline can be explained by reduced investment in the nation's highway system as the Interstate network nears completion and in education facilities, as the period of increased enrollment ends. Nonetheless, there has been a marked long-term decline in public works investments, even when highways and education are excluded. Moreover, even when investments associated with the assumption of responsibility for some public works by the private sector are included, there still has been an absolute decline in the percentage of GNP committed to capital investment in the nation's public facilities.[13]

The decline in public works investments has touched virtually every public works activity. As measured in non-inflationary 1972 purchasing power, during the period 1965-1978 there was more than a 50 percent drop in highway and street construction (Table 4). Conservation and development investments declined over 12 percent. Investments for improved water supply facilities also declined—even though the population substantially increased and water quality standards have become more rigid. The few areas of real growth in public works investments were in hospital construction, industrial facilities, and sewer systems. In each of these categories actual growth has been modest.

There are several reasons for these declines—a decrease in the nation's birth rate and the maturation of the "baby boom" have helped reduce the need for some kinds of investments. But the greater part of the decline reflects the growing habit of government at all levels to cut back on construction, rehabilitation, and maintenance in order to balance budgets, hold down the rate of tax growth, and finance a growing menu of social services. While such approaches keep budgets in balance and meet near-term needs, they impose serious long-term costs. Public facilities wear out and become obsolete.

Well-conceived public works are not a "pork barrel." This is a

Table 3
Public Works Investment in the United States
1965–1978
(1972 Constant Dollars)

Category	1965	1970	1971	1972	1973	1974	1975	1976	1977
Gross National Product (billions)	926	1,075		1,171	1,235	1,218	1,202	1,271	1,333
Population (millions)	194	204	207	209	210	211	213	215	217
Total Gross Capital Investment All Units of Government (billions)	38.6	37.5	36.9	35.9	36.2	36.8	34.8	32.0	30.4
Federal Investment	7.0	3.7	3.8	3.8	3.8	3.8	3.9	3.9	4.3
State and Local Investment	31.6	33.8	33.2	32.2	32.4	33.0	30.9	28.2	26.1
Public Works as a Percent of GNP	4.1	3.4		3.0	2.9	3.0	2.9	2.5	2.3
Per Capita Public Works Investment ($)	198	183	178	172	172	173	163	148	140

Source: Calculated from data found in the *Statistical Abstract of the United States, 1979*: Bureau of the Census, (100 edition), Washington, D.C., 1979: Table 479, p. 288; Table 715, p. 437; and Table 2, p. 6.

Table 4
Value of New Construction Put into Place
1965–1978
(Constant 1972 Dollars, millions)

Item	1965	1970	1975	1978
Total new construction	109,678	107,009	97,229	117,358
Private sector construction	75,948	75,113	68,628	91,189
Percent of total	69	70	71	78
Public sector construction	33,730	31,896	28,601	26,169
Percent of total	31	30	29	22
Buildings	12,245	12,008	11,207	9,151
Educational	6,693	6,336	5,607	3,779
Hospital	813	947	1,216	1,106
Industrial	576	561	663	718
Housing, redevelopment	856	1,239	572	578
Other public buildings	3,307	2,925	3,104	2,970
Highways and streets	11,651	11,282	7,269	5,685
Conservation, development	2,956	2,160	2,286	2,589
Military facilities	1,272	817	992	862
Other	5,606	5,629	6,847	7,883
Sewer systems	1,871	1,872	3,369	3,849
Water supply facilities	1,767	1,270	1,187	1,508
Miscellaneous	1,968	2,487	2,292	2,526

Source: U.S. Bureau of the Census, *Statistical Abstract of the United States: 1979,* (100 edition), Washington, D.C., 1979, page 774.

too-glib label attached to many investments that are essential. Deteriorating public facilities reduce the quality of life of virtually every American by diminishing essential community services. Investment in public works is as essential for national and local economic renewal as investment in our industrial plant itself. Indeed, economic development is dependent upon a sound public infrastructure.

FOOTNOTES TO CHAPTER 1

1. Federal Highway Administration, United States Department of Transportation, "1981 Federal Highway Legislation: Program and Revenue Options," Washington, D.C., June 26, 1980, pp. 2–3.

2. United States Department of Transportation, "Draft Transportation Agenda for the 1980s: The Issues," Washington, D.C., March 25, 1980, p. 15.

3. "1981 Federal Highway Legislation: Program and Revenue Options," pp. 3–9.

4. "1981 Federal Highway Legislation: Program and Revenue Options," p. 43.

5. General Accounting Office, *Additional Federal Aid for Urban Water Distribution Systems Should Wait Until Needs are Clearly Established,* Washington, D.C., November 24, 1980, p. 40.

6. United States Environmental Protection Agency, *The Cost of Clean Air and Water Report to Congress,* Washington, D.C., August, 1979, p. vii.

7. Goldin, Harrison J., *Deteriorating Infrastructure in Urban and Rural Areas,* Subcommittee on Economic Growth and Stabilization, Joint Economic Committee, Congress of the United States, Ninety-Sixth Congress, First Session, U.S. Government Printing Office, Washington, D.C., 1979, pp. 42–53.

8. Humphrey, Nancy; Peterson George E; Wilson, Peter, *The Future of Cleveland's Capital Plant,* The Urban Institute, Washington, D.C., 1979, pp. 52–73.

9. Wilson, Peter, *The Future of Dallas's Capital Plant,* The Urban Institute, Washington, D.C., 1980, pp. 27–40.

10. Business Week, "New Jails: Boom for Builders, Bust for Budgets," McGraw-Hill, February 9, 1981.

11. Choate, Pat, *The High Plains Project,* Economic Development Administration, United States Department of Commerce, Washington, D.C., 1978, pp. 1–3.

12. General Accounting Office, *Ways to Resolve Critical Water Resources Issues Facing the Nation,* Washington, D.C., April 27, 1979, pp. 23–25.

13. United States Department of Commerce, *A Study of Public Works Investment in the United States,* Washington, D.C., April, 1980, p. 19.

2

PUBLIC WORKS AND THE ECONOMY

Public works play a crucial role in the creation of national wealth and productivity growth. Education, research and development, and public works are the only real supply side *investments* the public sector makes in our economy.

Together with an aging industrial plant, deterioration of our public infrastructure has contributed to the decline in American productivity. Our *rate* of productivity improvement has fallen for almost 15 years and *absolute* levels of productivity have declined since 1979.[1] As national productivity weakens, so, too, does the nation's ability to finance private consumption, additional private capital investment and a diverse array of necessary governmental expenditures.

A number of recent studies suggests that these productivity reversals are the cumulative effect of: (1) a slowing rate of technological innovation and utilization; (2) inadequate rates of improvement in labor productivity; and (3) inadequate capital investment by both the public and private sectors in new and existing plants.[2] Attention has focused on technological decline, the quality of labor, and inadequate private capital investment. The role of public works in national development recently has been virtually ignored and dangerously regarded as the "pork barrel." While some public works have been misguided and can be labeled as "pork," it is both unwise and dangerous to castigate all public works as falling into that category.

A primary objective of public works investment is to provide basic public services, such as water supplies, waste water treatment, and transportation that underpin the operation of the national and local economies. Simultaneously, $80 billion in annual public works investments can also be used to:

■ assist in national economic stabilization (achieving a desired level of employment, output, income, and prices);

■ assist in stabilizing state and local budgets; and

■ assist specific geographic areas, economic sectors or population groups, in eliminating the problems of economic obsolescence.

PUBLIC WORKS AND JOBS The construction industry is a major sector in the U.S. economy. In 1977, over 477,000 firms were directly engaged in construction activity. They employed over 4.2 million persons in a variety of activities and trades, of which some 3.5 million were con-

11

struction workers (Table 5). These workers earned in excess of $43 billion.

Public works investments account for a substantial share of construction activity. Of the $223 billion in new construction put in place in 1980, over $56.7 billion was public works—more than 24 percent of the total investment (Table 6). Furthermore, the public sector invested an additional $30 billion in the purchase of right-of-ways, existing buildings, and equipment.[3]

Table 5
Firms and Employment in the Construction Industry
1977

Contract Construction	472.5	4,212	3,542
General Building Contractors	133.1	1,150	938
Heavy Construction Contractors	28.0	827	709
Special Trade Contractors	288.6	2,158	1,846
Plumbing, Heating, and Air Conditioning	56.5	458	368
Painting, Paperhanging, and Decorating	27.3	133	121
Electrical Work	36.8	366	305
Masonry and Stonework	24.8	152	143
Plastering, Drywall and Insulation	16.8	186	164
Terrazzo, Tile, Marble, and Mosaic Work	3.9	22	19
Carpentering	24.3	124	114
Floor Laying and Floor Work	9.0	41	34
Roofing and Sheet Metal	20.6	172	146
Concrete Work	18.4	139	125
Water Well Drilling	4.3	22	19
Structural Steel Erection	2.6	48	41
Glass and Glazing Work	3.2	24	18
Excavating and Foundation Work	16.2	103	91
Wrecking and Demolition Work	1.0	9	7
Subdividers and Developers	5.3	43	19
TOTAL	477.8	4,254	3,561

Source: U.S. Bureau of the Census, *Statistical Abstract of the United States: 1979,* (100 edition), Washington, D.C., 1970, page 776.

12

Table 6
New Construction Put in Place: Trends and Projections 1978–81
(in millions of current dollars)

Type of construction	1978	1979	1980¹	Percent change 1979–80	1981*	Percent change 1980–81
Total new construction	205,457	228,950	228,300	0	270,330	18
Private construction	159,556	179,948	171,600	-5	206,700	20
Residential buildings	93,424	99,030	84,000	-15	109,800	31
New housing units	75,808	78,587	60,800	-23	83,000	37
Additions and alterations	16,349	18,236	20,000	11	23,000	15
Nonhousekeeping	1,267	2,206	3,200	45	3,800	20
Nonresidential buildings	36,293	47,298	53,100	12	60,700	14
Industrial	10,994	14,950	13,800	-8	15,200	10
Office	6,574	9,461	13,200	40	17,200	30
Other commercial	11,991	15,463	17,800	15	19,600	10
Religious	1,248	1,548	1,600	5	1,700	5
Educational	729	806	1,200	50	1,300	10
Hospital and institutional	3,347	3,530	3,500	0	3,500	0
Miscellaneous	1,410	1,540	2,000	30	2,200	10
Farm, nonresidential	5,253	5,700	5,700	0	5,700	0
Public utilities	23,302	26,467	27,300	3	28,900	6
Telephone	5,418	6,343	7,300	15	8,400	15
Electric light and power	14,384	16,009	15,200	-5	13,700	-10
Gas	1,929	2,266	2,700	20	4,300	60

13

Table 6 (*Continued*)
New Construction Put in Place: Trends and Projections 1978–81
(in millions of current dollars)

Type of construction	1978	1979	1980[1]	Percent change 1979–80	1981[1]	Percent change 1980–81
Railroad	1,037	1,259	1,500	20	1,800	20
Petroleum pipelines	534	591	600	0	700	10
All other private	1,283	1,452	1,500	0	1,600	10
Public construction	45,902	49,003	56,700	16	63,600	12
Buildings	15,241	15,857	18,100	14	20,100	11
Housing and redevelopment	1,051	1,211	1,600	35	2,000	28
Industrial	1,184	1,411	1,800	30	2,300	30
Educational	6,264	6,903	7,700	12	8,500	10
Hospital	1,822	1,648	1,600	0	1,600	0
Other public	4,919	4,684	5,400	15	5,700	5
Highways and streets	10,712	11,915	15,500	30	17,800	15
Military facilities	1,512	1,640	1,700	5	2,000	20
Conservation and development	4,457	4,587	5,000	10	5,500	10
Other public construction	13,989	15,003	16,400	9	18,200	11
Sewer systems	6,765	7,298	7,700	5	8,500	10
Water supply facilities	2,661	2,490	3,500	40	4,200	20
Miscellaneous	4,563	5,215	5,200	0	5,500	5

1. Estimated by Bureau of Industrial Economics.

Source: United States Department of Commerce, *1981 U.S. Industrial Outlook*, Washington, D.C., 1981, p. 6.

Source: Bureau of the Census and Bureau of Industrial Economics.

The construction industry and the public works component of that industry extends far beyond the 4.25 million persons employed in direct construction activities. It is closely linked with a set of industry and service institutions, each of which feels the effects when the construction industry declines (Table 7). The Rand Corporation and U.S. Department of Labor traced these industrial linkages for 22 types of public works projects. For each type of project, the distribution of funds was followed to final destination (either direct on-site construction labor or the acquisition of specific materials and equipment) (Tables 8 and 9). The conclusions drawn from this analysis are:

■ The most significant short-term impacts of public works projects are found in equipment, material and other industries rather than in on-site construction. For every direct on-site construction job created by public works projects, three additional jobs are created in the overall economy.

■ There are substantial variations in the number of on-site construction jobs created by various types of public works projects. Public school construction requires almost 25 percent less on-site labor than college housing construction. Highway construction uses less than one-half as much on-site labor as that of dam, levee and local flood control projects.

■ Substantial variations exist in the quantities and types of materials and equipment used in public works projects.

Such variations are important because we can take advantage of them to tailor public works investments to meet a number of objectives including stabilization of the economy, alleviation of structural unemployment, and helping places suffering from economic obsolescence to adapt to new economic development possibilities.

PUBLIC WORKS AND PLACES

A large and growing number of communities are now hamstrung in their economic revitalization efforts because their basic public facilities—their streets, roads, water systems, and sewerage treatment plants—are either too limited, obsolete, or worn out to sustain a modernized industrial economy. As a rule of thumb, when a community wastewater treatment system is operating at 80 percent of capacity, that community will not be able to add additional industrial load. This is particularly true for smaller communities where the 20 percent of excess capacity will, in actual quantitative terms, represent limited treatment abilities. The operating ratio for water treatment that indicates effective full capacity utilization is 70 percent. A Department of Commerce survey of 6,870 communities' wastewater treatment capacity reports that 3,133 (46%) of these systems are operating at 80 percent of capacity or higher. The same survey indicates that 1,844 of 5,622 places have water treatment systems operating at 70 percent or greater capacity. When deficient transportation,

Table 7
Distribution of Inputs and Outputs:
New Construction Industries
(SIC CODES: PARTS 1112, 1212, 148, 15–17)

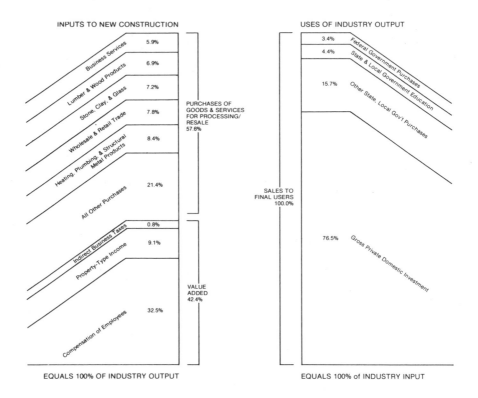

The new construction industry requires a high proportion of manufactured goods and services supplied by other industries (intermediate products) as inputs. As these flow through the construction process, value is added by the capital and labor employed to produce the industry output—buildings, highways, dams, etc.

Value added by construction labor and capital in the processing and resale of these inputs accounts for the remaining industry costs, with compensation of employees the largest component, as is the case for most industries.

The output of this industry is classified as fixed investment and all of it goes to final users such as purchasers of new housing, industrial plant and other business structures. The private sector takes three-fourths, and Governments—Federal, state and local— take about one-fourth of the total output.

Note: Percent distributions are based on the 1972 Input-Output table; shipments are valued at producer prices.

Source: U.S. Department of Commerce, *U.S. Industrial Outlook, 1980,* Washington, D.C., 1980.

publicly operated solid waste and toxic waste disposal sites, and other public facilities essential to private sector investment are also considered, at least one half (and more likely two-thirds) of the nation's communities are unable to support modernized development *until* major new investments are made in their basic facilities that undergird the economy.

A number of studies have attempted to measure the influence of public works on the location and investment decisions of individual firms. The most comprehensive was conducted in the mid-1970s by the Bureau of Census.[5] Over 2,000 firms operating in 254 distinct product classes were examined. Each firm was asked whether the availability of certain public works facilities were either: (1) critical; (2) significant; or (3) of minimal value in their location decisions. The survey indicated that for virtually all of the 254 categories studied, the availability of public works facilities was of either critical or significant importance to location decisions. The availability of public facilities was almost always a more important locational consideration than the existence of local tax incentives or local industrial revenue bond financing. Indeed, while public works in themselves are never a sufficient condition for economic development, they are almost always a necessary condition.

PUBLIC WORKS AND ECONOMIC STABILIZATION
It has long been a standing assumption that public works investments can be modulated to help stabilize the ups and downs of the economy. However, in practice, the U.S. has given little attention to such uses of annual public works expenditures.

The present recession is the sixth such decline in the economy since the end of World War II. As with previous recessions, the 1980–81 economic decline has created substantial unemployment and under-utilization of production capacities in the construction, materials, and equipment industries. The national unemployment rate in the construction industry averaged 17 percent in 1980; it rose as high as 40 percent in some regions. The steel industry, heavily related to construction, operated at approximately 50 percent of its capacity throughout 1980, creating 80,000 unemployed steel workers.

Economic policy might reduce the impact of such a severe recession by using the nation's annual $80 billion public works investments as a counter-cyclical economic tool for providing employment in the construction, materials and equipment industries. However, public works investments in the United States have long been made in a perverse pro-cyclical pattern, increasing during the expansionary phase of economic cycle and decreasing during its contractionary phase. This pro-cyclical management of public works investments creates many adverse consequences:

17

Table 8
Construction Costs, by Type of Building Construction, Allocated for Industrial Sectors and On-Site Labor
(in dollars per $1000 of total contract cost, 1974)

SIC	Sectors Description	Private One-Family Housing	Public Housing	Schools	Hospitals	Nursing Homes	College Housing	Federal Office Buildings
14	Mining, non-metallic metals, except fuel	2.60	—	—	—	—	—	—
22	Textile mill products	3.70	—	—	—	—	—	—
26	Paper and allied products	1.70	—	—	.40	2.20	.80	#
28	Chemicals and allied products	4.20	4.60	2.50	3.20	3.70	2.40	1.70
29	Petroleum products	4.60	5.70	6.60	2.30	5.10	2.50	2.00
30	Rubber and misc. plastic products	3.80	—	—	.30	.40	#	#
	Total Non-durable Goods Manufacturing	18.00	10.30	9.10	6.10	11.40	5.70	3.70
24	Lumber and wood products	117.50	40.20	33.50	16.00	30.50	33.20	9.10
25	Furniture and fixtures	.20	.60	7.70	1.00	.60	.70	.70
32	Stone, clay, and glass products	44.20	47.90	60.90	47.60	56.90	50.40	38.90
33	Primary metal products	14.40	15.90	7.20	15.80	10.70	7.10	10.40
34	Fabricated metal products	26.70	68.20	83.90	77.90	81.70	77.90	60.00
35	Machinery, except electrical (and excluding construction machinery)[a]	4.20	6.40	8.60	30.70	21.30	7.80	31.70
	Construction equipment[a]	5.40	13.90	13.60	11.80	10.10	12.50	15.20
36	Electrical equipment and supplies	14.70	21.90	24.80	37.00	26.00	19.40	30.00
37	Transportation equipment[a]	2.40	NA	NA	NA	NA	NA	NA
38	Instruments and related products	.20	#	4.30	5.70	3.60	1.30	3.40
	Total Durable Goods Manufacturing	233.70	222.10	251.40	245.60	243.00	211.70	200.70

Other Materials not otherwise classified[b]	3.80	7.10	7.00	2.10	1.60	1.50	1.30
Transportation	11.20	7.50	9.40	8.00	8.80	11.60	9.00
Wholesale and retail trade	183.20	184.10	255.60	238.20	240.60	271.00	280.30
Total Material, Equipment and Supply Cost	448.80	424.00	525.50	497.90	503.80	500.00	493.60
Total On-Site Labor Cost	214.60	359.40	303.60	338.20	332.70[c]	377.40	374.40
Total Unallocated Cost[d]	336.50	216.60	170.80	163.90	163.60[c]	122.60	131.80
Total Project Cost	1000.00	1000.00	1000.00	1000.00	1000.00	1000.00	1000.00
Ratio of total on-site labor cost to total project cost	.21	.36	.30	.34	.33	.38	.37
Ratio of total on-site labor cost to total cost of materials, equipment, and supplies	.48	.85	.58	.68	.66	.75	.76

SOURCES: Ball, Claiborne M. "Employment Effects of Construction Expenditures," *Monthly Labor Review*, February 1965, pp. 154-158; *Labor and Material Requirements for College Housing Construction*, BLS Bulletin 1441, May 1965, pp. 7, 28-31; *Labor and Material Requirements for Construction of Private Single-Family Houses*, BLS Bulletin 1755, 1972, p. 9, 17-20; *Labor and Material Requirements for Hospital and Nursing Home Construction*, BLS Bulletin 1691, 1971, pp. 11, 39-42, 48-50; *Labor and Material Requirements for Public Housing Construction*, BLS Bulletin 1821, 1974, pp. 8-10; *Labor and Material Requirements for School Construction*, BLS Bulletin 1588, June 1968, pp. 6, 19-21.

NOTES: NA means not available. — = not applicable. # means less than $.20 and more than zero. Columns may not add to total because of rounding. Data in the table are expressed in 1974 dollars. The year of survey for each type of project is as follows: private one-family housing—1969, public housing—1968, schools—1965, hospitals and nursing homes—1966, college housing—1961, and federal office buildings—1959.

[a] Where no separate data were available for the cost of transportation equipment, this cost has been included in the cost of construction equipment. The data under both categories are rental costs—i.e., the cost of owning (depreciation) and maintaining the equipment.

[b] Includes nursery products and materials not itemized by the contractors.

[c] On-site labor and unallocated costs for nursing homes have been estimated using data for hospitals.

[d] Includes warehousing, some off-site salaries, supplemental wage benefits, administration and clerical work, expenses of the central office, and yard operations.

Table 9

Construction Costs by Types of Heavy Construction Allocated to Industrial Sectors and On-Site Labor

(in dollars per $1000 of total contract cost, 1974)

SIC	Description	Highways	Sewer Works — Lines	Sewer Works — Plants	Large Earth Fill Dams	Small Earth Fill Dams	Local Flood Protection	Pile Dikes	Levees	Revetments	Power-house Construction	Medium Concrete Dams	Lock and Concrete Dams	Large Multiple Purpose Projects	Dredging	Misc.[a]
14	Mining, nonmetallic metals, except fuel[b]	—	—	—	#	15.00	25.10	77.30	45.30	208.70	6.10	1.20	42.50	24.80	#	14.70
22	Textile mill products	NA	—	—	NA	NA	NA	NA	NA	NA	NA	NA	NA	NA	NA	NA
26	Paper and allied products	NA	—	—	NA	NA	NA	NA	NA	NA	NA	NA	NA	NA	NA	NA
28	Chemicals and allied products	2.80	.90	2.40	NA	NA	NA	NA	NA	NA	NA	NA	NA	NA	NA	NA
29	Petroleum products	59.10	8.30	5.20	NA	NA	NA	NA	NA	NA	NA	NA	NA	NA	NA	NA
30	Rubber and misc. plastic products	—	—	—	NA	NA	NA	NA	NA	NA	NA	NA	NA	NA	NA	NA
	Total Non-durable Goods Manufacturing	61.90	9.20	7.60	65.60	77.80	23.70	33.00	61.90	34.30	5.90	13.70	14.30	17.50	72.60	85.80
24	Lumber and wood products[c]	5.30	2.70	5.70	6.80	5.10	9.90	46.90	.80	42.60	12.20	4.20	4.30	4.90	#	17.20
25	Furniture and fixtures	—	—	—	NA	NA	NA	NA	NA	NA	NA	NA	NA	NA	NA	NA
32	Stone, clay and glass products	79.30	123.30	39.60	9.30	6.60	44.20	—	.70	#	11.10	60.70	80.90	38.10	—	36.20
33	Primary metal products	NA	27.00	37.00	1.80	3.50	4.30	3.60	.90	3.90	13.90	28.70	60.90	30.00	40.40	32.50
34	Fabricated metal products	67.70	6.70	47.10	39.40	21.70	85.90	11.30	6.90	6.90	34.70	57.10	37.30	52.00	14.90	3.60
35	Machinery, except electrical (and excluding construction machinery)	—	6.50	60.90	11.40	10.60	2.20	5.30	.80	#	232.70	34.10	44.10	31.30	.80	7.70
	Construction equipment[d]	83.60[e]	95.80	69.00	83.40	120.20	31.90	48.30	56.80	16.60	23.10	65.80	89.10	33.90	25.90	87.00
36	Electrical equipment and supplies	—	1.10	16.10	.90	.90	.40	—	#	—	153.20	1.30	8.40	19.20	#	#
37	Transportation equipment[d]	NA	NA	NA	43.40	41.90	11.50	26.60	12.70	12.30	2.70	11.60	12.10	3.20	85.70	28.50
38	Instruments and related products[f]	—	—	3.00	NA	NA	NA	NA	NA	NA	NA	NA	—	NA	NA	NA
	Total Durable Goods Manufacturing	301.60	264.10	281.10	196.30	211.10	190.30	142.00	79.50	82.20	486.30	263.40	337.20	213.90	167.70	213.40
	Other materials, not elsewhere classified[g]	65.80	1.10	2.70	#	.70	#	—	#	—	2.50	#	—	1.30	#	.70
	Transportation[h]	6.60	9.00	7.00	19.10	36.80	44.00	105.50	63.40	251.50	31.60	22.20	74.30	44.70	20.50	42.40
	Wholesale and retail trade	177.20	252.60	246.20	149.20	149.30	103.00	89.80	71.40	103.30	140.30	106.40	130.90	75.90	73.20	139.30

20

Total material, equipment and supply cost	547.40	534.90	542.00	430.20	490.00	386.10	441.70	321.60	679.90	570.10	406.90	599.20	376.90	334.00	495.70
Total on-site labor cost[j]	226.00	304.80	330.80	434.00	441.80	510.70	415.10	494.90	192.60	297.50	486.30	368.70	555.20	511.70	391.90
Total unallocated cost[j]	226.60	160.30	127.10	132.80	68.10	103.20	135.20	183.60	127.30	32.40	106.90	32.00	67.90	154.40	112.40
Total project cost	1000.00	1000.00	1000.00	1000.00	1000.00	1000.00	1000.00	1000.00	1000.00	1000.00	1000.00	1000.00	1000.00	1000.00	1000.00
Ratio of total on-site labor costs to total project cost	.23	.30	.33	.43	.44	.51	.42	.49	.19	.30	.49	.37	.56	.51	.39
Ratio of total on-site labor costs to total cost of materials, equipment and supplies	.41	.57	.61	1.00	.90	1.32	.93	1.54	.28	.44	1.20	.62	1.47	1.53	.79

SOURCES: Claiborne M. Bell, "Employment Effects of Construction Expenditures," *Monthly Labor Review*, February 1965, pp. 154–158; Robert Ball, "Labor and Materials Required for Highway Construction," *Monthly Labor Review*, June 1973, pp. 40–45; Diane S. Finger, "Labor Requirements for Federal Highway Construction," *Monthly Labor Review*, December 1975, pp. 31–36; Robert H. Haveman and John V. Krutilla, *Unemployment, Idle Capacity, and the Evaluation of Public Expenditures: National and Regional Analyses*, Johns Hopkins Press, Baltimore, 1968, pp. 20–21; *Labor and Material Requirements for Construction of Federally Aided Highways, 1958, 1961 and 1964*, BLS Report 299, p. 5; *Labor and Material Requirements for Sewer Works Construction, 1968*, BLS Bulletin 1490, pp. 6, 24–25.

NOTES: NA means not available. — = not applicable. # means less than $.20 and more than zero. Columns may not add up to total because of rounding. Data in the table are expressed in 1974 dollars. The year of survey for each type of project is as follows: highways—1963; sewer works—1963; and civil works—1960. (The data for civil works have been inflated from 1958 prices.)

a. Miscellaneous includes four projects not elsewhere classified under the Civil Works heading: Bayou Macon Channel Improvement (Louisiana); Jetties, Gold Beach (Oregon); Outlet Channel, Sardis Dam (Mississippi); and Sea Wall Extension, Galveston (Texas).

b. The data given for civil works projects include metal, coal, and crude petroleum mining.

c. The cost of lumber products includes the cost of furniture and fixtures; (SIC 25) for all civil work projects. However, very little is spent on furniture and fixtures in the construction of civil works projects.

d. Where no data are given for the cost of transportation equipment, it has been included in the cost of construction equipment. The data under both categories are rental costs—i.e., the cost of owning (depreciation) and maintaining the equipment.

e. The cost of construction equipment for highways has been estimated from data for similar projects completed in an earlier year.

f. For civil works projects, SIC 38 is included in "Other Materials, not elsewhere classified."

g. Includes nursery products and, except for civil works projects, materials not itemized by the contractors. For civil works projects, this category also includes SIC 38, Instruments and Related Products, and SIC 39, Miscellaneous Manufacturing. For highways, it also includes some paints and other chemicals, aluminum, and paper products.

h. In the data for civil works projects, transportation costs include warehousing. For all other projects, warehousing is included in unallocated costs.

i. Estimates of costs for contractor-employed inspectors and engineers are included in on-site labor costs for civil works projects. For all other projects, these costs are included in the "Total Unallocated Cost" category.

j. For civil works projects, include contractor's tax payments, earnings from payments for rents and interest, corporate profits after taxes, overhead (including mobilization and demobilization costs), and services. For all other types of projects it includes, in addition, warehousing, some off-site salaries, supplemental wage benefits, administration and clerical work, expenses of the central office, and yard operations.

Table 10
Municipal and Industrial Wastewater and Water Treatment by Capacities by State

State	Wastewater Treatment			Water Treatment		
	Number of Places Surveyed	Number of Places Using 80 Percent or More of Capacity	Percent of Total Surveyed	Number of Places Surveyed	Number of Places Using 70 Percent or More of Capacity	Percent of Total Surveyed
Alabama	156	63	40.3	121	54	44.6
Alaska	11	6	54.5	22	10	45.4
Arizona	62	29	46.7	18	5	27.7
Arkansas	112	57	50.8	75	15	20.0
California	369	229	62.0	271	70	25.8
Colorado	95	45	47.3	80	5	6.2
Connecticut	90	34	37.7	56	18	32.1
Delaware	11	3	27.2	19	8	42.1
Florida	231	85	36.7	177	54	30.5
Georgia	215	83	38.6	132	55	41.6
Hawaii	29	6	20.6	3	1	33.3
Idaho	41	18	43.9	27	10	37.0
Illinois	363	188	51.7	386	177	45.8
Indiana	133	72	54.1	176	85	48.2
Iowa	124	60	48.3	129	35	27.1
Kansas	144	66	45.8	104	15	14.4
Kentucky	114	55	48.2	122	72	59.0
Louisiana	155	66	42.5	157	49	31.2
Maine	57	29	50.8	81	30	37.0
Maryland	76	22	28.9	50	N/A	N/A
Massachusetts	92	30	32.6	200	48	24.0
Michigan	203	N/A	N/A	165	21	12.7
Minnesota	117	42	35.8	168	15	8.9
Mississippi	96	25	26.0	129	67	51.9
Missouri	186	71	38.1	124	43	34.6
Montana	39	19	48.7	16	5	31.2
Nebraska	59	28	47.4	56	8	14.2
Nevada	22	8	36.3	15	3	20.0
New Hampshire	33	17	51.5	55	15	27.2
New Jersey	242	126	52.0	218	101	46.3
New Mexico	45	15	33.3	31	5	16.1

Table 10 (Continued)
Municipal and Industrial Wastewater and Water Treatment by Capacities by State

State	Wastewater Treatment			Water Treatment		
	Number of Places Surveyed	Number of Places Using 80 Percent or More of Capacity	Percent of Total Surveyed	Number of Places Surveyed	Number of Places Using 70 Percent or More of Capacity	Percent of Total Surveyed
New York	363	187	51.5	N/A	N/A	N/A
North Carolina	163	73	44.7	240	21	8.7
North Dakota	23	11	47.8	N/A	N/A	N/A
Ohio	400	212	53.0	498	276	55.4
Oklahoma	166	65	39.1	157	17	10.8
Oregon	96	20	20.8	158	18	11.3
Pennsylvania	461	198	42.9	288	177	61.4
Rhode Island	14	4	28.5	18	4	22.2
South Carolina	202	105	51.9	120	30	25.0
South Dakota	27	16	59.2	31	2	6.4
Tennessee	136	56	41.	113	30	26.5
Texas	486	285	58.6	121	57	47.1
Utah	48	30	62.5	38	5	13.1
Vermont	45	25	55.5	33	15	45.4
Virginia	137	65	47.4	122	43	35.2
Washington	102	36	35.2	113	6	5.3
West Virginia	77	39	50.6	110	37	33.6
Wisconsin	176	101	57.3	60	2	3.3
Wyoming	26	8	30.7	19	5	26.3
TOTAL	6,870	3,133	45.5 $(46.3)^2$	5,622	1,844	32.7 $(33.0)^2$

Source: Reid, George; Martin, Ralph; and Pulliam, J. Gordon, University of Oklahoma and Pulliam Associates under contract to the Economic Development Administration, United States Department of Commerce. *Report on Municipal and Industrial Wastewater Treatment Systems: A Statistical Compendium,* June 1978, and *Report on Municipal and Industrial Water Treatment Systems: A Statistical Compendium,* January 1978, Norman, Oklahoma, 1978.

1. As a rule of thumb, when a community wastewater treatment system is operating at 80 percent of capacity, that community will not be able to add additional industrial load. This is particularly true for smaller communities where the 20 percent of excess capacity will in actual quantitative terms represent limited treatment abilities. The operating ratio for water treatment that indicates effective full capacity utilization is 70 percent.

2. Excludes the N.A. (not available) states in the computation of percentages. Otherwise, the totals reflect percentage of those actually reported communities.

23

■ By increasing public works investments during the expansionary phase of the economic cycle, costs (materials, equipment, and labor) become artificially high and contribute to inflation; and

■ By decreasing public works investments during the contractionary phases, under-utilization of labor and industrial facilities increase in the construction, materials and equipment industries—worsening the recession.

Since 1960 Congress has enacted three public works counter-cyclical programs—the $1.9 billion Accelerated Public Works Program, (APW) in 1961–1962; the $130 million Public Works Impact Program (PWIP) in 1972–1973; and the $6 billion Local Public Works Impact Program (LPW) in 1976-1977. A number of studies have concluded that the three temporary programs fell far short of meeting their *stated* objectives, i.e., stimulating employment for the structurally-unemployed in distressed areas during an economic downturn. Evidence suggests that these shortcomings lay in the timing and administration of these expenditures and in the narrowness of the goals of the program.[6]

The temporary counter-cyclical Local Public Works program of 1976–1977 did nothing to relieve the 1974–1977 recession until late 1976. Over 80 percent of the direct employment generated by the LPW projects did not occur until the recovery phase of the cycle had begun. These time lags reflect less on the efficacy of public works as a counter-cyclical device than they do on the sclerosis of the executive and legislative process. Lags occurred because of delays in securing passage of legislation, Presidential approval, appropriation of funds, selection of projects, and construction. Two years after the onset of the 1974 recession, the Ford Administration continued to resist adding to the budget deficit by refusing to use counter-cyclical public works for economic stabilization, relying instead on traditional fiscal and monetary measures until the summer of 1976.

Occasional recessions are inevitable. The annual $35 billion federal public works expenditures can exert major economic stabilizing influences. Thus, it is both timely and prudent to devise policies and administrative techniques for managing public works investments in anticipation of the economic cycle.

A Permanent Counter-Cyclical Use of Public Works—If public works investments are to be used as a flywheel on the economy, we must make a choice between the relatively small-scale temporary programs of the past and a more permanent policy that governs the timing of investments of all federal public works programs. The federal government has a large array of permanent public works programs which could be used as a counter-cyclical tool. Several are directly federal, such as the public works construction of the Corps of Engineers. However, approximately 80 percent of the funds that the federal government invests in public works are in grants-in-aid to state and local governments.[7] Some of these federal funds are in the form of revenue sharing or by block grants such as the Community Development Block Grant Program (CDBG). Most are made available through categorical programs such as those of the Environmental Protection Agency, the Federal Highway Administration, the Farmers Home Administration, and the programs of the Economic Development Administration, among many others. Federal transfers of funds and direct investments constitute 50 percent of all financing of public works construction in the U.S. Much of the remaining 50 percent of construction financing represents matching grants by state and local governments to meet federal requirements or mandated federal investments.

There are many possible advantages to the use of these public works funds as a counter-cyclical tool. The first, and perhaps most important, is to reduce the adverse consequences created by the present pro-cyclical pattern of these investments. In many ways present pro-cyclical investment patterns for public works are akin to loose cargo in a ship in turbulent waters. As the ship sways side-to-side the cargo shifts and accentuates the sways. The counter-cyclical management would directly address this issue, something temporary programs cannot, by their very nature, accomplish.

A large portion of the benefits of counter-cyclical public works projects can be generated during the contractionary phase of the economy cycle if political and ideologically generated delays are eliminated. Also, economic recovery in the initial phases of the expansionary phases of the cycle can be accelerated. After all, there is little merit in having massive unemployment and unused production capacity in a slow recovery period. A number of reforms are worth discussion including (1) stand-by authorities; (2) the identification of a backlog of projects which would serve both counter-cyclical purposes and long-term national and local development; and (3) the creation of purchasing techniques which would permit stockpiling of materials and equipment for use in future projects.

A permanent, more systematic counter-cyclical policy for public works programs would also reduce the "crisis" management atmosphere which has existed in temporary programs, such as LPW, funded on a "crash" basis. Temporary funding created very strong political pressures when applicants realized the existence of a "now or never," one-time-only project funding opportunity. For example, in LPW there were over $22 billion of applications for $6 billion of funds. The crisis management approach of "get out the money," with quality often a secondary consideration, would also be obviated. In a permanent program, administrators would be able to better meet their responsibility to choose worthy projects. By advancing projects or adding projects to permanent programs, many of the political pressures created in temporary programs can be substantially reduced—

25

particularly the very intense pressure generated around marginal projects.

A third advantage to permanent programs would be a reduction in lags between the beginning of a recession and the time when benefits would begin to flow. Since the end of the Second World War the nation has gained substantial experience in economic policy. The tools of economic analysis have been substantially improved. The use of permanent programs would permit the acceleration of projects at a very early stage in the economic decline and would permit a timely reduction of effort as the economy moved to advanced recovery. The use of permanent programs would facilitate advance purchase programs for a wide array of equipment materials.

A fourth advantage to the adoption of a permanent, counter-cyclically administered public works policy would be to help ensure that federal funds are not used to replace state and local funds. In permanent programs, the source of local matching funds is generally mandated as a federal funding requisite. By advancing the pipeline, this fiscal integrity can be maintained. However, when it is desirable to waive matching requirements in order to aid state and local fiscal stability, such actions could be taken explicitly.

A fifth advantage would be to facilitate better targeted investments in order to address regional and sectoral variations in the economic cycle. Roger Vaughan has documented how regionally disparate these cycles often are. By the use of advance purchases in specific industries located in specific places, economic stimulus can be achieved. Conversely, in the expansionary phase of the cycle, purchases can be deferred or placed in specific sectors or places needing stimulus. Vaughan has also described how state stabilization funds could be created to finance such projects.[8]

A sixth advantage of a permanent counter-cyclical program would be the improved fiscal stability it could help bring to state and local public works expenditures. Public works constitute a significant component of most state and local budgets, averaging about 15 percent.[9] Public works funds are often cut back during a contractionary period, especially in major urban areas the fiscal base of which is already deteriorating. Forestalling state and local cutbacks in essential maintenance and rehabilitation through a counter-cyclical federal spending pattern would help state and local governments avoid even larger capital replacement investments in the future. And such a program could be more effectively targeted to help the unemployed as well.

Targeting—In the past, federal public works programs adopted to put the structurally unemployed back to work in economically distressed places yielded disappointing results.

Past experiences of the LPW and PWIP programs indicate that relatively little of the employment they created went to the long-term unemployed, the unskilled, or even to those persons living in places where individual projects were constructed. Indeed, construction wages constitute only a minor share (22 percent) of total public works expenditures. Vaughan and the Office of Management and Budget have analyzed the targeting of counter-cyclical public works to distressed areas and to structurally unemployed persons.[10] They conclude:

■ The majority of the expended funds for PWIP and LWP projects did *not* go to direct employment for on-site construction but rather to the related materials, equipment and associated industries;

■ Employment directly created by these projects did not greatly affect the unemployed. In the PWIP program, the unemployed accounted for only 27 percent of the total jobs generated and accounted for less than seven percent of the program budget. The LPW program employed even fewer. Only 12 percent of the jobs went to the unemployed, a total of two percent of the overall budget;

■ The duration of employment created for workers was short. Under the PWIP program, the average project employment period for unskilled workers was 3.7 weeks; for skilled workers it was only 4.2 weeks. Under the LPW program the average project period of employment for unskilled workers was 3.9 weeks; and for skilled workers 3.6 weeks. Since their experience tenure was brief, most unskilled workers did not receive adequate on-the-job training to prepare them for other employment.

Evaluations of the LPW and PWIP programs by the Economic Development Administration and the Office of Management and Budget also concluded that much of the on-site construction employment went to persons not residing in the area, many of them employees of construction firms located outside the area where the public works project was constructed.

However, by careful planning, government *can* target benefits to help both people and specific industries. Studies by the Rand Corporation concluded that in the recessions since the end of the Second World War, there has been excess capacity in the materials and equipment industries in the contractionary phases of the economic cycle. In this present cycle, the steel, aluminum, fabricated metals, concrete, equipment and related industries find themselves operating at substantially less than full capacity. To address this economic sluggishness, the present $100 billion backlog of funded, but unspent, public works funds could be used to purchase needed materials and equipment in advance of actual construction. This would produce many benefits. For example, purchasing steel at a time when that industry is operating at 54 percent of capacity would avoid ensuing price rises; permit the industry to operate closer to normal levels of production; improve conditions of certainty in that sector; create jobs for laid-off workers, many of whom reside in distressed areas; and eliminate almost $10

27

million per week in unemployment payments. Tables 8 and 9 identify the range of industries that could be similarly assisted.

Targeting specific sectors can be an effective means for addressing major regional variations that exist in the economic cycle. Pre-purchasing would also provide a stimulus to basic industries operating at low capacity with high unemployment in distressed places.

ECONOMIC STABILITY OUT OF PROGRAM CHAOS In a decade of severe fiscal constraint, when we face the major necessities of economic revitalization, we cannot pursue the open-ended, excessively fragmented approaches to policy so typical of the past. Fiscal and economic austerity is the order of the day. The benefits of each dollar must be stretched as far as we can take them. We now face the need to shift from a purely legislatively-dominated approach to public works at the national level to one in which the Executive Branch provides a disciplined base of analysis and priorities designed to ensure public works expenditures that meet the long-term needs of national economic renewal in phase with the shorter-term needs of economic policy dictated by the rise and fall of the economic cycle. Such reforms are possible, will save money, and make the capital we have go further.

But how can we find the capital we need to meet all of the competing demands in the 1980s?

FOOTNOTES TO CHAPTER 2

1. Schwartz, Gail Garfield and Choate, Pat, *Being Number One: Rebuilding the U.S. Economy,* Lexington Books, Lexington, Massachusetts, 1980.

2. U.S. Bureau of Labor Statistics, *Productivity and the Economy,* Bulletin 1926, Washington, D.C., 1979.

3. *Statistical Abstract,* 1979, p. 288.

4. Vernez, George; Vaughan, Roger; Burright, Burke; and Coleman, Sinclair, *Regional Cycles and Employment Effects of Public Works Investments,* The Rand Corporation, Santa Monica, California, January, 1977, pp. v–xx.

5. United States Department of Commerce, *Industrial Location Determinants,* 1971–1975, Washington, D.C., 1973.

6. Sulvetta, Anthony, *Public Works as Countercyclical Assistance,* Office of Management and Budget, Executive Office of the President of the United States, Washington, D.C., November, 1979.

7. *A Study of Public Works Investment in the United States,* pp. 14–18.

8. Vaughan, Roger, *Public Works as a Countercyclical Tool,* Joint Economic Committee of the Congress of the United States, September, 1980.

9. *Statistical Abstract,* 1979, p. 292.

10. *Regional Cycles and Employment Effects of Public Works Investments, and Public Works as Countercyclical Assistance.*

3

FINANCING PUBLIC WORKS IN THE '80s: THE COMPETITION FOR CAPITAL

In the 1980s, the competition for financial capital will be intense. The private sector will require substantial investment in order to regain its competitive edge in both domestic and international markets. The re-tooling and modernization of many of our basic industries is imperative. General Motors alone is now engaged in a five-year re-tooling effort that will cost over $40 billion. The capital requirements of high technology firms that will create a large portion of the jobs of the future will be still greater. But at the same time, our public infrastructure must be renovated and upgraded. Otherwise many of our efforts in economic renewal will be thwarted and community services will deteriorate even further.

At present it is difficult to even estimate the range of potential investments that will be required for public facilities. This reflects:(a) the absence of national capital budgeting; (b) the absence of common standards for public works facilities and the services they provide; (c) inadequate information on the inventory and condition of existing facilities and the costs of repair; and (d) the lack of a political consensus on what types of projects should receive priorities.

Even though the magnitude of the problem cannot be specified, it is obvious the public works investment requirements for the 1980s will far exceed the investment levels of the 1970s. Clearly not all needed projects can be funded. Too many other compelling public and private uses of capital exist. A number of difficult strategic choices must be made. The first is to determine how much of the Gross National Product (GNP) is to be allocated to consumption and how much encouraged into savings for new capital investment. The second is to determine how much of that capital investment will be used by the public sector and how much by the private sector. The third set of choices involves the allocation of what will inevitably be limited public works funds among specific places and classes of projects.

INVESTMENT VERSUS CONSUMPTION

For at least two decades, in both the public and private sectors, we have favored consumption over investment. Relative levels of the GNP devoted to real

30

private sector investment in production have declined. So too have real levels of investment in public works. While the nation has been able to live off its past accomplishments for a brief period of time by deferring capital investment to subsidize current consumption, we have come to the point when maintaining even the status quo will require substantial increases in both the real levels of investment, public and private, and the share of GNP devoted to it.

Since the end of the Second World War, private sector fixed capital investment has been approximately 10 percent of the annual GNP.[1] But this figure masks a decline in real productive investment as the private sector has been forced by regulation to divert some of its capital into non-productive activities. For example, environmental investments made by private firms in the United States in 1979 exceeded $23 billion—10 percent of the total capital investment made that year by the private sector. Occupational safety and other regulations similarly diverted capital.

The diversion of this capital away from production-related activities would be of secondary consequence *if* there had been corresponding increases in the relative levels of the GNP devoted to capital investment. Unfortunately, there have not been. The share of GNP devoted to private sector fixed capital investment has not appreciably changed in recent years. As discussed in Chapter 2, the rate and levels of capital investment in public facilities has continuously dropped since the mid-1960s. Investment in public facilities accounted for 44 percent less of the GNP in 1977 than in 1965.

Increasing the shares of the GNP used for investment will strike hard at both public and private consumption. Many individuals will experience deferred growth in wages, dividends and other income and thus postponed personal consumption, while those resources flow into new facilities. Progress in environmental protection might also have to be slowed in order to increase the allocation of capital to productive investment. As distasteful as such sacrifices might be, they are certain to be much less painful than the long-term consequences that will result from the continued deterioration of the economy and the public facilities that undergird it.

CAPITAL ALLOCATIONS BETWEEN THE PRIVATE AND PUBLIC SECTORS

The allocation of investment capital between public and private uses raises a nettlesome challenge for the decade. Traditionally, government has been able to determine its share of capital through the preemptive use of its taxing and borrowing powers. Over the past five decades, government has also increased its role in promoting and enforcing a hierarchy of uses of capital *within* the private sector. Mandated safety and environmental investments

31

are only a few of the many examples of government-encouraged or directed uses of private capital.

Rationalizing capital allocations among and between the private and public sectors will be difficult because: (1) public and private capital investments are intertwined; and (2) the present government interventions that influence capital allocations are random. In the 1980s, the federal government must reduce many of its influences over private investment decisions, let the "market" better work its will, and simultaneously define and adopt more coherent policies and management practices to guide those interventions affecting capital allocations that it must, of necessity, continue.

In a decade of intense competition for capital, governments at all levels will have to carefully assess the consequences of their interventions for economic productivity in general. They will also find it essential to carefully plan and budget the claims they must make in the capital market to finance the renovation and construction of public infrastructure essential to bolster that private productivity and provide essential community services.

Several actions will be necessary to meet these objectives:

■ Better uses of existing financing mechanisms and new approaches to the long-term financing of capital improvements will have to be explored.

■ To help establish true priorities for public works improvements, financing and use of facilities may have to be more clearly related to each other. Too often under the pluralism of our federal system, those who benefit from an improvement and those who pay are not the same. In some cases, that is defensible public policy. But often it is not.

■ Inefficiencies and fraud that waste a substantial share of each public works dollar must be substantially reduced or eliminated.

■ Rigorously drawn long-term capital budgets that can accommodate shorter-term counter-cyclical policies are essential if public facilities investments are to be disciplined so that they do not subvert private investment requirements in capital markets.

■ A clear definition of who is responsible for what will be essential to ensure full accountability and effectiveness. (What public facilities might be provided more effectively and efficiently through private firms? What are the public works responsibilities of the federal government that are distinct from those of state and local governments?)

CAPITAL ALLOCATION AMONG PLACES

The final and perhaps most sensitive—even volatile—sets of allocation choices concern the division of public works funds among places. In allocating public works funds among places two issues appear relevant. First, public works investments in themselves can do little to reverse structural economic change or induce individuals back to places they have left. Too many other forces are involved.

For example, even with decades of investment in rural areas, little was accomplished by attempts to alter the flow of persons and economic activity back into those areas. When such change finally did occur, it was largely the consequence of other more powerful demographic and economic forces such as people desiring retirement homes in warm climates and structural shifts in economic production due to alterations in factors of production such as costs of labor. These structural forces must be carefully identified and analyzed to determine their implications on public works policies. For example, rebuilding or even rehabilitating much of the infrastructure in many cities will not in itself offset such broader structural forces as the availability of energy, the costs of labor, or the transportation differentials created by shifting markets. In such circumstances strategies are required to help accommodate to smaller populations and different forms of economic growth. Such strategies should guide market forces by smoothing out their rough edges, rather than by attempting to reverse them. Public works investments should support new realities. This will not only ease the pains of transition and speed it along, it will also reduce the backlog of public works investments.

Setting priorities in the use of public works funds will be a neccesity in an era of increasingly scarce public resources. For example, should the nation complete the remaining 1,500 miles of the Interstate Highway System at approximately $75 billion of cost or use part of those funds to do all or some of the $33 billion of bridge repairs now needed, accelerate industrial water and waste water treatment facility construction, or some combination of these and other alternatives? Or should new construction with federal funds be de-emphasized to provide more balance with needs for rehabilitation, maintenance, and operations? While some parts of the nation, such as the South and West, require new facilities, other regions need funds for rehabilitation and maintenance.

FINANCING OUR PUBLIC WORKS NEEDS

Many states and localities have fallen back on the "soft" option—deferring maintenance in order to meet current operating costs and to balance their budgets. Now we are compelled to deal with the inevitable result of delayed upkeep: replacement, reconstruction, or abandonment.

As cities and states became dependent on intergovernmental grants-in-aid for capital investment (federal grants provided ten percent of state-local capital expenditures in 1957, but now exceed 40 percent), they grew highly susceptible to the biases reflected in federal programs.[2] The most pronounced of these biases has been towards new construction. Many federal programs do not permit the use of funds for maintenance. Substantial under-maintenance has resulted in many fiscally stressed cities. Pagano and Moore found that those public works activities financed by user charges are far less susceptible to inadequate maintenance than those financed from general funds, particularly in fiscally distressed cities.[3] Boston and New Orleans, with dedicated revenue sources, were better able to maintain water services and facilities than other cities using general revenues.

The choice of mixes in the use of limited funds among types of public works projects and among the various public works functions is made difficult in the absence of: (1) a framework for decisions; (2) basic information on the existence of facilities, the quality of services they provide, and construction/service standards; and (3) cost estimates. Such limitations seriously cripple efforts to assess the consequences of these decisions on both the private sector and other government functions.

The potential sources of public works financing such as privatization, user charges, debt financing, and tax-based federal, state, and local financing require a careful re-examination. For example, substantial increases in certain forms of local taxes to finance public works may deter private sector investment. Conversely, an increase in federal public works expenditures may require reductions in other federal state and local expenditures unless better modes of financing are developed.

The federal government finances many of the public works for which it is directly responsible through direct appropriations, such as those for the Corps of Engineers. Others it finances out of capital markets such as those of the Tennessee Valley Authority. Many cities are being forced out of the bond market because of high interest rates, a "tightness" caused by the sale of pollution control bonds, and the expanded and often promiscuous use of industrial revenue bonds. Many smaller communities are also finding that small bond issues present such high transaction costs (law fees, underwriting expenses, printing, etc.) that they are effectively excluded from the market. A number of ways exist to facilitate access to private bond markets by smaller communities. One is the creation of consolidated bond sales (several communities going together in order to reduce transaction costs). A number of states, such as Florida, have supported such efforts and have established the necessary financing mechanisms to achieve this goal.

National, regional, or state "development banks" have been proposed from time to time to improve access to capital markets and lower transaction costs. The National Public Advisory Committee on Regional Development reviewed the diverse array of options for creating a National Development Bank and a potential Reconstruction Finance Corporation. After public hearings and analysis, that body of public officials, bankers, and public administrators concluded that such a mechanism is needed and if created should operate much like the Federal Land Bank. It should provide *access* to capital markets for communities and states (particularly smaller places), should *only* be used for capital construction or rehabilitation, and should charge interest rates which reflect *market* prices. The advantage of such a mechanism would be *guaranteed* access to monies for needed facilities, reduced transaction costs, a long-term pay back schedule, and the longer-term capitalization of some interest in order to provide "patient" capital in the early years of a project's life.[4]

Since about half of all federal funds for public works are disbursed to state and local governments for improvements, administrative requirements under these programs must be evaluated to determine their influences on the renovation of vital infrastructure. Requirements that investments be targeted on needy neighborhoods under the Community Development Block Grant Program have prevented the use of these funds for renovation of urban infrastructure on any scale significant to economic renewal.[5]

Increased Application of User Charges   While user charges are an accustomed method of financing many public services, there are many instances in which their expanded and creative use could result in more effective financing and more efficient management.

The General Accounting Office's (GAO) analysis of the need for additional federal aid for urban water distribution systems concluded that, where fee-for-service financing existed, as in Boston and New Orleans, management was better.[6] Actions were taken to improve conservation, reduce leakage, and control other non-revenue producing water uses, such as illegal hydrant openings and meter underregistration. Conversely, cities such as Washington, D.C., whose water programs are financed from general revenues, give little attention to leakage or even such issues as more consistent collection of existing water fees. For example, the GAO found that in 1972, 35 percent of Washington, D.C.'s water distribution mains needed replacement, cleaning, or lining. By 1980, over 50 percent of these mains required reconstruction.

In the southwestern United States, the sale of municipal water is often a principal source of community revenues—particularly in smaller communities.

The use of fee-for-service charges improves access to capital markets because of a dedicated, guaranteed flow of revenues. They also have the virtue of more directly relating prices to consumption and real costs. Many cities, such as New York City, do not meter sales of water. Metering would eliminate much waste and could obviate some of the demand for construction of expensive, supplemental supply systems. Where the cost of providing meters is prohibitive, other alternatives can be devised. User charges can adversely affect low income citizens, but in those circumstances, special income adjustments for the poor can be created.

Privatizing Public Still another alternative worthy of consid-
Facilities eration is private operation of some
facilities that in recent decades have been
the responsibility of the public sector. Earlier in this century, the private construction and operation of water supply systems was common. More recently, we have seen private contractors as alternatives in the delivery of many services to public agencies. Competition in garbage collection, fire protection, street cleaning, and parcel delivery are examples. This model can apply to the construction and operation of many kinds of public facilities as well.

The Advisory Commission on Intergovernmental Relations (ACIR) and the International City Managers Association (ICMA) have both conducted surveys to measure cities' reliance on and preference for the use of private sector firms to provide select public services.[7] Of 2,650 cities surveyed by ACIR, over 36 percent of the respondents indicated a preference for contracting with a private firm for the provision of services rather than shifting or giving the responsibilities to government agencies. The ICMA survey of 379 cities determined that 225 respondents were already using private firms in their productivity programs—particularly in solid waste collection and disposal; street maintenance and construction; hospital construction and operation; and public transit.

The use of private firms is influenced by a number of historical, political, and economic considerations. Many cities are using private firms for waste collection and disposal because private firms can secure necessary capital funds irrespective of local expenditure limits. In the past many hospitals were established by or purchased by communities because of the inability of the private sector to raise necessary capital. Today, with revenue generating abilities of government increasingly constrained, such facilities are starting to revert back to private ownership and operation.

Private firms provide a means to escape the excessive rigidities of overly-bureaucratized public agencies and public labor-management problems. Private firms can sometimes be more efficient and operate at less cost than public agencies because of their ability to swiftly introduce new technology; their greater flexibility in the use of worker incentives; their ability to eliminate or reduce an unneeded service by simply not continuing a contract; and their often superior understanding of economies of scale and specialization. The ability of private firms to provide better, less costly services will vary between specific functions and areas.

The potential for privatizing public services must be gauged realistically. It is wise to remember that many facilities and services once privately and now publicly provided were converted because of abuse and corruption in the private sector and many private sector operations are inching slowly toward the public sector today. The conversion of many of the bankrupt railroads into quasi-public entities such as CONRAIL and AMTRAK are but two of the more glaring reminders. Federal loan guarantees to major corporations in economic trouble provide more evidence of this drift in the other direction.

Privatization is not an option in all circumstances. There will always be situations in which the private sector is unable to provide profitably many basic services such as water, electricity, or waste disposal. The arguments most often advanced against the use of privatization include:

■ Poorer service and greater consumer expense because of the need for profits.
■ Problems of controlling, monitoring and evaluating the performance of contractors.
■ Private sector graft—collusion among bidders and bribery of public officials.
■ Problems of preparing enforceable contracts.
■ The often fierce opposition from government workers and unions.

The U.S. Chamber of Commerce suggests five basic steps for exploring the potential of privatization:
■ Identify to what extent federal, state and local laws restrict or promote the use of private firms for the provision of select services.
■ Determine if there are a sufficient number of firms qualified to provide the service under reasonable terms.
■ Ascertain whether bidding and procurement procedures are so formidable that private firms will be deterred.
■ Determine whether public authorities are given preference over private firms.
■ Determine if adequate and reasonable performance measures have been identified. If performance or incentive contracts are to be used, such standards are absolutely necessary. However, without such standards, any firm providing such services would either be at risk or the public sector would risk not getting their money's worth.[8]

There is limited information on the effectiveness of privatization and the specific circumstances in which it is most appropriate. There is also limited agreement on which types of facilities and services should be provided by the private sector. Yet privatization offers a potentially important means for government to move toward a system in which public facilities and services receive priorities reflected in the realities of what the market will support. It also has the virtue of relating more directly those who pay with those who benefit.

Interim Privatization   There are other alternatives. One is to grant licenses and rights of eminent domain to an authority or private company to permit them to finance and construct a facility, operate it with user charges until the investment is returned and a profit is secured, and then turn ownership over to the public. The major highway between Dallas and Fort Worth, Texas was financed, built, and operated in this manner.

A more extensive privatization scheme has been suggested by *The Economist* for use in Great Britain.[9] It is applicable in the United States as well. The private sector would construct, rehabilitate, maintain, and operate a city's sewers or streets or municipal buildings with debt which is privately raised and held. The city would repay the cost of the debt over a fixed period of time, such as 10 or 20 years, at the end of which the government would own the facility.

This arrangement could be attractive to the private sector—and not only for its likely tax advantages by collateralizing select facilities and income flows. By earmarking user fees and being willing to guarantee where necessary limited annual supplemental payments, the private firms would be assured of securing excellent financial ratings and lowered borrowing costs. For cities with poor bond ratings, these savings could be substantial.

Such an approach would be attractive to communities for several reasons. First, necessary capital expenditures could be made more quickly than otherwise possible, particularly in hard-pressed places. Second, assigning a private firm the responsibilities to collect user charges and maintain the facility would likely result in both a higher collection rate and better maintained facilities. Third, such financing could reduce the financing burdens placed on city budgets.

But it is unlikely that the public sector will be willing to accept departures in present policies unless it can be assured of more effective uses of public works dollars than the present policies and practices have yielded.

FOOTNOTES TO CHAPTER 3

1. *Being Number One: Rebuilding the U.S. Economy.*

2. *A Study of Public Works Investment in the United States,* p. 15.

3. Pagano, Michael, A., and Moore Richard J., "Emerging Issues in Financing Basic Infrastructure," an unpublished paper, 1980.

4. United States Department of Commerce, *Recommendations of the National Public Advisory Committee on Regional Development,* Washington, D.C., 1977.

5. Henry, Patrick J., "Removing Internal Restrictions in the CDBG Program to Permit More Creative Uses by Local Governments," an unpublished paper, the Academy for Contemporary Problems, Washington, D.C., November, 1980.

6. *Additional Federal Aid for Urban Water Distribution Systems Should Wait Until Needs are Clearly Established.* p. i–v.

7. The Chamber of Commerce of the United States, *Improving Local Government Fiscal Management,* Washington, D.C., pp. 32–35.

8. *Improving Local Government Fiscal Management.*

9. The Economist, "How to Privatise Public Investment," London, United Kingdom, December 5, 1980, p. 20.

4

GETTING MORE FOR THE PUBLIC WORKS DOLLAR: REDUCING THE COST OF DELAY

The nation can get much more from the public works dollars it is spending. To do so, we must attack:

■ The losses resulting from delay (about one-fifth of the $80 billion in annual public works appropriations);

■ The losses resulting from the misuse of funds; and

■ The losses resulting from wasteful management and bad planning.

THE COSTS OF DELAY   In the 1960s, an electric power plant could be constructed in less than five years. Today, more than 12 years are required. The Tennessee Valley Authority (TVA) is currently experiencing an average eight-year delay in seven major power plants—a delay which has almost trebled construction costs by raising costs an additional $11 billion.[1] This is a good example of what happens when we neglect the consequences of mismanaging time. Time is, indeed, money.

The time consumed in building major projects is increasingly determined by government regulations and requirements. Yet, public administrators have tended to be ignorant of or insensitive to the costs and consequences of delays in their administrative, financial, regulatory and legal decisions. Unnecessary delays are decreasing real capital investment as funds are diverted to the nonproductive task of financing increased interest charges generated when projects take longer to put into operation. Additional funds are required to keep pace with inflation-devalued public works purchasing power as delays put off construction. Financing delay has become a major levy on available monies for public works. About 20 percent ($16 billion) of the nation's annual public works appropriations are now used for such financing—a major and unnecessary waste of shrinking public capital.[2]

Yet, in the past, government and business have often successfully met tight schedules. An American was placed on the Moon in less than a decade. The new Smithsonian Air and Space Museum was constructed on time and under budget. But to ensure that such performance becomes the norm rather than the exception, major reforms are needed.

There are no reliable statistics on the time allocated to the many

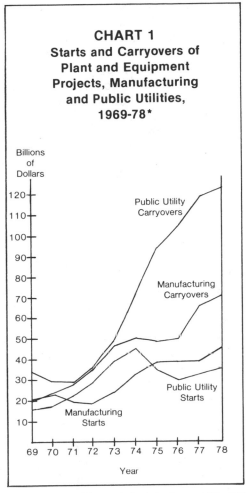

CHART 1
Starts and Carryovers of
Plant and Equipment
Projects, Manufacturing
and Public Utilities,
1969-78*

Source: Bureau of Economic Analysis, **Survey of Current Business**, June, 1969—78.

*Starts represent new construction. Carryovers represent expenditures to be incurred for plant and equipment at the end of the first quarter of each year.

phases of public works projects, i.e., research, design financing, and approval. However, there is reliable information on the construction phase in both the public and private sectors. Since the mid-1960s, the Bureau of Economic Analysis of the Department of Commerce has annually reported the aggregate value of public and private construction starts, as well as the cumulative value of uncompleted construction carried over into each new year (Chart 1).

41

In the period 1969-1978, the Bureau reported substantial increases in the value of annual construction carry-overs, which reflect (1) increases in the cost of starts; (2) increases in the costs of projects; and (3) the additional time required to complete projects.

The most spectacular increase of carry-overs compared to the value of starts has been in public utility construction. In 1969, there were about $19 billion in carry-overs from 1968 and about $15 billion in new public utility starts. This represented a ratio of carry-overs to starts of 1.2 to 1. By 1978, there were approximately $122 billion in carry-overs from 1977, and $35 billion in new starts. Thus, within a decade, the carry-over-to-starts ratio in this industry has almost tripled, rising to 3.5 to 1. In large measure these delays were due to the dramatic expansion of time required to complete new electric generating plants—five years in the late 1960s as compared with 12 years a decade later.

Another measure of delay can be obtained by analyzing the time lags in the disbursements of funds for public construction programs. Presently, many agencies require six or more years to disburse a single fiscal year's appropriations—even after the funds have been committed to specific projects (Table 11). For example, although the Economic Development Administration has one of the federal government's better construction management programs, projects now require one year between approval and construction bids. By contrast the GAO found that of the 77 projects for which the Corps of Engineers completed survey investigation or design phases during fiscal years 1975, 1976, and 1977, an average of *26 years* was required after initial authorization before construction began. Over 12 years were used for planning and 14 years for reviews and appropriations.[3] HUD's Community Development Block Grant Program has a construction backlog equal to three years of that program's annual budget for construction.[4] The Environmental Protection Agency has a backlog of construction projects exceeding $8 billion—a backlog equal to two full years of appropriations.[5] Many public works projects funded at least a decade ago are still unfinished.

Similar delays are found in virtually all federal, state, and local public works construction programs. In aggregate, the value of projects in the public works pipeline now exceeds over $100 billion (Table 12).

CAUSES OF DELAY In a complex world, some delay is justified to allow the consequences of an action to be adequately considered. But managerial indifference is too often the cause. This indifference is often equated with "prudence," or with being a "part of the system." Consequently, little is done to bring delay under control. Instead, poor planning, unbounded time consumed in decisionmaking, changing regulations, increased

42

Table 11
Disbursement Rates for the Community Development Block Grant Program, Local Public Works, and the Economic Development Administration's Title I Public Works Programs

Year	CDBG[a]	LPW[b]	EDA - Title I[c]
	Rate at Which One Year of Funding is Disbursed		
1	2.6	9.75	4.2
2	30.2	50.95	29.9
3	48.3	29.00	39.9
4	15.4	5.97	4.4
5	5.5	3.33	7.7
6	0	1.0	5.7

a. The Department of Housing and Urban Development's Community Development Block Grant Program. These data include both construction and non-construction activities. At present, this program has a backlog of approximately $6 billion—about one-third of the total funds appropriated since FY 1974. Of this backlog approximately 55 percent are earmarked for construction. Since this program invests only 25-30 percent of its annual appropriations in capital items, the backlog represents almost three years of capital funding.

b. LPW disbursement rates are calculated from the budgetary data presented in the *Budget of the United States* for the years 1977-81. Since the LPW program was initiated in the middle of two different fiscal years, these data are an aggregate of the speed with which funds were expended.

c. EDA Public Works drawdown rates are calculated on the basis of EDA disbursements as of January 15, 1980. Since these calculations are based upon the first quarter of FY 1980, these estimates slightly overstate the disbursement rates of the program. The EDA totals do not add to 100 since there are funds as yet undisbursed for fiscal years prior to FY 1974.

litigation, and chaotic administration are the real culprits in expanding the time required to plan and construct necessary public works projects.

Pre-Construction Delays

The primary source of construction delays is found in the pre-construction stage of projects. Essentially the sources of these construction delays are:

■ *Lack of Specific Time Limits*—Many regulatory functions are conducted with virtually no time limits. For example, licensing or zoning applications may pend for years before decisions are rendered. Government actually encourages delay, since there are high penalties for government officials if mistakes are made in accelerating projects.

■ *Institutional Fragmentation*—Often, more than one government agency is involved in a specific project or activity. For example, most

Table 12
The Value of the Public Works Pipeline
(Billions of Dollars)

Fiscal Year	Value of Public Works	Present Value of Backlog
1980	$ 45.0	$ 43.7
1979	45.0	30.2
1978	45.0	10.4
1977	43.4	5.6
1976-70	249.1	14.9
TOTAL	$487.5	$101.8

SOURCE: These are estimated values. The base value of the public works pipeline is the actual amount of capital construction expenditures as reported by the U.S. Bureau of the Census in the *Statistical Abstract of the United States, 1979* for all governments (federal, state, and local)—Table 478. This value does not include land costs or most equipment included in these projects. The value of public works construction for 1978 is unpublished data supplied by the Census. Values for 1979 and 1980 are estimates.

The present value of the national public works backlog is calculated on the basis of the following disbursement rates: Year 1—3 percent; Year 2—30 percent; Year 3—44 percent; Year 4—10 percent; Year 5—7 percent; and Years 6-10—a residual rate of 6 percent. These disbursements rates are the average of those found in public works programs of the Department of Commerce's Economic Development Administration and the Department of Housing and Urban Development's Community Development Block Grant Program.

These estimates are based on the value of the backlog as of 1 October 1980.

public works projects require at least 16 federal certifications—many from a variety of agencies and many of which have different procedures and criteria for decisionmaking.

Also decisions are often made at different managerial levels and in different geographic locations. The conflicts created by this fragmentation are almost always left to the state and local governments to resolve.

■ *Documentation Delay*—All levels of government require documentation for public works projects. Often state and local requirements are more time consuming than their federal counterparts.

■ *Judicial Delays*—A wide array of legislation gives citizens and public interest groups easy access to court action. Often suits are filed by opponents of projects to delay construction and to shift costs so as to assure that a project never leaves the drawing board.

Although responsibility for pre-construction delays is shared by all levels of governments, an increasing body of evidence suggests that much of it is at the local level. An analysis of delays in the construction grants program of the Environmental Protection Agency has identified four fundamental sources of pre-construction delays: (1) real property acquisitions (including easements); (2) lack of local funding; (3) difficulty in negotiating service agreements; and (4) slow historical resource investigations.[6]

The Department of Housing and Urban Development's Community Development Block Grant (CDBG) has experienced similar delays with local governments, and has concluded that the primary causes for delays were (1) inadequate local project planning; and (2) local bureaucratic red tape (Table 13).

The delays caused by inadequate planning reflect the fact that at the local level many federal grants for specific local public works projects are made on the basis of "concepts" rather than actual projects. More specifically, funds are provided for a project idea; the community then produces a detailed plan, secures architectural and engineering designs, gets clearances and approvals, secures local funds, buys land, lets bids, and awards contracts. During this preparatory period, the project funds remain warehoused, and lose purchasing power as inflation erodes their value.

Implementation of the CDBG program at the local level has been hindered by numerous interagency procedures, local approval requirements, and local political conflicts. HUD also found most local governments to be well-versed in the requirements of the federal government, such as Bacon-Davis standards and environmental protection rules, but often ignorant of their own local and state laws and regulations.

Delays in the Construction Process

Actual delays in constructing a project are a minor source of the overall delay. There are exceptions, of course, such as the construction of the new Hart Senate Office Building, which will require seven to ten years to complete. However, the majority of the public works projects require only 6 to 21 months to complete once construction begins. (Table 14).

THE CONSEQUENCES OF DELAYED PUBLIC WORKS CONSTRUCTION

Unnecessary delays have many direct and and indirect effects on the national economy, including diminished purchasing power and productivity growth; postponed benefits; uncertainty and a loss of confidence in the public sector.

45

Table 13
Principal Delay Factors in the Community Development Block Grant Program

Factors Associated With Project Start Up	Factors Associated With Project Approval	Factors Associated With Project Operation
Local approval requirements (e.g., commission and legislative bodies)	Local political debate over project (e.g., involving major/council/commissioners)	Civil rights compliance
Condemnation process preceding acquisition	Citizen complaints	Davis-Bacon requirements
Environmental review process	Lawsuits	State requirements
Citizen participation process	Negotiations with HUD	Staff capabilities
Administrative factors (inter-agency cooperation, contracting procedures, etc.)		Project costs
Arrival of other federal funds to match		Local bookkeeping methods for transfer of funds
Need to secure private financial commitments		Urban county procedures for reimbursing cooperating jurisdictions
Planning, design, and implementation after HUD approval		
Urban renewal local approval requirements		
Weather		

Source: Unpublished data, U.S. Department of Housing and Urban Development, Washington, D.C., 1980.

Diminished
Purchasing Power
Delay diminishes purchasing power during a period of inflation. For at least the past decade the rate of inflation in the construction industry has been higher than general price increases. Thus delayed projects become more costly to build—diverting funds from other potential uses. At present the backlog of public works in the United States that have been funded, but are not yet completed or under construction, represent a $100 billion pool of funds that is diminishing in value every day. In such a circumstance delay is very expensive in terms of lost purchasing power.

Postponed Benefits
When delay postpones the benefits of projects, economic and social side effects can be serious. For example, as the TVA has had to postpone its construction of new power plants, it has both substantially increased capital costs and deferred the operation of a major source of nonpetroleum electric generation.

San Bernadino's experience in delaying construction of a series of community and service centers for the elderly is another example of postponed benefits *and* the loss of purchasing power. In 1975, that county government decided to build the centers for the elderly, but elected to accumulate construction funds for them at the rate of one-third of total project costs per year. By the time the funds were accumulated, the county found the monies it had set aside were inadequate to finance the program—inflation had done its magic. Thus, the county was obliged to decide whether to reduce the size of the centers, to cancel some of them, or to divert funds from other projects to complete the project.

Uncertainty and
Loss of Confidence
Major public works projects are increasingly affected by litigation, by changing social and political conditions, by changing technology, by changing public regulatory actions, and by inflation. As the time required to complete a project is extended, the project is exposed to increasing uncertainties and risks.

The construction of any major waterway, flood control project, mass transit system, reservoir, or highway provides examples of projects initiated and constructed under conditions of growing uncertainty. As time needed for pre-construction activities continues to expand, construction cost containment is virtually impossible. Construction firms cannot negotiate long-term, fixed-fee contracts because of inflation. Also regulatory requirements change and there is little assurance that today's requirements will be the same tomorrow.

Moreover, major projects require political, social and economic accord which is difficult to maintain when conditions of uncertainty exist.

47

Table 14
Duration of Construction, by Type of Public Works Project

	Construction time distribution (months)	Total Duration in Months	Total On-site Man-hours[a]	Range of Construction Time
Building Construction				
Private one-family housing		4.8	37.5	NA
Public housing	10.4, 21.6, 27.3, 23.2, 15.1	14.8	52.9	NA
Schools	15.6, 26.9, 32.6, 22.2	12.0	39.3	NA
Hospitals	6.5, 12.4, 16.5, 19.3, 17.6, 14.9, 9.8, 3.0	21.0	43.4	10-47
Nursing		13.4	42.0	NA
College housing	11.1, 22.4, 31.3, 25.4, 9.6	13.4	43.7	4-22
Federal office buildings	6.8, 15.3, 20.5, 23.0, 21.8, 12.0, .6	16.8	41.9	9-31
Heavy Construction				
Sewer lines	27.0, 41.1, 26.4, 5.5	9.5	45.0	NA
Sewer plants	45.7, 47.3	6.5	43.4	NA
Land operations[b]	27.5, 33.5, 26.0, 13.0	11.1	52.2	2-30
Dredging[c]	39.5, 44.0, 16.5	6.7	82.3	2-16

Axis (months): 3, 6, 9, 12, 15, 18, 21

48

Sources: *Labor and Material Requirements for Construction of Private Single-Family Houses, 1972*, BLS Bulletin 1755, p. 5; *Labor and Material Requirements for Public Housing Construction 1968, 1974*, BLS Bulletin 1821, pp. 6-7; *Labor and Material Requirements for School Construction, June 1968*, BLS Bulletin 1586, pp. 7, 17; *Labor and Material Requirements for Hospital and Nursing Home Construction, 1971*, BLS Bulletin 1691, pp. 14-15; *Labor and Material Requirements for College Housing Construction, May 1965*, BLS Bulletin 1441, pp. 24-25; *Labor Requirements for Federal Office Building Construction, 1962*, BLS Bulletin 1331, pp. 26-27; *Labor and Material Requirements for Sewer Works Construction, 1966*, Bulletin 1490, p. 18; *Labor and Material Requirements for Civil Works Construction by the Corps of Engineers, 1964*, BLS Bulletin 1390, pp. 19-20.

NOTES: Figures in italics indicate percentage of total on-site man-hours spent in quarter. NA means not available.

a. For each $1000 of contract costs, measured in 1974 dollars.

b. Land operations, as defined by the Bureau of Labor Statistics, include 28 civil works projects: large earth-filled dams (3 projects), small earth-filled dams (1 project), pile dikes (5 projects), levees (7 projects), revetments (5 projects), and four miscellaneous projects—channel improvement, jetties, outlet channel, and sea wall extension.

c. Dredging includes 15 projects, of two different types: hydraulic, in which a dredge equipped with a cutterhead pumps soft material through a pipeline to a disposal area, usually on-shore; and the second type, in which soft or broken hard material is loaded into scows and taken to a disposal area, usually in deep water. The sample projects are the same as those used in the Haveman and Krutilla study.

Source: Vernez, Georges; Vaughn, Roger; Burright, Burke; and Coleman Sinclair, *Regional Cycles and Employment Effects of Public Works Investments*, The Rand Corporation, Santa Monica, California, January 1977.

The private sector is affected by uncertainty as well. Firms are reluctant to invest in ventures dependent on public infrastructure that is either nonexistent or in poor repair. Ultimately, uncertainty causes a loss of public confidence in government and in government leaders.

REFORMS Unnecessary delays can be eliminated. Several basic reforms are necessary to control time management—some of them can be accomplished quickly; others will take time. All are important.

Short-Term Actions The first and most needed short-term action is to reduce the $100 billion backlog in the public works pipeline. Since the majority of the funds in this backlog represents appropriated, but unused federal funds, the principal responsibility for identifying and initiating reforms resides with the Office of Management and Budget and the respective federal agencies. State and local agencies should be involved when appropriate. The following actions might be taken:

1. Identify the backlog of public works obligations by fiscal year, by specific project, and by specific funding agency.

2. Divide these obligated, but undisbursed, funds into five categories:

A. Projects which are permanently stalled.

B. Projects which are salvageable, but are stalled due to a variety of factors (lack of local matching funds; inability to meet regulatory requirements; rising construction costs; etc.).

C. Projects under construction but which could be accelerated in order to reduce or eliminate further delay.

D. Projects that are on schedule but which require no action.

E. Projects on schedule but which could be accelerated.

Those projects already funded which appear to be terminally stalled should be closely assessed by the individual funding agencies. If there is no, or only a remote, possibility that these individual projects will enter the construction stage within a specific time, such as nine months, the funds allocated to these projects should be de-obligated and re-programmed so that other projects can make use of these funds.

In order that communities with stalled projects are not unduly penalized, the funding agency could create procedures for re-funding the project within a specified period of time, such as two years. During that period, the community would have the right to re-assess the project. If it is determined to be still feasible and all requirements for construction are met, the de-obligated project would be given priority status for re-funding consideration.

Funds freed under such a de-obligation process could then be channeled to other projects ready for construction, could be used to fund new projects, or could be used to supplement existing programs which have been halted by inflation.

The backlogs under block grant programs, such as the CDBG of HUD and facilities grants from EPA, could be reduced through the use of a forward-funding concept. Using such an approach, communities able to use construction funds expeditiously could request and receive advance funding based on their future entitlements. Advance funds would come from the agency's existing backlog.

The expenditure of funded block grant programs, such as HUD's CDBG program and the construction programs of EPA, would produce substantial benefits including:
■ Increased purchasing power.
■ Improved services to the public.
■ Counter-cyclical employment in construction and construction-related industries.

A sound management action that can be taken is to identify systematically impediments to the construction of funded projects. These impediments should be analyzed to determine:
■ Their nature and source.
■ Organizations responsible for the delays.
■ Actions necessary to reduce or eliminate delays.
■ A timetable for project completion.
■ Actions necessary to change legislation, policies and operating procedures to eliminate future delays.

Such analysis could be rapidly completed given the expertise that does exist in the public works agencies.

Long-Term Actions   A number of long-term policy and administrative reforms to improve time management are both possible and appropriate. This can (1) reduce delay, and (2) minimize the cost of those delays which do occur.

Improved time management will involve many actions, some of which may seem unimportant but which in aggregate will reduce delay. For example, HUD has prepared a guide for local officials on streamlining land use regulations.[7] This guide identifies many small but important steps local officials can take to simplify land development reviews at the pre-application stage, at the staff review stage, and at the public official review stage. Many of these actions are simple, commonsense approaches—such as arranging an early pre-application conference between the applicant and staff persons from the reviewing departments of local government. The identification and resolution of dozens of small impediments can substantially reduce delay.

The following basic measures, coupled with dozens, even hundreds, of other ingenious implementing actions, can make substantial contributions to reducing government-induced delay.

51

■ *Creation of Public Works Time Management Standards and Monitoring Procedures.* Time management standards and procedures are needed throughout government. Reliable and consistent indicators for decisionmaking and government action can be established relatively inexpensively. When such information is available to administrators, to the Congress, and to the public, it will be possible to identify policy and administrative changes which can enhance program effectiveness and efficiency. A number of basic indicators are required for the creation of effective standards:

a. Chronological data are needed on time requirements for construction of various types of public works projects. These data will help in finding the causes for delay.

b. Time limitations for all applications for government funds should be established.

c. Deadlines should be established and monitored for the time consumed between project funding and actual expenditure.

d. Unexpended balances of funds in each program for present and past fiscal years must also be monitored. Using this information, accurate norms for expenditure rates could be created. Deviations would indicate the need for policy or administrative changes. These data are already available in each public works agency, but a standard format and reporting system are lacking.

■ *Create Personal and Institutional Incentive.* Among other considerations, public managers and employees must be rewarded or penalized according to how well they manage time.

Beneficiaries of federal and state grant-in-aid programs also need incentives for expeditious use of grants and other funds. Several such incentives are possible, and could include "use it or lose it" provisions linked to specific time frames and qualitative considerations. The impediment to such "either/or" incentives is legislation which does not permit reallocation of funds. For example, if EDA makes a public works grant commitment and the fiscal year ends before the funds are expended, those funds cannot be reallocated. If reprogramming were permitted, communities with inordinately slow expenditure rates could lose their grants and the unused monies transferred to areas where funds could be put to immediate use. The very existence of reprogramming possibilities could serve as an incentive to action. The effectiveness of this approach has been demonstrated in the Appalachian Regional Development Program.

Another possible means for creating incentives and simultaneously ensuring the efficient expenditures of funds is the use of previously described "forward-funding." Forward-funding would permit well managed communities to complete projects more rapidly, thus avoiding cost overruns caused by inflation. Slow draw-down communities would not be penalized more than they already are by their delays since they would retain the right to their entitlements. Their penalty would be the receipt of inflation-ravaged funds. At present levels of inflation, EPA would secure at least $1 billion of increased purchasing power annually from its $8 billion backlog by such an improved money management plan. This approach can be adapted by virtually every federal grant agency.

Agencies should also limit the amount of their funds that can be used for overruns. In most federal public works programs, over ten percent of all new public works funds are used to finance overruns on prior commitments. If the financing of overruns is shifted to state government and local communities, incentives for the expeditious use of funds are created. However, where delay is caused by the federal government, it should bear overrun costs.

■ *Improved Planning of Government Actions.* Government activities are often poorly planned. Short time horizons are the norm rather than the exception. Often little attention is given to indirect consequences of policies or actions. A major reform in HUD programs has been to require communities receiving CDBG funds to prepare a threeyear plan for projected use of these monies. This improved planning permits better citizen participation, better project consideration, and the more expeditious use of funds when they do become available. This form of planning is one of several reasons why HUD in the past two years has been able to accelerate the use of its funds.

The creation of two-step funding is another major innovation that would expedite the use of actual project funds. Small amounts of funds—as little as two percent of project costs—can be set aside very early for engineering, preliminary regulatory requirements and securing local matching funds. Major project funds would not be extended until these requisites had been met. Thus, when major funds are made available, they can be immediately used rather than being stored for one to three years. This pre-planning can significantly reduce delay and assist government to keep its money at work in projects—thus getting more for each dollar committed.

■ *Creation of Mediation Processes.* The federal government has long sponsored the Federal Mediation Service in the Department of Labor. This service uses both staff and consultants to assist in neutral mediation between management and labor. Using a variety of techniques they have assisted in resolving conflicts in hundreds of situations which otherwise would have been long delayed.

The mediation service is needed for public works and other projects which are stalled because of conflict. Examples of the range of disputes which can be settled through mediation are found in the experiences of the Institute for Environmental Mediation located in Seattle,

Washington. For example, a 1977 mediation process broke a six-year port development stalemate between development and environment advocates and the Port of Everett, Washington and a comprehensive development plan was created which was acceptable to all parties.

■ *Time-Bound Regulatory, Certification, Compliance and Permit Procedures.* Regulatory, certification, compliance, and permit procedures *must* have time limits. These limits must be reasonable, publicized, and firmly applied. When the limits are exceeded, the direct and indirect costs of delay should be calculated and individuals and organizations held responsible.

The federal government should require that *all* bureaucratic procedures be accomplished within specific time frames. This requirement, if further reinforced by legislation, would eliminate the burden of open-ended governmental decisionmaking on the construction industry in particular and on the business community in general.

■ *Simplify Government Regulatory, Certification, Compliance and Permit Procedures.* Regulatory, certification, compliance, and permit procedures need simplification. New York State has simplified the permit process for the private sector through the creation of an Office of Business Permits. This Office has a central inventory which identifies individual regulatory bodies in New York State, the types of activities for which permits are required, criteria for approval, costs involved, and the time required to secure permits. It also provides assistance to firms in meeting these requirements. Simultaneously it works with all state agencies, reviewing their permit processes in order to further simplify procedures and eliminate outmoded and burdensome requirements. Actions to create a simplified public works construction permit could include:

a. Creation of Office of Business Permits in most states to assist contractors in quickly meeting their requisites.

b. Simplification of federal, state and local certification and compliance requirements. This is an area with much potential for reducing delay. Presently, individual government agencies often have differing compliance requirements for the same legislation. Communities and businesses bear the direct expense and the cost of delay involved in meeting these multiple compliance and assurance standards which should be standarized so one certification is accepted by many agencies. Several federal agencies have begun this process in their funding of rural water and sewer projects. This overall responsibility would best be performed by OMB. It should be made one of the top priority items on OMB's agenda.

■ *Simplify and Streamline Appellate Procedures.* The appeals process requires simplification and streamlining. Under present laws and practices, motions to appeal government regulatory decisions are generally decided by the courts. Generally, these actions begin at the lower court level in the federal or state judicial system and work their way upward. Present appeals processes are time consuming, since fixed time schedules are rarely used. The process is made even more difficult and time consuming since appeals can be initiated in one of the many courts (scattered in several locations) with judges having little or no technical background on the questions at issue. There are a number of working models that could be adopted to expedite the appellate review process without sacrificing any quality of decisions—perhaps even improving the quality and consistency of decisions. For example, a streamlined appellate review process could be established. In such an approach, all appeals from permit or regulatory decisions in connection with a single development activity, such as land use regulation, could be combined in a single appellate review process. This would permit not only more expeditious decisions, but also the use of specialized staff and thus better decisions. Streamlined appellate processes can be structured while assuring access to all interested parties and therefore significantly reducing unnecessary and costly delay.

FOOTNOTES TO CHAPTER 4

1. Choate, Pat, *As Time Goes By: The Costs and Consequences of Delay,* The Academy for Contemporary Problems, Washington, D.C., 1980.

2. This is a calculated value based on a backlog of construction of $100 billion, an average delay per project of one year, construction and related inflation at 12 percent per year and interest rates for interim construction at 12 percent.

3. General Accounting Office, *Ways to Resolve Critical Water Resources Issues Facing the Nation,* Washington, D.C., p. 7.

4. United States Department of Housing and Urban Development, *CDBG Program Status by Government Unit,* Working Report, Washington, D.C., January, 1980.

5. United States Environmental Protection Agency, *Construction Grant Projects Not Under Construction,* Washington, D.C., June, 1980.

6. United States Environmental Protection Agency, *An Internal Analysis of the Causes of Construction Delays in the Construction Grant Projects,* (unpublished), Washington, D.C., 1980.

7. United States Department of Housing and Urban Development, *Local Capital Improvements and Development Management,* Washington, D.C., June, 1980.

5

GETTING MORE FOR THE PUBLIC WORKS DOLLAR: REDUCING FRAUD AND ADMINISTRATIVE WASTE

The precise magnitude of the funds lost through fraudulent practices or poor construction is impossible to estimate. The number of indictments and convictions for public works related fraud suggests that such fraud is widespread. Its reduction would be a major means of increasing the usable funds for public works projects. Any fraud or substandard construction is too much.

The problems include: (1) pay-offs, price-fixing, and influence peddling in the pre-construction stage; and (2) defective work, exhorbitant costs and extortion in the construction stage.

PRE-CONSTRUCTION FRAUD There are many kinds of illegal practices involved in zoning, land purchases, architectural/engineering awards, and construction contracts. In 1980 the Justice Department obtained indictments against 34 companies and 41 individuals in four states for conspiring to raise prices and allocate highway construction contracts. That investigation is continuing in other states.

Awards of architectural/engineering contracts on the basis of "contributions" to political parties is virtually institutionalized in many states and communities. The *Tennessee Journal* reports that architects and engineers seeking state business have known for decades that professional competence is not enough: political acceptability—as gauged by money contributions for gubernatorial and legislative races—is also required.[1]

In Massachusetts, the corruption commission found several instances of architectural firms generating substantial "political" funds from corporate monies—even though such corporate contributions have been illegal since 1946.

When firms "buy the job" through political contribution, the public can have little expectation that either the best firm has been chosen or that the public interest will be paramount in the subsequent construction. Such practices need not exist. Upon becoming Governor of Tennessee in 1979, Lamar Alexander reformed the process selection for architects and engineers used in state projects. By adapting selection guidelines prepared by the American Institute of Architects, a board chosen from professional organizations makes recommendations for the selection of architects and engineers. The state has also begun providing a public notification of proposed state construction projects. Previously, firms learned of potential projects from individuals and the relevant agencies on an ad hoc basis. The Commonwealth of Massachusetts is adopting major reforms in management of its public works expenditures, including creation of an independent inspector general.

CONSTRUCTION FRAUD AND POOR CONSTRUCTION   Fraudulent construction practices inflate project costs or result in deficient construction or both. A blue ribbon panel investigating bribery and corruption in award of public construction contracts in Massachusetts recently reported that over $6.4 billion of state and county building construction in the period 1968-1980 is defective, requiring repairs costing more than $2.1 billion (over $857 per Massachusetts resident).[2] The panel cited a variety of examples of defective work: At the University of Massachusetts, a toilet fell through a new, poorly-constructed floor when a student sat on it; an incompleted parking garage in Haverhill is already falling down, prompting local residents to demand its demolition; in Worcester, the county jail was built with cells that don't lock.[3] Although more than 60 percent of the state and county building work in Massachusetts in the period 1968-1980 was defective, such a high rate is probably not the norm for the nation as a whole. Corruption exists because of the lack of oversight by public agencies or collusion by responsible public officials.

Although the nation badly needs additional funding for public works projects, it will be difficult to secure voter approval for such funds if fraudulent activities are widespread and reform efforts are few. Thus, a prerequisite to national, state, and local efforts to build or rehabilitate essential public infrastructure is the elimination of fraud.

It will not be easy. The continued identification and prosecution of firms and individuals that engage in fraudulent activities are a minimal step. Indeed, a comprehensive review of the adequacy of present federal and state justice activities as to level and focus of effort is clearly needed. Resources put into such investigations will undoubtedly be cost effective in terms of reducing fraud.

Other measures should be taken to preclude the *opportunity* for many corrupt practices. The following actions would be a good beginning:

1. Standards for construction of various types of public works projects are required. Since the federal government supplies almost one-half of the funds for the nation's public works projects, and thus has the largest vested interest in preventing fraud, it should take the

lead in involving state and local government units, professional associations, and the construction industry in designing and applying such a set of standards. (In some public works areas, such standards already exist.) Such standards are necessary to provide an analytical framework for architectural/engineering design competition, funding decisions, and construction contract awards.

2. Public notification should become a standard procedure for *all* public works design, engineering, and construction contracts. Ad hoc notification approaches create the climate for fraud and favoritism.

3. Multiple oversight of public works activities is required. Such oversight should include funding agencies, independent inspector generals and local, state, and national legislative bodies. Perhaps the best and most easily replicable example of effective agency oversight of public works projects is found in the Economic Development Administration's public works program. Since its inception in 1965, that agency has had *no* scandal due to fraudulent public works design, engineering, or construction practices with its regular programs. At the same time EDA is a very small federal agency with total staffing of less than 1,000 persons. Its success is due to the following procedures:

a. The agency permits the recipients of its funds to use up to six percent of project funds to employ private architects and engineers. EDA engineers perform expert reviews of all projects at all stages.

b. At the pre-funding state, EDA engineers review proposed plans and cost estimates. If costs or designs are unreasonable, the project is rejected.

c. After a project is funded, the EDA Construction Review Division gives the community and architects/engineers a specific procedure to follow that includes competitive bidding for construction and ongoong detailing of expenses. EDA delegates to the private architects/ engineers construction oversight responsibility. However, at regular intervals, EDA engineers do full and partial review inspections of work *on-site,* and EDA staff commonly attend sessions when the principal competitive bids are opened.

The EDA procedures are both effective and efficient. Moreover, they are popular with project recipients and with architects and engineers because they are clear and equitably enforced.

In addition to oversight by agencies, increased Congressional oversight of fraudulent practices is needed.

4. Warranties on work are required. In addition to prosecuting individuals and firms that abuse the public through shoddy work, the public needs the assurance that defective projects will be replaced at little or no public cost. The $2.1 billion cost of repairing shoddy work in Massachusetts indicates the need for substantial warranties on public construction. Moreover, warranties are worthless unless enforced. Procedures are required for explicit and public waiving of warranty by public officials when they are *not* to be exercised.

A side benefit of design, engineering, and construction warranties will be reviews of firms and practices by insurance firms (much as they now do in private construction activities). While warranties may add a small amount to project costs, in the long term they will be a major deterrent to fraud and thus ultimately inexpensive. Certainly the people of Massachusetts would be better off today if their many defective projects had been covered with warranty insurance.

5. Standards are required to hold public officials *personally* accountable for their oversight of public works projects. Such accountability should include *financial* responsibilities for inadequate oversight and related derelictions of duties. Public officials can best be expected to put their heart into meeting their oversight responsibilities when they are personally liable for any incompetence or corruption associated with their work.

6. In Massachusetts the creation of a state corruption commission provided a mechanism for identifying and analyzing fraudulent practices that required reform. A similar *national* effort is required. Because of the prevalence of fraudulent public works activities and the need to reduce such abuses, a temporary Federal Commission of Public Works Design and Contracting should be established by the President and the Congress to identify specific actions necessary to reduce fraudulent public works activities.

WASTEFUL PROGRAM ADMINISTRATION Present administrative practices for public works are wasteful. There is no coherent approach to public works policy in the Executive Branch of the federal government. Policy setting has been dominated by individual Congressional committees, each pursuing different and sometimes inconsistent goals.

The GAO reports that there are wide variations in the capital budgeting procedures used by the individual agencies. No standards now exist for federal programs. Fundamental information used to guide the nation's public works investments is either non-existent, incomplete, or incomparable. For many types of service provided by public works there are no uniform service standards. The nation has neither an inventory of its capital stock nor assessments of its conditions—basic information that is necessary to establish priorities for future public works investments, rehabilitation, maintenance, and operation—nor any basis for making such assessments. The three agencies of the federal government which do collect information about public works are located in the Department of Commerce, but use different definitions, different geographic boundaries for reports, and different time periods. This reflects both their differing uses of the data and the lack of focus brought to public works data collection (Table 15).

Table 15
Summary of Public Works Data Strengths and Weaknesses by Source

Source	Strengths	Weaknesses
Bureau of the Census Governments Division	Data are centrally compiled Comprehensive governmental coverage Distinction between PWI expenditure types Grouping by functional category Spatial detail on state and local PWI Comparability between revenues and expenditures	Absence of quality control measures Absence of spatial detail on Federal PWI Lack of functional detail for PWI below national level Imprecise functional definitions Missing linkage between governmental revenues and PWI Measurement in current dollars only Measurement on fiscal year basis Changes in functional detail over time Construction PWI is not value put-in-place Lack of a consistent time series on individual small local governments Use of obligations to measure Federal equipment PWI
Bureau of Economic Analysis	Data are centrally compiled Comprehensvie governmental coverage Distinction between PWI expenditure types Detailed functional breakdown at national level for state and local PWI Measurement on calendar year basis Measurement in both current and constant dollars Compatibility of PWI with national income and product accounts Construction measured as value put-in-place	Absence of quality control measures Lack of functional detail for Federal PWI Absence of spatial detail Missing linkage between governmental revenues and PWI Exclusion of land purchases Use of obligations to measure Federal equipment PWI

Table 15 (Continued)
Summary of Public Works Data Strengths and Weaknesses by Source

Source	Strengths	Weaknesses
Federal Information Exchange System	Data are centrally compiled Consistent with OMB reporting procedures Conducive to analysis by • Function • Location • Type of Assistance • Agency	Federal obligation data only PWI not separately identified Absence of quality control measures Measurement in current dollars only Measurement on fiscal year basis Reliability of data below state level Changes in functional classifications over time
Independent Surveys: a. On-Site Visits	Precision control over data collection and management Linkage between revenues and PWI expenditures Identification of maintenance and renovation expenditures	Limited spatial coverage Measurement in current dollars Measurement on fiscal year basis
b. Mail/Phone Surveys	Precision control over data collection and management Spatial and temporal coverage	Limited agency coverage Incomparability between different types of outlays Measurement in current dollars Measurement on fiscal year basis

SOURCE: U.S. Department of Commerce, *A Study of Public Works Investment in the United States,* Washington, D.C., 1980.

Senator Robert Stafford of Vermont has declared federal policies on the construction, leasing, alteration and repair of government buildings that house federal workers to be in such an advanced state of disarray that they are actually "attracting confusion and influence, if not exorbitant waste; favoritism and scandal."[4]

Two examples illustrate Senator Stafford's point: (1) Present federal lease practices permit private entrepreneurs, often at virtually no risk, to finance, construct, and lease to the government for up to 20 years buildings having useful lives far in excess of these lease periods. Yet at the end of these leases, the entrepreneur owns the building and, as Senator Patrick Moynihan has commented, "the government is left with a stack of rent receipts." During the past decade, this practice has expanded—federal office space under lease has increased 117 percent to over 102 million square feet, and the amount of government-owned space under the management of the General Service Administration (GSA) has declined.[5] (2) A major portion of the GSA lease obligations are not reported in any budget. For example, the budget submitted to the Congress by the President in January 1980 requested $112 million in budget authority for GSA to make or renew leases on buildings. Upon investigation, the State Committee on Environment and Public Works determined that approval of this request would actually obligate the government to rental payments of approximately $1.03 billion during the fiscal year 1981 and the succeeding years of these lease commitments. This "omission" of $925 million of future obligations is altogether unreported anywhere—neither in the regular budget nor elsewhere "off-budget."[6] Although billions of dollars of federal funds are involved, the aggregate amount of GSA lease obligations from commitments of prior years remains unreported in the budget process. Reform of these practices has been a major agenda item of this Senate Committee, but obstacles have delayed progress.

There is also an absence of policy and administrative coherence for the annual $40 billion plus of public works assistance the federal government provides to state and local governments as well. Single-year funding and divergent criteria for the financing of similar types of facilities among the many federal funding agencies imposes major burdens on recipient state and local governments. For example, state and local capital budgeting is made dependent on annual changes in priorities, commitments, and funds from federal sources; excessive administrative obstacles are created in the use of federal funds; bureaucratic rigidity prevents the pooling of scarce public resources from several federal agencies to finance common projects; and, often there are duplications in some projects, while in other cases critical national and local projects are omitted.

For example, the federal financing of public works is heavily biased towards new construction. Many federal programs do not permit the use of funds for maintenance and rehabilitation. This bias induced many communities that are dependent on federal financing to forego maintenance and rehabilitation of basic facilities. Consequently, many existing public works facilities are allowed to deteriorate when limited funds for rehabilitation could restore them at a substantially lower cost than required for new construction. For example, the General Accounting Office reports that the old cast iron water mains in many cities could often be restored to an almost "new" condition through in-place scraping and relining at a cost between 30 and 50 percent of replacement expense.[7] In many cases not restoring these facilities results in wasting past investments that could be salvaged at less cost than new expenditures.

Attempted   Many studies have documented the ad-
Management Reform   ministrative confusion, excessive burdens, impediments to private sector
investments, barriers to the use of multiple financing sources, and lack
of priority-setting procedures in a variety of public programs, including those involving public works expenditures.

Efforts have been made to correct these deficiencies—reorganization; introduction of planning requirements; interagency task forces
and interagency cooperation agreements (such as the Under-
Secretaries and Assistant Secretaries Working Groups); centrally
directed program simplification efforts; A-95; intergovernment review
processes; and legislative coordination. Almost all have failed.

Reorganization and Public Works—One of the most attractive,
most often attempted, and least successful options to bring policy and
administrative coherence to the functions of government—including
public works—have been efforts to reorganize. Since 1948, there have
been 28 *major* but unsuccessful attempts to restructure and consolidate
federal economic policymaking—now delegated to 33 separate
departments and agencies *outside* the Executive Office of the
President.[8] None were successful.

Salamon suggests that reorganization is nothing more than the
continuation of politics by other means.[9] Reorganization for economy
or efficiency is rarely successful—the sums saved are often small in
comparison to the cost of the effort; increased efficiencies are either
miniscule or impossible to measure; and those savings which are
achieved generally come from programmatic changes that could have
been made without reorganization in the first place, rather than from
the reorganization itself. Efforts to achieve policy effectiveness
through reorganization always seem to slowly wind up concentrating
on institutional fragmentation as the primary impediment to coherent
policymaking—which it rarely is. Salamon concludes that most
reorganizations are used to:

> downgrade or get rid of an unwelcome official, to secure a change in
> Congressional venue, to bury a program, to change an agency's image,
> to give the appearance of action, to convey an impression of managerial
> confidence, to pay off a political debt, to forestall more radical change,
> to remove an agency from the budget or put it in, to shield an activity
> from congressional scrutiny or gain access, representation, visibility,
> and a secure institutional niche for a particular interest.

Interagency Coordination—Federal administrators have frequently
resorted to the use of working groups composed of senior officials
(career and appointed) representing various agencies involved in
common or shared responsibilities as a means of solving policy and
operational problems and "negotiating" working arrangements. Such
groups have included the Under-Secretaries Groups, Assistant

Secretaries Councils and other special purpose task forces. Recent efforts include the 1978 Urban Policy; the 1979 Rural Policy; and the 1980 Economic Renewal Policy.

Such approaches consume time and often substitute form for substance; are "fragile" because of the ascendancy of personal influence over such substantive matters as budgeting or policy objectives; and are operationally ineffective, for they generally fail to include regional, state, and local federal offices in policy, planning or budgetary decisions. Even when effective such relevance is generally short-lived because personalities that make such approaches work often change.

Program Simplification—There have been many attempts to simplify the administration of federal programs, including the block grant approach. Yet, considerable divisiveness and duplication exist even in those programs which have been "simplified." The Joint Funding Simplification Act of 1974 (Public Law 93-510) provided means for several federal agencies, state and local governments, and private (or even non-profit) organizations to negotiate and operate programs under a single formal and binding agreement that simultaneously committed several agencies to a common program of work.

However, during the period 1974-1978 the Act was used only 10 times. OMB, in an analysis of the Act, concluded that the Joint Simplification Act was not successful because: (1) federal agencies were not committed to using joint fundings and often refused to relate their own programs to common objectives; (2) there was a widespread ignorance of the Act and few persons knew how to use it at either federal, state, or local levels of government; (3) since the Act was permissive, many federal agencies ignored it; and (4) OMB itself had not provided adequate or timely leadership, support or oversight to assure implementation of the Act by federal agencies.[10]

Another attempt at simplification of federal requirements, the Rural Facilities Simplification Process, adopted in 1978, attempted to consolidate many of the federal administrative and application procedures that small, non-metropolitan communities must follow to secure funds from various federal programs. This effort, unlike many others, has successfully reduced and simplified many of the application requisites for joint projects and for determining which of several agencies will accept responsibility for a particular project. To date, however, concentration has been in pre-funding phases of projects and little attention has been given to simplifying and accelerating construction of projects once funding has been made.

The Intergovernmental Review and Comment Process—More than 200 federal programs now require that individual projects be reviewed by the concerned State and areawide planning institutions before sponsoring federal agencies will fund them. While this regulation has been beneficial as an information exchange, it has done nothing either to reduce duplication among federal and state programs or to standardize multiple planning and administrative requirements. Also, the federal government is frequently unresponsive to negative reviews of projects, effectively discouraging substantive comments. If this program is to be effective, even as an information exchange, a number of improvements are needed, including: full compliance by federal agencies; improved cooperation among areawide planning bodies; clearer and more timely information about projects and their impacts; more funding for the A-95 clearinghouses; better training for A-95 staff; and a substantial reduction in paperwork involved in the A-95 process.

Convening Authorities—Another attempt to bring policy and program focus has been the use of convening and coordination authorities; the Congress and a succession of Presidents have passed legislation and issued Executive Orders giving Presidential appointees the "right" to call meetings with their peers to coordinate their mutual actions. Specifically, the Department of Housing and Urban Development has been given the authority to call meetings of the federal agencies engaged in urban development; the Department of Commerce has such authority for multi-state or regional development; and the Department of Agriculture has such authority for rural development. Upon closer examination, however, these authorities are meaningless. They only authorize the agency officials to call meetings—a prerogative they had without legislation. More importantly, these agencies are not empowered to enforce decisions.

Planning and Public Works—During the past two decades, there has been an increasing reliance on planning programs financed by the federal government but conducted by state or local institutions. In 1978, the Advisory Commission on Intergovernmental Relations (ACIR) inventoried federally sponsored planning programs.[11] The ACIR found:

■ There are 40 federal planning assistance programs in the fields of economic and community development; environmental protection; transportation; energy development; social services; public safety; and general policy development and management;

■ Federal planning requirements are now attached to approximately 150 federal aid programs.

The net effect of most federal planning programs is to impose on state, regional and local agencies duplication, disorder, and discord. As a result, most public planning is done chiefly to meet federal regulatory requirements or to secure federal funds. Planning requirements per se have proven to be neither an effective means of coordinating various federal programs, nor an effective link between federal, state and local management because: (1) The federal and state grants-in-aid programs operate separately without overall specific

65

goals or objectives. Accordingly, agencies define their goals and objectives in terms of parochial, political, bureaucratic, and ideological considerations which often reflect agency wishes rather than the need of the public. (2) Virtually no attempts are made in planning to focus the many functional programs that may exist in a particular public works arena, such as water treatment, where there are seven district federal programs operating independently of each other. (3) Planning does not take into account the often disruptive, significant side effects and unintended consequences which result in the long term.

All of these efforts by Congress and the Executive Branch were attempts to achieve rationality and coordination among federal programs that do similar or related things in the same places. They were not sufficient to overcome the core problem that federal public works policy is made in a disjointed way by many individuals in many agencies and many legislative committees.

All of the tools were "band aids." The time has come for a more sweeping and difficult approach but one that has some chance of success—a capital budget.

FOOTNOTES TO CHAPTER 5

1. Smith, M. Lee, a series of articles in the period 1977–1980 on abuses in the use of architect-engineer contracts. The Tennessee Journal, Nashville, Tennessee.

2. State of Massachusetts, *Report of the Special Commission Concerning State and County Buildings,* Boston, Massachusetts, December, 1980.

3. Karagianis, Maria, "Defects: A Sad Slapstick Tale," The Boston Globe, Boston, Massachusetts, January 1, 1981.

4. Stafford, Robert, *Report to the Senate on Several Public Building Proposals,* Submitted by the General Services Administration, Committee on Environment and Public Works, United States Senate, Ninety-Fifth Congress, Second Session, Washington, D.C., 1978, p. 14.

5. Committee on Environment and Public Works, United States Senate, Ninety-Sixth Congress, Second Session, *Report to the Senate Committee on the Budget,* Washington, D.C., 1980, pp. 31–32.

6. Ibid.

7. *Additional Federal Aid for Urban Water Distribution Systems Should Wait Until Needs are Clearly Established,* GAO, pp. 8–19.

8. Office of Management and Budget, Executive Office of the President, "An unpublished report prepared for the President's Reorganization Project," Washington, D.C., 1978.

9. Salamon, Lester M., "In Pursuit of Reorganization: the Question of Goals," a paper delivered at the Administration Conference of the United States, Washington, D.C., 1980.

10. Office of Management and Budget, Executive Office of the President, *Report to Congress, Implementation of the Joint Funding Simplification Act of 1974 (Public Law 93-510),* Washington, D.C., February, 1979.

11. The White House Conference on Balanced National Growth and Economic Development, *Proceedings,* Washington, D.C., 1978.

6

A CAPITAL BUDGET FOR THE UNITED STATES

The federal, state and local governments have long used budgets as a device for bringing policy and administrative coherence to their operations. Virtually all major corporations, all state governments, and most local governments use capital budgets as basic policy and administration tools. Some states such as Pennsylvania and some cities such as Cincinatti, Ohio now include life-cycle costing in their capital budgets.

A major flaw in federal public works policymaking and program administration is the absence of national public works investment policies and a supporting capital budget.

This omission is no accident. It is the consequence of explicit decisions not to have a capital budget. It is explained in the *Special Analysis: Budget of the United States Government—1981* as follows:

> The Federal Government has never produced a capital budget in the sense of one in which capital or investment-type programs are financed separately from current expenditures. One major reason is that a capital budget could be misleading as a measure of the government's effect on the demand for economic resources. Another is that such a budget might favor programs with intensive expenditures for physical assets, such as construction, relative to other programs for which future benefits cannot be accurately capitalized, such as education or research. Likewise, physical assets might be favored relative to current operations in any given program, since deficit financing for capital would be easier to justify. A capital budget would also pose formidable accounting problems involving the measurement of depreciation on government property—[and] there are also inevitable classification difficulties.[1]

The annual Federal Budget of the United States submitted to the Congress each year presently contains three fundamental components: (1) the basic budget in overview; (2) a detailed budget appendix; (3) the special analyses. The special analyses are designed to highlight specified program areas or provide other significant presentations of federal budget data. These special analyses help bring policy and administrative overviews to 12 areas of major federal concern.

The preparation of one of these analyses, the special budget analysis of federal credit programs, demonstrates how useful a comprehensive annual accounting of fragmented federal activities can be. The federal government is engaged in numerous credit activities, including financing housing, rural electrification, support of rail programs, and the Export-Import Bank among others. These credit activities have major effects in both national and world credit markets. However, the assessment of these impacts was not possible until a standardized classification and accounting system was created to provide an overview of: (1) direct loans from the federal government; (2) federal guarantees of private lending; and (3) lending by privately-owned government sponsored enterprises. Once this analysis was created, the magnitude of these credit activities became clear. For example, the aggregate value of the federal government's loan guarantees now exceeds $239 billion. In fiscal year 1980, the on-budget and off-budget direct loan activities of the federal government exceeded $50 billion.[2] With accurate data, OMB is now able to better manage federal credit activities.

A thirteenth special analysis is now needed. The creation of a national capital budget analysis would permit a similar overview of the federal government's capital expenditures and commitments. As with the annual Federal Credit Analysis, it would permit consideration of public works activities in light of other national needs such as funding for social programs or for defense. It would also permit construction, rehabilitation, maintenance, and operational requisites to be explicitly considered.

The technical success of OMB in annually creating 12 special and complex budget analyses demonstrates that OMB can surmount the accounting and classification problems which might arise in creating a national public works capital analysis and a national public capital budget.

The Congress has demonstrated concern about the need to bring structure and focus to the federal public works investments. For example, the House of Representatives' Public Works Committee in 1974 sponsored research and hearings resulting in a call for the creation of a National Public Works Investment Strategy.[3] In 1976, the Congress directed the Department of Commerce to prepare what eventually became the 1980 report, *A Study of Public Works Investment in the United States*. The Congress held hearings and ordered that the studies be conducted on the use of public works as a counter-cyclical device in both 1978 and 1980. In 1980 the Committee on Environment and Public Works introduced legislation to create a systematic Federal Public Buildings Policy.[4] Numerous other committees of the House and Senate have conducted hearings and have sponsored studies on the deterioration of the nation's public infrastructure.

The time has come to annually prepare a special capital analysis in the President's Annual Budget and to create a national public works capital budget.

ELEMENTS OF A CAPITAL BUDGET   A national capital budget would consist of three essential components: (1) current and projected capital needs and expenditures; (2) current and projected operation and maintenance needs and expenditures; and (3) sources of financing.

Capital Expenditures   The budget would identify capital investment needs and (1) proposed federal investment in facilities to be used by federal government; and (2) proposed federal grant-in-aid financing of public works for state and local governments. Priorities would be identified. Both current and future (perhaps up to ten years) investments would be identified. To be useful for policymaking and program management, this information would ideally be disaggregated in a variety of ways, including:

(1) A division of investments by types of facilities such as aggregate investment in transportation, water treatment facilities, flood control facilities, airports, etc. This would be further divided by region or state. These two types of classifications could be used to prepare priority lists for investment both by types of facilities and areas. Among other information required to make such decisions would be analysis of the condition of existing facilities, quality of services provided, projections of future demand and estimates of alternative future investment costs.

(2) The identification of proposed public works investments by individual federal agencies. This would permit analysis of the roles of agencies when more than one makes the same type of investment. (For example, seven federal agencies now invest in water treatment facilities, each using differing policy and administrative criteria).

(3) The breakdown of capital expenditures between new construction, rehabilitation, land purchases, purchase of existing buildings, etc. (Such a breakdown would permit an assessment of where existing programs favor new construction over rehabilitation, and would facilitate life-cycle costing).

(4) A distinction between economic development investments and those public works related to basic community services (for example, industrial parks versus creation of recreation facilities).

Operation and Maintenance Expenditures   A national capital budget would include projections of the funds needed for operation and maintenance of federally-financed public works—by program, by type of project, and by area. Capital stock create demands for operation and maintenance funds. To avoid deferring maintenance and to insure funds to operate essential facilities, a number of cities, such as Cincinatti, Ohio, and Waco, Texas, will not consider making new capital construction unless there is a long-term assurance of long-term operation and maintenance funds. Similar standards are necessary for facilities whose construction and rehabilitation are wholly or partially funded by the federal government.

Sources of Financing   A national capital budget would classify public works investments (i.e., construction, rehabilitation, maintenance, and operation) and identify the responsible level of government for financing both specific categories of public works projects (roads, water supply, etc.) and the specific activities associated with those projects (construction, rehabilitation, maintenance, and operation).

POLICY AND MANAGEMENT USES OF A NATIONAL CAPITAL BUDGET

A national capital budget could bring new coherence to public works policy-making and program management by providing a framework for legislative and administrative decisions.

A capital budget would permit public works policymaking and program administration to be considered within a consistent framework of topics and subtopics. It would permit a greater degree of simplicity, and would lend validity and significance to decisions. Among other issues a national capital budget would provide a framework for analyzing in a systematic manner:

1. The aggregate requirement for domestic non-defense public works investments in the face of such other pressing claims such as national defense and social programs.

2. The relationship of public works investments to national defense, social, and economic development objectives.

3. The impacts of government regulatory actions on public works investments and operations. For example, mandated investments to assist the handicapped on public transportation threaten to bankrupt some public transportation systems such as those in New York City.

4. The consequences of allocations of limited public works funds as between new construction, rehabilitation of existing facilities, and operation maintenance.

5. The social and equity issues associated with the distribution of public works funds among and between various regions.

6. The sources, consequences, and alternative financing sources of public works projects and their operation.

Capital budgeting is ultimately a political process through which resources are allocated to meet a variety of objectives. The creation of such a budget would provide a framework in which: (a) the advocates

71

for federal investments in public works would negotiate these potential expenditures against other uses of federal funds such as national defense and education; (b) funds would be allocated among such programs as transportation, water treatment, and navigation, etc.; and (c) funds would be allocated among construction, operation, maintenance, and rehabilitation activities.

A capital budget would ultimately serve as a device by which the President and the Congress could bring necessary control to the present "free form" investment and management practices of the various federal public works agencies and permit effective Congressional management, especially of Congress's own committee actions which have been a major contribution to duplication and inconsistency.

Public works investments reflect a history of choices, decisions, bargains, compromises, and allocations which provide a foundation for present and future actions. A capital budget could chronicle this important set of information. It could also articulate a statement of the future, specifying goals and resources needed to attain those goals. States and communities, now dependent on federal public works funding, operate on a year-to-year basis with the ever present possibility that federal "commitments" will be altered or regulations changed. State and local governments need more certainty than a one-year federal budget. The private sector similiarly would also profit from improved certainty. For example, the private sector could have adjusted more efficiently to ever-changing air and water control standards if in the early 1970s, the federal government had more clearly specified their intentions in this field.

The creation of any public facility places a variety of demands on other public programs and services. A national capital budget could provide a mechanism for identifying and quantifying these relationships.

Choosing Basic Goals and Objectives

Clearly stated goals and objectives for federal public works investments are required to give a common direction to policymaking and program investment.

These goals will necessarily be influenced by the availability of resources and must accord with other social, area development (urban, rural, and regional), sectoral, industrial, and macro-economic policies. Among goals which require specification are: (1) the basic levels of public works services to be provided for specific populations and specific geographic areas; and (2) the extent the public sector will finance infrastructure to support economic development.

Once these and other goals have been articulated, they can serve as the basis for motivating the bureaucracy (thus creating a sound management control system), providing a realistic framework within

72

which programs can be evaluated and, a solid foundation for creating a public works management philosophy relevant to the needs and political/financial realities of the 1980s.

Research, Analytical Although all levels of government have
Evaluation, and long made substantial annual investments
Data Requirements in public works, there has been an
amazingly small amount of research and analysis on the topic. Thus, many significant information gaps exist, including:

■ *Data.* Data on public works are fragmented and often incomparable among the various data series. There is no inventory of the nation's capital stock, virtually no estimate of the condition of individual facilities or the quality of service they provide, no estimate of future capital needs, and no estimate of the funds that will be required to maintain and operate existing and proposed facilities. Limited data exist on the fiscal capacities of governments to finance these expenditures.

■ *Replacement/ Repair.* There are no standardized replacement/ repair analytical techniques—techniques which systematically determine when it is economically feasible to replace or repair facilities.

■ *Demographics.* There are virtually no analyses of the role of public works in stimulating shifts in population and economic activity among and between regions of the nation.

■ *Counter-cyclical Spending.* The studies on the use of counter-cyclical public works have been limited to temporary programs. Virtually no attention has been given to the use of the nation's $80 billion of annual public works investments as a major tool for economic stabilization.

■ *New Technology.* There are only limited analyses of how new techniques can be implemented to extend the life of existing facilities or how to provide the same service in a better, less expensive way.

■ *Financing.* The alternative financing of future public works investments has received little attention, and has focused only on the introduction of limited purpose tools such as national urban banks or selected application of user charges. There has been no overall analysis of the impact of future financing requirements on capital markets in general or on available alternatives.

■ *Operational Data.* Operational data necessary for managing programs, such as temporary public works, either do not exist or are inadequate.

■ *Funded Projects.* Information on the status of projects already funded but not yet constructed is not collected in a systematic manner. This oversight has contributed to the creation of the $100 billion backlog of funded but uncompleted public works projects.

■ *Evaluation.* No systematic system for evaluating the nation's public works policies or programs exists.

Financing

A basic function of a national public works capital budget is the identification of sources and uses of financing. The creation of such a new policy tool will necessarily involve a complete review of present and future financing options, including, federal, state and local fiscal capabilities.

Personnel Policies

The recent studies on public works investments have consistently excluded personnel considerations. Yet, a major cause of the rapid deterioration of many public works facilities is inadequately trained personnel. Thus, a major element in the creation of a national public works investment strategy or a national budget is the identification of personnel needs and an assessment of the efficacy of present recruitment and training procedures. For example, the federal government must seriously consider whether or not it should make capital investments when communities cannot demonstrate that they will have well-trained personnel to operate these facilities.

A second personnel consideration involves federal managers. Presently, the federal agencies rarely school even senior managers in the logic and techniques of strategic management. If a national capital budget is to be created, training programs in these techniques of strategic management are essential for participants. (Private firms such as IBM, General Electric, and Control Data regularly invest substantial funds in training even the most senior management in strategic management techniques. The federal government should do no less).

A third personnel improvement that is required is training of federal, state and local officials in the techniques and economics of real estate and public works development and management. Given the quantities of public funds involved, and the impact of these funds on the quality of life of the nation and its cities, their physical structure and economic development, such training should be a basic requisite for individual employment and advancement. Given the large numbers of officials now in position of responsibility who have not had such training, remedial courses should be made mandatory—starting with the most senior officials *first*.

REQUISITES FOR SUCCESSFUL CREATION OF A NATIONAL CAPITAL BUDGET

Many attempts have been made to bring policy and program coherence to the operations of government through budgeting, such as Zero-Based Budgeting (ZBB) and Planning, Programming, and Budgeting Systems (PPBS). However, such approaches to improved decisionmaking have most often failed because of: (1) the complexity of the systems themselves; (2) internal resistances to change; and (3) the manner in which these systems were introduced. Perhaps most importantly, these systems failed because the budget instrument itself was seen as the mechanism for change rather than the result of a larger, overall process of policy and administrative reform.

If a national capital budget is to be created and successfully used as a policy and management tool, a number of conditions are necessary. Steiner identifies a number of those needed elements for successful budgeting in the private sector.[5] Slightly modified they are equally, if not more, applicable to capital budgeting in the public sector:

■ The leadership of the President and Congressional support are essential, particularly in the early stages.

■ The budget process must cover all the federally financed public works activities—construction, rehabilitation, operation, maintenance, and financing.

■ The budget process must be directly tied to the planning process overall and for specific programs. Although the budget is not the only planning process, it is the major device for formalizing plans and translating them into operations. This linkage must be recognized and accommodated.

■ The responsibility for creating and operating the national capital budget must be clearly assigned. This assignment will define who is expected to do what, by when, and what standards are to be met. In the Executive Branch there is only one logical choice for administering the national capital budget—the Office of Management and Budget. The Office of Management and Budget has overall budgeting responsibilities; the expertise necessary to prepare a national capital budget; and the power necessary to integrate this budget with other claims on resources.

■ As with the Executive Branch, the responsibility for capital budgeting should be assigned to a specific committee of the Congress. Among other logical choices are the public works committees and the budget committees. Irrespective of which committee is given such a responsibility, the Congressional Budget Office should prepare a special annual analysis of the federal government's long- and short-term capital investments.

■ The capital budget should contain a degree of flexibility. Circumstances change and fixed budgets will at times require modification to accommodate these changes. The knowledge that unusual circumstances can be accommodated will permit the creation of a capital budgeting process responsive to both anticipated and unanticipated needs—a basic requisite for effective management and on-going support from those involved in the budgeting process.

■ The language of capital budgeting must be kept as free of complex accounting terms as possible. One of the present difficulties with the various public budgets is the use of "jargon." What may be "state-of-the-art" terminology to budgeteers confuses policymakers and others who are essential to creating and carrying out an effective budgetary process. Thus, a common terminology should be uniformly applied; this will permit communication not now possible.

■ The budgeting system itself should be kept as simple as possible. As Steiner points out, "Budgets are tools for management, not management itself . . . too much complexity and restriction will create frustration, then resentment and finally inertia."

■ Capital budgets must have clear standards upon which performance will be based and evaluated. Such standards must be fair, clear, and firmly applied.

■ The final and most important requisite is the initial and on-going participation of principals—at both policy and operational levels—in the budget process. Although there are limits to such participation, the degree of support for the capital budget process will generally rise proportionately to the degree of participation. Such participation will permit the identification of problems that often go unnoticed until remedial action is required. A capital budget can be a basic tool for creating an overall design for policies and actions. It is not a punitive device for frustrating the functions of an organization. Nor can it in itself serve as a means to good performance. Other management tools are available for purposes of incentive.

This budget could serve as an initial guide for coordinating federal actions with those of state and local governments. It would necessarily represent the culmination of an intensive and close interaction between the Executive Branch and the Congress, with state and local governments, and with the private sector.

The nation needs clearer definitions about which level of government is accountable for what. Present confusion within the system accounts for much of the existing waste and the deterioration in our public works.

FOOTNOTES TO CHAPTER 6

1. Office of Management and Budget, Executive Office of the President, *Special Analyses: Budget of the United States,* Washington, D.C., January, 1980, p. 91.

2. *Special Analyses: Budget of the United States,* pp. 141–207.

3. Committee on Public Works, U.S. House of Representatives, *A National Public Works Investment Policy,* Ninety-Third Congress of the United States, Second Session, Washington, D.C., December, 1974.

4. United States Senate, Ninety-Sixth Congress, Second Session, S.2080 "Public Buildings Act of 1980," Washington, D.C., 1980.

5. Steiner, George A., *Top Management Planning,* Macmillan Publishing Company, New York City, New York, 1969.

7

ALLOCATING PUBLIC WORKS RESPONSIBILITIES WITHIN THE FEDERAL SYSTEM

Since every dollar must count in the 1980s, it does behoove us to re-examine and reallocate public works responsibilities and authorities among the various levels of government. Over the past 20 years, with the enthusiastic support of most state and local governments, the role of the federal government in financing local public works has steadily increased. In 1957, the federal government funded ten percent of state and local public works investments; by the late 1970s, over 40 percent of these expenditures were federally financed.[1] Today, funding from federal appropriations has eclipsed state and local debt financing as the primary source of investment in state and local public facilities.

DILUTED ACCOUNTABILITY An assessment of what level of government should be responsible for financing each type of public facility would go to the heart of the complex and frequently duplicative network of inter-governmental relationships that has evolved since the Second World War. In the decade of economic and fiscal constraints that lies ahead, it may prove necessary to simplify these relationships in order to ensure that accountability at each level of government for the responsibilities allocated to it are consistent with its fiscal, territorial, and statutory capacities.

There are at least 100 separate federal agencies, 50 state governments, (each with their separate agencies), the District of Columbia, Puerto Rico, the protectorates, 3,042 counties, 35,000 general purpose local governments, 15,000 school districts, 2,000 areawide units of government, over 200 interstate compacts, and nine multi-state regional development organizations all engaged in public works planning and construction.[2] Although responsibilities and authorities within these governments are intertwined, neither their public works policy-making nor their administration reflect a coherent focus. Indeed, they are often engaged in fierce competition for resources and bureaucratic turf—a competition which too often results in an actual reduction of effort and increased waste.

Equally significant, their relationships are vertical. Highway agencies at each level are closely linked. So, too, are water and sewerage agencies, community development organizations, etc. These vertical alliances of functional agencies are the heart of the new "Administration State." But there are no politically-accountable horizontal decisionmaking and planning institutions that cross-cut these vertical kingdoms in the Administrative State to ensure that their separate actions add up to coherent results over-all. It is too much to expect that the President, a Governor, a Mayor, or a County Commissioner can surmount the vertical fragmentation that has been generalized over the last three decades.

The existing fragmentation creates a number of bureaucratic perversions, including: the loss of accountability for the elected officials of general government; limited pooling of public resources; duplication of some facilities and services and the omission of others; contradictory and redundant activities and conflicting program procedures; divergent delivery systems and eligibility criteria; and a lack of clarity as to the assignment of specific authorities and responsibilities for financing construction, rehabilitation, maintenance and operation.[3] The policy and program disorders which have resulted greatly exceed the planning and administrative capacities of the federal, state and local governments to correct without fundamental changes.

Fragmentation is not solely the product of special interests or bureaucratic expansionism; it also mirrors the fragmentation which inevitably results when Congress is heavily dependent upon the work of its Committees to produce legislation. Recent budget reforms in Congress have provided the basis for horizontal, cross-cutting procedures by means of which Congressional leadership can judge proposed legislative initiatives against the back-drop of statutes already on the books and proposals emerging from other standing committees. But the potential of the new budget process to promote legislative coherence is yet to be fully realized. As a consequence, executive agencies are all too often blamed for duplication and conflict that is not really their own doing, but is the result of fragmentation on the legislative process itself. At present, national capital budgeting, coupled with the Congressional Budget reforms, offers a practical and effective means to confront much of the present fragmentation.

ALLOCATION OF POWERS AND FUNCTIONS

No clear allocation of responsibilities and functions exists among and between the various levels of government. Prior to the 1960s, the division of powers and functions between national and state governments for provision of public works activities was relatively definable.

The federal government funded and operated projects that were in the national interest and were beyond the fiscal capacities of the states and private sector—projects such as flood control and navigation on the Mississippi River. Such federal aid to state and local governments as did exist, as in aid for highway construction, was based on the premise of partnership in which each partner put up approximately half of the funds. The assumption was that the facilities being built served both national and local needs.

However, as James Sundquist, of the Brookings Institution has noted, the early 1960s brought a distinct change in the evolution of American federalism.[4] The national government aggressively embarked on a course of using state and local governments as vehicles to achieve federally-defined national objectives. The categorical grant assistance programs became the most influential tools the federal government could use to pursue this new activist role. To induce state and local participation, matching requirements were lowered or even eliminated. Close federal administrative control was introduced and numerous projects were funded on an individual basis with decisions centralized in Washington. The fundamentals of American federalism were altered. Recipients of aid often dealt directly with federal agencies. State and local policymakers were designed out of the system. Indeed, in some programs, federal funds were provided to recipients to enable them to face city hall and the state house as adversaries. Non-profit organizations of many kinds were created to be recipients of federal funds in order to bypass local and state governments.

Continuing this trend toward centralism, regulation became an increasingly powerful tool used by the federal government to mandate state and local actions in the 1970s. While in 1969 there were fewer than 30 federal regulatory agencies, there were approximately 100 such agencies in 1980.[5] And during the 1970s, another departure was taken from the presumed principles of American federalism when the federal government began to impose general mandates upon state and local governments that were not tied to specific federal programs, but were imposed as general requirements that state and local governments were expected to meet without federal financial recompense. These included requirements such as providing full access to buildings and services for the handicapped, requirements that wages paid to workers on public projects be consistent with the Davis-Bacon Act, and requirements levied on all projects under a variety of environmental protection acts. Such general mandates effectively bypassed the legislative responsibilities of local and state governments. They "appropriated" state and local funds outside their legislative processes at either level.

There have been efforts over the past decade to address some of the problems resulting from this drift toward a more unitary or centralized system. Attempts have been made to consolidate many categorical programs into block grants to provide more state and local flexibility. Revenue-sharing went still further by untying grant requirements from the state and local use of federally-raised funds. These reforms have been partially effective. By 1980, 22 percent of the federal grants were either block grants or revenue sharing ($18.4 billion out of $82.9 billion). Nonetheless, over 78 percent of federal assistance still remains categorical.[6]

As useful as the creation of block grant and revenue sharing programs have been, they do not answer the question of who should be responsible for what within our federal system. Which types of public works should be the responsibility of the federal government? Which should be the responsibility of the state and local governments? Which should be a shared responsibility? Which types of financing, (construction, rehabilitation, maintenance and operation) should be the responsibilities of which levels of government? For example, if the federal government finances construction of sewerage treatment facilities, which level(s) of government should assume responsibility for maintenance and operational expenses and under what conditions? We cannot afford the redundancy and diluted accountability of our present system under the special financial constraints we will face in the 1980s.

The point was articulated by then Governor Ronald Reagan in 1972:

> Do we have the will and the courage to look at our government structure; to evolve a practical plan whereby tasks and services performed by the government will be assigned to those levels of government best qualified to handle them regardless of what has been the pattern of the past; to construct a revenue system that matches with sufficient tax resources the tasks assigned to each level of government?[7]

During the past two decades, as responsibilities for various governmental functions or components of functions have been shifted from one governmental unit to another, there have been a growing number of attempts to redefine appropriate functional responsibilities. The Advisory Commission on Intergovernmental Relations reports that most of these shifts have been vertical—between levels of government. The trend of these shifts has been to elevate responsibilities to higher levels of government reflecting: (1) the conclusion of many local leaders that many services can best be performed by larger units of government where economies of scale are possible; (2) the need to shift fiscal responsibilities to levels of government with a more productive fiscal base; and (3) the political attractiveness of using sources of financing for which local leaders are not responsible.

In the past two decades there has been an increase in the number of special interest groups (many of which are federally financed) that are skilled in bringing political pressure to bear on all levels of government. They have been successful in shifting emphasis to social and other programs at the sacrifice of public works activities. Even within the sphere of public works expenditures, special interest groups have been able to convince political leaders to allocate funds to specific types of projects and activities irrespective of their implications for the long-run viability of the national and regional economies.

The use of public works funding as a tool of power politics has been as American as cherry pie. At all levels, the extension or withholding of specific public works projects has always been used to entice or force decisions on other, often unrelated, issues. Public works policy has been almost entirely a Congressional prerogative since the founding of the Republic and federal public works projects have been the progeny of legislative "rough and tumble."

In an era of tight economic and financial constraints, when public works must be viewed as fundamental to the long-term health of the national economy and the provision of services essential to social stability, we can no longer afford the luxury of pork or special interest politics. We must construct at each level of government both executive and legislative procedures that imbue public works investment with the long-term perspectives required for a sound, long-range, carefully timed capital investment program.

IMPROVING ACCOUNTABILITY: REALLOCATING FUNCTIONS

In this bicentennial decade of our Constitution, it is singularly appropriate that we undertake a major assessment of the drift that has been occuring in our federal system and to redefine, in the context of the coming decades, the roles and responsibilities of each level of government. To the extent that some functions, such as welfare, can be nationalized, resources may be freed up at the state level to renovate and modernize infrastructure.

Such an assessment is beyond the scope of this book. It can be undertaken best by the Advisory Commission on Intergovernmental Relations or a new national commission created for the purpose.

But in the field of public works, several principles are worth setting forth:

1. *The level of government mandating a requirement must be prepared to pay for it.*

Mandated public works investments are a major source of the fiscal stress on state and local governments. The federal government has mandated a broad array of investments for state and local governments (at least 1,500), and state governments have imposed an equal or larger number on local governments. The fiscal and economic strains placed on state and local governments can be highly disruptive, forcing postponement of investment that may be vital in the long-run. To reduce the fiscal and economic strains on local governments, a reassessment of mandating by the federal and state governments is essential. The ACIR has identified a number of steps for such an evaluation:[8]

- Inventory existing mandates;
- A review procedure is needed to identify, eliminate, postpone, or alter unnecessary or overly restrictive mandates;
- Create federal and policy statements and review procedures for all proposed mandates;
- Full federal and state reimbursement for mandates that intrude into issues that are essentially state and local concerns, such as working hours and working conditions;
- A procedural safeguard to insure an equitable and efficient reimbursement process.

2. *Functions that are in the national interest should not be imposed on inappropriate levels of jurisdiction lacking the capacity to deliver. To the extent that state and local jurisdictions are used as vessels of administrative convenience to meet a national need, the federal government must finance the cost from national tax revenues.*

3. *On the other hand, federal financing of public works should not supplant local or state responsibilities or capacities. It should be used to finance those necessary works clearly beyond the financial responsibilities and capacities of the jurisdictions involved.*

Existing grants-in-aid should be evaluated from a number of points of view.

a) Does a particular grant-in-aid promote capital substitution or is it too stimulative? The 50/50 matching ratio used in the federal highway programs of the past permitted states to construct roads then desired by the states and also met national needs. Given the political pressures that always exist with road construction, the states were almost without exception anxious to raise their 50 percent matching funds. Thus, a stimulative effect was created. When these ratios were increased to 70-90 percent, the relative stimulative impact was diminished and funding responsibilities and control increasingly passed to the federal government.

b) Is it intended to equalize capacity or simply underwrite operations? The choice of intentions or mix is important to any reform of the system. For example, revenue sharing is less unlikely to result in public works construction than either block grant programs or categorical assistance given these latter programs' restrictions. For example, GAO reports that in Fiscal Year 1977, only 1.2 percent of total General Revenue Sharing funds went to municipal water projects ($79 million of $6.55 billion), while 23 percent of EDA's $300 million were so allocated. Conversely, revenue sharing would more likely result in operation and maintenance expenditures than construction oriented categorical programs.

4. *Public works financing must promote the maintenance of the*

nation's infrastructure once built rather than focus solely on construction.

The preponderance of federal programs fund new construction without concern for long-run maintenance and replacement. Future assistance should also focus on life-cycle costing and maintenance.

5. *Federal public works policy must accommodate the diversity of regional needs and problems and not impose rigidly standardized approaches irrelevant to the realities of national development.*

Sectionalism has long been a divisive force in American politics. the allocation of public works funds is politically sensitive. *At present, when all public works funds are considered, there is a fairly even per capita allocation between regions.*[10] The West and South receive more funds through the Corps of Engineers and the Bureau of Reclamation than the Northeast and Midwest, but industrial Midwest and Northeast receive more funds from other categorical public works programs.

Each region of the country faces quite different problems in meeting national economic objectives. Many Northeastern cities require funds for rehabilitation of obsolescent facilities. Many Southern and Western cities require funds for new construction. Rural regions such as the Great Plains and large areas of the Southwest face acute water problems that will affect the nation's agricultural and energy output.

The nation has a stake in resolving these development problems in all of its regions, for they serve as major impediments to national economic renewal.

6. *State and local governments must lessen their growing dependence on federal aid by reassuming responsibility for the financing and delivery of those functions which are clearly assigned to them in terms of their capacity, responsibility, and jurisdiction.*

The states are given a crucial role under the Constitution. They alone have the power to form the boundaries and define the functions of local units of government. They possess all the powers which were not explicitly extended to the national government through the Constitution. And, of course, they have the ability to revise their own constitutions at will. All of these powers have been used erratically. Through legislation and a series of constitutional amendments, the states have constrained their own ability to provide necessary public works through tax, borrowing and expenditure limitations. As a result, they have been forced to reduce essential services, abandon certain functions altogether, and to rely even more heavily on federal financing. Indeed, the increasing role played by the federal government in the construction of basic public works is as much the result of these self-inflicted federalist wounds as the aggressiveness of an ambitious national government.

Just as the national government must re-examine its own functions and responsibilities in light of the economic realities of the 1980s, so, too, must the state governments and thereby the local governments they have created.

Basic systems of local government functions, organization, and finance require fundamental assessment. To match the evaluation of appropriate federal functions, a reallocation of functions between the state and local governments will prove just as necessary. States may have to assume financial and operating responsibilities for certain facilities and services hitherto provided by municipalities. Counties may have to be granted legislative charters and some municipal responsibilities in order to encompass the patterns of economic and social life that have expanded beyond the reach of municipal boundaries.

Dependence upon the local property tax may have to be replaced by increased use of other, progressive taxes. While states ease fiscal restrictions on their local jurisdictions, they may have to assume increased responsibility for auditing and overseeing the financial integrity of their own jurisidictions.

But most important, states working closely with their local jurisdictions will find it essential to shift more of their resources toward investment in capital infrastructure. And in many states, that will require new approaches to state capital financing.

State governments and most municipal governments use capital budgeting, but in the overwhelming number of cases such budgeting represents the compilation of project listings from individual agencies rather than within an overall framework. Project management techniques in the public sector significantly lag behind those in the private sector construction.

Reform is needed in public works activities at all levels of government.

FOOTNOTES TO CHAPTER 7

1. *A Study of Public Works Investment in the United States.*

2. *Statistical Abstract,* p. 283.

3. Office of Management and Budget, Executive Office of the President, *Reorganization Study of Local Development Assistance Programs,* Washington, D.C., December, 1978.

4. Advisory Commission on Intergovernmental Relations, *Categorical Grants: Their Role and Design,* Washington, D.C., 1978, p. 31.

5. *Being Number One: Rebuilding the U.S. Economy.*

6. *Special Analyses: Budget of the United States Government,* Fiscal Year 1981, pp. 239–277.

7. Advisory Commission on Intergovernmental Relations, *State Planning of Local Expenditures,* Washington, D.C., July, 1978.

8. Ibid.

9. *Additional Federal Aid for Urban Water Distribution Systems Should Wait Until Needs are Clearly Established,* p. 38.

10. *A Study of Public Works Investment in the United States—Summary.*

8

RECOMMENDATIONS

At this critical juncture, when much of the nation's attention must be focused on economic renewal, can we find the resources needed to renovate, replace, or construct the public facilities needed to underpin the industrial economy? Can we institute the practices and procedures required to make the most effective use of whatever resources we have?

It is possible so long as we are not tempted to fall back upon ineffective tinkering. Wholesale revolution is not necessary either. But it does mean that the Executive Branch must share responsibility for creating and managing public works policy more coherently than in the past.

A NATIONAL CAPITAL BUDGET A systematic and orderly approach to public capital investment must replace the loose, give-and-take procedures of the legislative process we have known in the past.

(1) Congress should require the preparation of a *Special Analysis* to accompany each annual budget outlining the nation's public works needs as they affect national economic performance.

(2) Congress should direct the Executive Branch to undertake an inventory of national public works needs as they affect the economy.

(3) With the inventory as a starting point, Congress should then require preparation of a Capital Budget that proposes phased capital investments matched to both short-term cyclical and long-term national economic needs. The budget would display preconstruction, construction, maintenance, and operating costs.

(4) Congress should direct the Executive Branch to begin preparation of the required data bases required to make national capital budgeting feasible. The data systems should be designed to enable Congress and the Executive Branch to manage federal public works investments so that they are counter-cyclical rather than pro-cyclical. The systems should identify back-logged projects in the inventory, the construction of which can be accelerated when economic circumstances indicate.

The systems should also display:

■ Economic linkages—The linkages between specific types of public works construction and the purchase of related materials and employment. Such data are essential for targeting public works investments to specific economic sectors and work forces *outside* of on-site construction activities.

■ Improved Industrial Capacity Data—If public works purchases are to be made on a cyclical basis, better data must be prepared on utilization rates of key industries involved with public works construction and more detailed monthly capacity utilization data than are now available.

■ Data for Triggering Devices—The major weakness found by virtually every analysis of the LPW program was the inadequacy of unemployment and other data used in triggering decisions. Rather than patch together disparate and unsatisfactory data sources which result in an inadequate counter-cyclical public works triggering device, a more productive and less expensive course of action would be to create specific data series which meet specific triggering objectives.

MAKING THE PUBLIC WORKS DOLLAR GO FARTHER

(5) Congress should direct the Executive Branch to report by an appropriate date steps by means of which delays in public facilities construction can be reduced through reforms in federal, state, and local administrative procedures. Similar efforts in reducing other regulatory delays are already underway at the direction of the President.

(6) Congress and the Executive Branch should consider undertaking a series of reforms designed to minimize corruption and waste connected with public works expenditures.

(7) The Executive Branch should undertake an administrative evaluation of the scattered public works activities of the federal government and be prepared to consummate consolidated reforms simultaneously with the proposed Public Works Report to Congress.

CLARIFYING RESPONSIBILITIES

(8) Congress or the Executive Branch should direct the Advisory Commission on Intergovernment Relations or a new body constituted for the purpose to review the public works responsibilities of each level of government and propose appropriate guidelines for allocating functions and responsibilities.

CONCLUSION

It would be all too tempting to avoid the difficulties of disentangling the knotted threads of intergovernmental complexity and to assume that federal public works expenditures must be drastically curtailed in the face of current economic conditions. But such a course would contravene the very purposes of economic policy now being formulated.

Economic renewal must be the premier focus of domestic policy in this decade. Our public infrastructure is strategically bound-up in that renewal. Without attention to deterioration of that infrastructure, economic renewal will be thwarted if not impossible.

We have no recourse but to face the complex task at hand of rebuilding our public facilities as an essential prerequisite to economic renewal and maintenance of our quality-of-life.

BIBLIOGRAPHY

Abt Associates, Inc., *National Rural Community Facilities Assessment Study*, Boston, Massachusetts, 1980.

Advisory Commission on Intergovernment Relations, Washington, D.C.

1. A Catalog of Federal Grant-in-Aid Programs to State and Local Governments: Grants Funded FY 1975. (A-52a), October, 1977

2. *Improving Federal Grants Management.* (A-53), February, 1977.

3. *The Intergovernmental Grant System as Seen by Local, State, and Federal Officials.* (A-54). March, 1977.

4. *Community Development: The Workings of a Federal-Local Block Grant.* (A-57). March, 1977.

5. *The States and Intergovernmental Aids.* (A-59). February, 1977.

6. *Federal Grants: Their Effects on State-Local Expenditures, Employment Levels, and Wage Rates.* (A-61). February, 1977.

7. *The Intergovernmental Grant System: An Assessment and Proposed Policies.* (B-1). 1978.

8. *Restructuring Federal Assistance: The Consolidation Approach,* Bulletin No. 79-6. October 1979.

9. *Categorical Grants: Their Role and Design.* (A-52). May, 1977.

10. *Pragmatic Federalism: The Reassignment of Functional Responsibility.* July, 1976.

11. *State Involvement in Federal-Local Grant Programs.* (M-55).

12. *State Mandating of Local Expenditures.* (A-67). July, 1978.

13. *Measuring the Fiscal Capacity and Effort of State and Local Areas.* (M-58). March, 1971.

14. *Multistate Regionalism.* (A-39). April, 1972.

Aldrich, Mark, *A History of Public Works in the United States,* 1790-1970, U.S. Department of Commerce, Washington, D.C., 1979.

Alexander, Governor Lamar, *The Five Year Capital Budget for the State of Tennessee. 1980–81, 1984–85.* The Government of the State of Tennessee, Nashville, Tennessee, January, 1980.

American Public Works Association, *A History of Public Works in the United States,* Chicago, Illinois, 1976.

Anthony, Robert N., *Planning and Control Systems: A Framework for Analysis,* Harvard University, Boston, Massachusetts, 1965.

Bryce, Herrington, J., *Small Cities,* Lexington Books, Lexington, Massachusetts, 1979.

Centaur Associates, Inc. *Economic Development Administration Title I Public Works Program Evaluation,* Washington, D.C., May, 1979.

Chamber of Commerce of the United States, *Improving Local Government Fiscal Management: Action Guidelines for Business Executives.* Washington, D.C., 1979.

Choate, Pat, "As Time Goes By: The Costs and Consequences of Delay." The Academy for Contemporary Problems, Columbus, Ohio. 1980.

Choate, Pat, *The High Plains Project,* Economic Development Administration, Washington, D.C., March, 1978.

Choate, Pat, "Urban Revitalization and Industrial Policy: The Next Steps." Testimony before the Subcommittee on the City, Committee on Banking, Finance, and Urban Affairs, U.S. House of Representatives on hearings on Urban Revitalization and Industrial Policy. Washington, D.C., September 17, 1980.

Committee on Environment and Public Works, United States Senate, 95th Congress, 2nd Session. *Report to the Senate of Several Public Buildings Proposals,* Washington, D.C., August, 1978.

Committee on Environment and Public Works, United States Senate, 96th Congress, 1st Session. *Report to the Senate Committee on the Budget.* Washington, D.C., March, 1979.

Committee on Environment and Public Works, United States Senate, 96th Congress, 2nd Session. *Report to the Senate Committee on the Budget.* Washington, D.C., March, 1980.

Committee on Public Works, United States Senate, 93rd Congress, 2nd Session, *Construction Delays and Unemployment.* Washington, D.C., 1974.

Committee on Public Works of the U.S. House of Representatives, *A National Public Works Investment Policy,* Washington, D.C., December, 1974.

Congressional Budget Office of the U.S. Congress, *Countercyclical Uses of Federal Grant Programs,* Washington, D.C., November, 1978.

Congressional Research Service of the Library of Congress, *Review of Title V Commission Plans,* Washington, D.C., 1977.

Consad Research Corporation, *A Study of Public Works Investment in the United States,* published by the U.S. Department of Commerce, Washington, D.C., April, 1980.

Devoy, Robert and Wise, Harold, *The Capital Budget,* The Council of State Planning Agencies, Washington, D.C., 1979.

Due, John F. *Government Finance,* The Richard D. Irwin Company, Homewood, Illinois, 1959.

The Economic Development Administration of the U.S. Department of Commerce, *An Updated Evaluation of the EDA-Funded Industrial Parks— 1968-74.* Washington, D.C., 1974.

Environmental Protection Agency, Unpublished working documents on the status of projects funded but uncompleted. Washington, D.C., June 11, 1980.

Executive Office of the President, "Small Community and Rural Development Policy," Washington, D.C., December 20, 1979.

Executive Office of the President, Office of Management and Budget, *Managing Federal Assistance in the 1980s,* Washington, D.C., March, 1980.

Executive Office of the President, Office of Management and Budget, *Public Works as Countercyclical Assistance.* Washington, D.C., November, 1979.

Executive Office of the President, Office of Management and Budget. *Reorganization Study of Local Development Assistance Programs,* Washington, D.C., December, 1978.

Executive Office of the President, Office of Management and Budget, *Special Analyses. Budget of the United States Government—Fiscal Year 1980.* Washington, D.C., 1980.

The Federal City Council, *Local Public Infrastructure in the District of Columbia.* Washington, D.C., August, 1980.

Getzels, Judith and Thurow, Charles. *Local Capital Improvements and Development Management: Analyses and Case Studies.* American Planning Association, Chicago, Illinois. June, 1980.

Grossman, David A., *The Future of New York City's Capital Plan,* The Urban Institute, Washington, D.C., 1979.

Grossman, David A., *Water Resources Priorities for the Northeast,* The consortium of Northeast Organizations, Washington, D.C., September, 1979.

Hatry, Harry, P., *Local Government Capital Infrastructure Planning: Current State-of-the-Art and "State-of-the-Practice."* The Urban Institute, Washington, D.C., 1980.

Hoyle, Robert S. "Capital Budgeting Models and Planning: An Evolutionary Process," Managerial Planning, November/December, 1978.

Hubbel, Kenneth L., editor, *Fiscal Crisis in American Cities: The Federal Response.* Ballinger Publishing Company, Cambridge, Massachusetts, 1979.

93

Humphrey, Nancy; Peterson, George E.; and Wilson, Peter. *The Future of Cincinnati's Capital Plant.* The Urban Institute, Washington, D.C., 1979.

Humphrey, Nancy; Peterson, George E.; and Wilson, Peter. *The Future of Cleveland's Capital Plant.* The Urban Institute, Washington, D.C., 1979.

Industrial Research and Extension Center, *Effects of Environmental Protection Regulation on Regional Economic Development,* University of Arkansas, Little Rock, Arkansas, September, 1977.

Joint Economic Committee of the Congress of the United States, 96th Congress, 2nd Session. *Public Works as a Countercyclical Tool,* 1980.

Kaynor, Edward R. "Uncertainty in Water Resources Planning in the Connecticut River Basin." American Water Resources Association, December, 1978.

Lapping, Mark B., "The State of Water Resources Planning and Management in New England: An Overview of Institutional Frameworks and Issues." The New England Federal Regional Council, Boston, Massachusetts, October, 1980.

Malone, Larry. *Coordinating State Functional Planning Programs: Strategies for Balancing Conflicting Objectives.* U.S. Department of Housing and Urban Development, Washington, D.C., 1977.

Milkman, Raymond H. and Toborg, Mary A., *Evaluating Economic Development Programs.* The Lazar Institute, Washington, D.C., 1978.

Morrison, Peter A., "Overview of Demographic Trends Shaping the Nation's Future." The Rand Paper Series, The Rand Corporation, Santa Monica, California, May, 1978.

National Conference of State Legislatures and the National Governor's Association, "Statement on Federalism Reform." November 25, 1980.

National Governors' Association, *Federal Roadblocks to Efficient State Government,* 1977.

National Governors' Association Center for Policy Research, *Bypassing the States: Wrong Turn on Urban Aid.* Washington, D.C., November, 1979.

Newman, William H. and Logan, James P., *Strategy, Policy and Central Management.* Southwestern Publishing Company, Dallas, Texas, 1976.

Oklahoma Water Resources Board, Oklahoma Comprehensive Water Plan, Oklahoma City, Oklahoma, April, 1980.

Pagano, Michael and Moore, Richard J. "Emerging Issues in Financing Basic Infrastructure," unpublished paper, September, 1980.

Pritchard, Allen, E., "Private Delivery of Public Services," The Academy for Contemporary Problems, Columbus, Ohio, 1976.

Reuss, Henry, S. *To Save Our Cities,* Public Affairs Press, Washington, D.C., Washington, D.C., 1977.

Salamon, Lester M., "In Pursuit of Reorganization: The Question of Goals," paper given at the Administrative Conference of the United States, Washington, D.C., 1980.

Schramm, Gunter, *The Value of Time in Environmental Decision Processes.* The University of Michigan, Ann Arbor, Michigan. November, 1979.

Schwartz, Gail Garfield and Choate, Pat. *Being Number One: Rebuilding the U.S. Economy.* Lexington Books, Lexington, Massachusetts, 1980.

Schwertz, Eddie L. Jr., *The Local Growth Management Guidebook.* The Southern Growth Policies Board, Washington, D.C., 1979.

Snelling, Governor Richard A., *Policy Statement on Capital Debt,* State of Vermont, February, 1979.

Stamm, Charles F. and Howell, James M. *Urban Fiscal Stress: A Comparative Analysis of 66 U.S. Cities.* Touche Ross and Company and The First National Bank of Boston, Boston, Massachusetts, 1979.

State of Colorado, *Private Choices, Public Strategies,* Denver, Colorado, February, 1980.

Steiner, George A., *Top Management Planning.* The MacMillian Company, New York City, 1969.

Subcommittee on Economic Development of the Committee on Public Works and Transportation of the House of Representatives, Ninety-Fourth Congress, 1st Session. *Public Works Project and Program Acceleration.* Washington, D.C., March 12, 1975.

Subcommittee on Economic Growth and Stabilization of the Joint Economic Committee of the Congress of the United States, 96th Congress, 1st Session, *Deteriorating Infrastructure in Urban and Rural Areas,* Washington, D.C., 1979.

Subcommittee on the City of the Committee on Banking, Finance and Urban Affairs, House of Representatives, 95th Congress, 2nd Session. *Small Cities: How Can the Federal and State Governments Response to Their Diverse Needs?* Washington, D.C., May, 1978.

The Urban Consortium, "Urban Infrastructure: Assessing Its Condition and Developing Policies and Methods for the Future." Washington, D.C., July, 1980.

U.S. Bureau of the Census, *Statistical Abstract of the United States: 1979.* (100 edition.) Washington, D.C., 1979.

U.S. Department of Agriculture, Rural Development Progress, January 1977-June 1979. Washington, D.C., 1979.

U.S. Department of Agriculture, *Social and Economic Trends in Rural America,* Washington, D.C., October, 1979.

U.S. Department of Commerce, "Establishment of a National Development Bank" National Public Advisory Committee on Regional Economic Development. Washington, D.C., 1976.

95

U.S. Department of Commerce, *Industrial Location Determinants,* Washington, D.C., 1973.

U.S. Department of Commerce, Industry and Trade Administration, *1980, U.S. Industrial Outlook,* Washington, D.C., 1980.

U.S. Department of Housing and Urban Development, *Advance Project Planning for Public Works: A Systematic Approach.* Washington, D.C., 1979.

U.S. Department of Housing and Urban Development. "Causes and Consequences of Delay in Implementing the Community Development Block Grant Program," Washington, D.C., June, 1980.

U.S. Department of Housing and Urban Development, "Streamlining Land Use Regulation: What Local Public Officials Should Know." Washington, D.C., 1980.

U.S. Department of Housing and Urban Development, *The President's National Urban Policy Report.* Washington, D.C., 1980.

U.S. Department of Transportation, *Draft Transportation Agenda for the 1980s: The Issues,* Washington, D.C., March, 1980.

U.S. Department of Transportation, Federal Highway Administration, *1981 Federal Highway Legislation:* Program and Revenue Options, Washington, D.C., June, 1980.

U.S. Environmental Protection Agency, *Clean Water: Fact Sheet,* Washington, D.C., April, 1980.

U.S. Environmental Protection Agency, *The Cost of Clean Air and Water: A Report to the Congress.* Washington, D.C., August, 1979.

U.S. General Accounting Office, *Federal Capital Budgeting: A Collection of Haphazard Practices.* Washington, D.C., February, 1981.

U.S. General Accounting Office, *Federally Assisted Areawide Planning Need to Simplify Policies and Practices,* Washington, D.C., March, 1977.

U.S. General Accounting Office, *Foresighted Planning and Budgeting Needed for Public Buildings Program.* Washington, D.C., September 9, 1980.

U.S. General Accounting Office, *Long-Range Analysis Activities in Seven Federal Agencies.* Washington, D.C., December, 1976.

U.S. General Accounting Office, *More Can Be Done to Insure that Industrial Parks Create New Jobs,* Washington, D.C., December 2, 1980.

U.S. General Accounting Office, *Perspectives on Intergovernmental Policy and Fiscal Relations.* Washington, D.C., June 28, 1979.

U.S. Senate, 96th Congress, 2nd Session S. 2080 (a draft bill), Washington, D.C., June 12, 1980.

U.S. Senate, 96th Congress, 2nd Session, *Standing Rules of the Senate,* Washington, D.C., March 25, 1980.

Vaughan, Roger J., "Countercyclical Public Works: A Rational Alternative." Testimony given before the Joint Economic Committee of the United States Congress, June 17, 1980. Washington, D.C.

Vaughan, Roger J., *Public Works as a Countercyclical Device: A Review of the Issues.* The Rand Corporation, Santa Monica, California, July, 1976.

Vernez, Georges and Vaughan Roger, J., *Assessment of Countercyclical Public Works and Public Service Employment Programs,* The Rand Corporation, Santa Monica, California, 1978.

Vernez, Georges; Vaughan, Roger, J.; and Yin, Robert K., *Federal Activities in Urban Economic Development.* The Rand Corporation, April, 1979.

Vernez, Georges; Vaughan, Roger, J.; Burright, Burke; and Coleman, Sinclair. *Regional Cycles and Employment Effects of Public Works Investments.* The Rand Corporation, Santa Monica, California, 1977.

Wallace, Holly, "Infrastructured: Maintain It Now or Pay the Price Tomorrow" *City Economic Development,* The National League of Cities, May 12, 1980.

White House Conference on Balanced National Growth, *Proceedings,* Washington, D.C., 1978.

Wildavsky, Aaron, Budgeting: *A Comparative Theory of Budgetary Processes,* Little, Brown and Company. Boston, Massachusetts, 1975.

Wilson, Peter. *The Future of Dallas's Capital Plant,* The Urban Institute, Washington, D.C., 1980.

Part II

REBUILDING AMERICA
FINANCING PUBLIC WORKS IN THE 1980s

Roger J. Vaughan

CHAPTER I

The "Infrastructure" Question: Meeting Needs or Efficient Investing?

IN 1973, a truck, heavily laden with road-repairing materials, plunged through the Westside Highway in New York City. The surprised driver escaped serious injury, but the event proved a precursor of an issue that now afflicts almost all Americans: the nation's public works are deteriorating.[1] Dams and bridges have been declared unsafe. Roads are impassable. Sewers are backing up. Hazardous wastes are leaking into water supply systems. The rate of public investment in maintaining existing physical infrastructure[2] and in building new facilities has fallen below 2½ percent of GNP—less than half the rate a decade ago. Net investment is close to zero.[3]

State and local officials seem powerless to address the problem. On the one hand, a growing volume of studies indicates that massive increases in public spending are necessary to arrest the rate of deterioration and to develop needed new facilities—perhaps a 300 or 400 percent increase from our present annual spending rate of $70 billion. At the same time, the money to pay for these investments is scarce. Federal aid for capital spending is being cut by 40 percent in real terms between 1981 and 1984. Recession has shrunk state and local tax revenues. Many states and localities face legislative or constitutional limits on debt issues, on revenues, or on both. Tax-exempt interest rates are at record levels. State and local governments must compete in bond markets with huge increases in federal borrowing. Escalating federal budget deficits render any increase in federal aid to states unlikely and make further cuts in aid almost inevitable.

To meet the needs that have been documented in recent studies, state and local governments would have to increase all taxes by about 40 percent. This would be constitutionally or legally impossible in many states, and politically impossible in all. Even if the money were available, it could not be spent efficiently. There are no reliable data concerning the condition of public works because few states, counties, or cities have measured the extent of under-investment, kept records of their capital investment needs, or determined their priorities.[4] In addition, responsibility is split between 100 federal agencies, 50 states, 3,042 counties, 35,000 general purpose local governments, 15,000 school districts, 26,000 special districts, and 209 multistate organizations.

Faced with an apparently insoluble dilemma, local governments have responded in an ad hoc fashion. In California, the aftermath of Proposition 13 has forced cities and counties to make residential developers pay for utility hook-ups. In Michigan, the economic depression in basic industries has forced across-the-board cuts in all public programs. From New York to St. Petersburg, fiscal problems have led to deferred maintenance of public works, which has accelerated the speed of deterioration. To stretch scarce dollars as far as possible, local governments have tried a number of financing gimmicks: in 1981, Massachusetts sold zero-coupon bonds to cut the cost of debt financing; Oakland, California, has sold and leased back its art museum to a private corporation to finance rehabilitation of its Coliseum; and New York City's subway cars will be owned, at least for tax purposes, by a communications corporation.

Innovative financing techniques, however, will not bridge the massive gap between needs and resources. At best, improved bond-marketing techniques, better planning, and innovative management techniques can help current capital spending buy 20 percent more capital investment in real terms. But that is less than 10 percent of the gap. There are no low-cost solutions to span the remaining 90 percent. If we continue with past policies of papering over the widening cracks in our public works, then economic recovery will stumble over ill-paved roads and ruptured water mains. A more comprehensive and radical strategy is required, a strategy that encompasses eight elements:

1. *Redesigning Engineering Replacement Standards and Improving Maintenance Procedures.* Many of the standards that are used by federal, state, and local governments to measure investment needs and to guide maintenance procedures can, with no harm, be modified to delay the replacement cycle and to ensure that what money is spent is allocated to high-priority projects. In an analysis of public investment financing policy, Peterson and Miller conclude:

> Although needs gaps are usually thought to be filled by additional spending, they can be closed by reconsidering and reducing the needs standards that have given rise to the investment gap. This is not a matter of redefining infrastructure needs to make them disappear, but of recognizing that needs always exceed resources and that, with budgets as tight as they now are, priorities must be selected even within "needs" categories (Peterson and Miller, 1981, p. 2).

The issue is not only defining replacement cycles that reflect realistic priorities but also designing engineering standards that are cost effective. For example, more than half the road bridges requiring replacement are on the list because the bridge is narrower than the approach roads, not because they are structurally unsound. Public investment, like private investment, must be guided by a careful comparison of costs and benefits, not by simple engineering algorithms.

2. *Reducing Subsidies to Private Investment.* State and local governments must cut back on using tax revenues and the proceeds from tax-exempt bond sales to finance private sector capital investments. In 1981, more than half the proceeds from long-term bond sales were used to finance projects that are not, traditionally, the responsibility of the public sector, including private hospitals, industrial development projects, pollution control facilities for private companies, convention centers, and university dormitories. State and local governments do not

103

have the resources to maintain and develop public infrastructure—roads, bridges, sewer and waste systems, schools, and parks—and to subsidize investments by private firms. The National Economic Recovery Tax Act of 1981 provided deep incentives for private investments while raising the cost of public borrowing. Using scarce state and local resources to provide further incentives is not fiscally prudent although it is politically difficult for a state to reduce these incentives unilaterally.

3. *Improving Capital Planning, Budgeting, and Management.* A comprehensive public investment strategy will require much more sophisticated planning and budgeting procedures and the design of more effective management techniques for disbursing funds and for operating public facilities. Shepard and Goddard summarize the need for better planning:

> Strategies and programs to restore the infrastructure to its role of providing efficient service to human and economic goals must be preceded by deliberation and the capacity to act—the country has learned all too well that massive doses of money, even if they were available, can contain the disease but cannot provide a complete cure. Time conscious planning and the capacity to analyze appropriate capital development strategies can be as valuable a step as the generation of the dollar resources needed for restoration and revitalization (Shepard and Goddard, *no date*, p. 18).

The failure to develop comprehensive needs assessment, planning, and budgeting techniques is reflected not only in the misallocation of resources among projects and the failure to prevent serious breakdowns, but also in increasing delays in undertaking projects. In *As Time Goes By,* Dr. Pat Choate (1979) documents a backlog of funded but unconstructed federal, state, and local capital projects of $80–$100 billion. With high inflation, these delays have escalated project costs by as much as 12 percent annually or over $1 billion each month. Not only do we need to develop effective planning mechanisms for capital projects, but we need to develop mechanisms to speed up the permitting and contract-letting procedures to avoid costly delays. New administrative structures will be needed to ensure that public facilities are efficiently managed.

104

4. *Project-Specific Cost Sharing Arrangements with Private Firms.* Some public capital projects are made for the exclusive benefit of major private sector developments. The most obvious examples are new towns constructed to house the labor force for large-scale energy developments in the West. Smaller examples include streets, sidewalks, and utility hook-ups for residential subdivisions, and highway and railroad spurs for new manufacturing facilities. The major beneficiary of these investments should be required to pay at least part of the investment costs.

5. *Charging for Public Services.* Bridging the infrastructure gap will require much greater reliance on "user fees" for public services, such as waste disposal and water supply, and recreation. User fees should not be regarded as merely a source of revenues. Efficient pricing encourages efficient use of services and will reduce the amount of new construction needed. For example, if water use is metered and charged for, supply capacity will not necessarily have to expand in proportion to population or employment growth. Paying for each gallon of water consumed encourages conservation, which means fewer new reservoirs and treatment plants. Less public capital spending will be needed if user fees are more widely applied, where the administrative costs are not prohibitive and equity issues are manageable.

6. *Improving Bond-Financing Mechanisms.* A little more than half of all state and local capital spending is financed through revenues from the sale of tax-exempt bonds—including general obligation and limited obligation issues. The disorganization and decentralization of the bond market in some states have contributed to high financing costs—there are over 1.5 million different tax-exempt issues outstanding. The costs of issuing these bonds can be reduced through state bond banks, state bond guarantees, and state loans to localities. In addition, new revenue sources can be found to service the debt and improve the credit rating.

7. *State Assistance to Local Governments.* Local governments—cities, counties, and special districts—directly invest about twice as much as state governments in capital projects, although many of the funds are provided from

105

federal and state sources. Many local jursidictions have reached statutory or constitutional bonding limits and are facing extreme fiscal pressures as a result of the economic recession and cuts in federal aid. Some increase in state aid (both dollars and planning assistance) will be necessary for those cities and counties with extensive infrastructure needs and slender fiscal resources. The state can help through technical and planning assistance, intrastate revenue sharing, direct loans, categorical project grants, or state assumption of local responsibilities.

8. *Increasing Public Capital Investment.* The final element in bridging the gap is for increased spending on public works. The revenues will come from user fees, increases in existing tax rates, and perhaps from reducing tax abatement and exemption programs for business. Although these steps will not be politically popular, taxpayers may be less hostile if the revenues from increased tax rates are directly committed to specific purposes and projects.

These eight steps are complementary elements of an effective program of public capital investment. They reduce the apparently overwhelming infrastructure crisis into a series of manageable policy issues. Instead of asking the unanswerable question—How do we finance a quadrupling of state and local infrastructure spending?—we must examine three questions. How should responsibility for infrastructure financing be shared between the public and private sectors? What is an efficient level of public investment in, and maintenance of, capital facilities? And, finally, What is the most efficient way of financing public investments? The goal is to make efficient investment decisions, not to meet ill-defined needs.

This book discusses financing options (steps 4, 5, 6, 7, and 8). In the companion volume, *Planning and Managing Public Works Investments in the 1980s*, planning, budgeting, and management issues are analyzed in detail (steps 1, 2, and 3). It is intended to assist state and local officials—those charged with planning, budgeting, and policy development—to think strategically about public capital investment policies. It reviews the alternative policies that can be pursued in designing user fees, improving the operation of the bond market, sharing responsibility with the private sector, and providing increased assistance to local governments. It is not intended as a technical manual in the arcane procedures related to bond sales, leasing, and negotiated investment strategies.

The following chapter describes current capital spending by federal, state, and local governments and their fiscal capacity to increase the level of spending. The third chapter provides a brief overview of the principles that must guide the design of a public capital investment strategy, including a discussion of the allocation of responsibility between the public and private sectors, and the selection of alternative financing methods. In chapter 4, user fees are discussed. The term *user fees* is applied to all fees, charges, and dedicated tax revenues (where the level of taxes paid is related to the use of a facility, e.g., gasoline tax revenues applied to road repair) that are used to finance the operating and maintenance costs of public works and new construction. The chapter opens with an examination of equity and efficiency issues and concludes with an analysis of opportunities to apply user fees to different types of public facilities.

Debt-financing issues are discussed in chapter 5. The opening sections describe the operation of the tax-exempt bond market and how recent changes in federal policy have influenced the market. The final section explores ways of reducing the cost of debt financing including technical assistance, state guarantees for local issues, bond banks, zero-coupon bonds, and state incentives for local capital investments. The sixth chapter analyzes the special problems that state and local governments face with respect to financing public infrastructure necessary for large-scale private resource development projects. It outlines how costs can be shared between the public sector and private firms, and how states can assist localities in avoiding the adverse effects of large development projects. Chapter 7 outlines how state and local governments can use leasing, service contracts, and the outright sale of public facilities to private firms to reduce the costs of public capital investments. Chapter 8 summarizes the major conclusions from the preceding chapters. It explores state-local fiscal relations and ways to increase state aid to localities for capital investments. It also briefly examines how alternative federal actions may influence the design of state and local capital strategies.

By carefully selecting financing techniques, and through complementary reforms in capital planning and management procedures, the infrastructure problem can be reduced to reasonable and tractable dimensions. A prudent state investment strategy can lay the foundation for stable and sustainable economic growth.

CHAPTER I NOTES

1. See Choate and Walter, 1981; Choate, 1982; Dossani and Steger, 1980.

2. The term *infrastructure* refers to facilities and equipment necessary or desirable for the delivery of services to meet social and economic needs. The most exhaustive classification is provided in a study conducted by Abt Associates for the U.S. Department of Agriculture. They identified thirty-seven categories under two major headings: service facilities and production facilities. These categories are reproduced below (see also Holland, 1972). Most studies focus on water systems, sewer systems, streets and highways, mass transit and bridges (see Dossani and Steger, 1980; U.S. Department of Commerce, 1980; Humphrey et al., 1979).

Categories of Public Infrastructure

I. SERVICE FACILITIES

Education

1. Elementary Schools
2. Middle Schools
3. Secondary Schools
4. Public Libraries

Health

1. Hospitals
2. Nursing Homes
3. Ambulatory (Outpatient) Care Facilities
4. Ambulatory Dental Care Facilities
5. Ambulatory Mental Health Facilities

II. PRODUCTION FACILITIES

Energy

1. Direct Power Suppliers

Fire Safety

1. Fire Stations
2. Vehicles
3. Communications Systems
4. Water Supply and Storage Facilities

Solid Waste

1. Collection Facilities and Equipment
2. Disposal Sites

6. Residential Facilities for
   a. orphans and dependent children
   b. the emotionally disturbed
   c. alcoholics and drug abusers
   d. the physically handicapped
   e. mentally retarded
   f. blind and deaf
7. Emergency Vehicle Services

Justice

1. Law Enforcement Facilities
2. Jails

Recreation

1. Community Recreation Facilities

Transportation

1. Railroad Facilities
2. Airports and Related Facilities
3. Streets and Highways (including bridges)
4. Inter- and Intra-Community Transit

Telecommunications

1. Cable Television
2. Over-the-Air Television
3. Disaster Preparedness

Waste Water

1. Sewer Mains and Collection Systems
2. Treatment and Disposal Systems

Water Supply

1. Community Systems
   a. Storage Facilities
   b. Treatment Facilities
   c. Delivery Facilities
2. On-Site Wells and Cisterns

---

3. See U.S. Department of Commerce, 1980, especially appendix A.

4. For a discussion of the data problems, see Abt Associates, 1980; Choate and Walter, 1981; Dossani and Steger, 1980; U.S. Department of Commerce, 1980.

Source: Abt Associates, National Rural Community Facilities Assessment Study: Pilot Phase, Final Report, March, 1980, p. 16. See also appendix A-1 for definitions used by others.

CHAPTER II

Public Capital Investments: Present Patterns and Fiscal Capacity

PUBLIC CAPITAL INVESTMENTS—in everything from schoolhouses to sewer systems—are made by all levels of governments, from federal agencies and state authorities to city and county governments and thousands of special districts. Funding sources are equally diverse and include appropriations from general revenues, intergovernmental grants, revenues from fees and charges, and the proceeds from tax-exempt bond sales. In some cases, private resources are used. The allocation of responsibility among different levels of government for raising the funds to pay for the maintenance and development of public works and for actually managing the process of capital spending varies among different types of projects and among different states. So, too, does the choice of financing mechanisms. Constitutional restrictions, legislation, and historical accident have all contributed to divergence in practice and capability among different governments. As state and local governments develop capital investment strategies, they must operate within these legislative and institutional constraints. What is efficient and feasible in one place may be impossible in another.

The purpose of this chapter is to provide a brief description of present public capital investment practices. It gives a context in which to place the more specific discussions and recommendations in the following chapters. The first section defines what is meant by *public capital investment* and its role in public service delivery. The sec-

ond section describes current patterns of public investments and how the responsibility for finance and management is allocated among different levels of government.
The third section provides an overview of recent fiscal patterns of state and local governments, including changes
in revenue sources and expenditures.

Definitions and Concepts

Economic development requires capital investments.
We must set aside some of our output of goods and services to expand our ability to produce in the future. Investment not only provides the machinery and resources necessary to generate new jobs for the growing labor force but
also increases the productivity of existing workers so that
real incomes will grow. Capital accumulation can take
many forms. It includes investments in research to develop new products and processes, in new plant and equipment, in maintenance and repair of existing machinery.
The acquisition of education and new skills by the work
force, the managing and development of natural resources, and the provision of the underlying public structures necessary to provide public services and to sustain
development are also forms of capital accumulation.

Neither public nor private capital investments are
ends in themselves. Both are necessary to expand production of goods and services demanded by households. Although it has become fashionable to downplay the usefulness of public spending, the difference between public and
private capital spending does not arise because of differences in their contributions to economic development.
A sound transportation system is as important to our economy as modern steel-producing facilities. The difference
is that, while the returns to a private investment accrue
in most part to the private investor, the benefits of a public
investment accrue to a much broader population and are
less easily measured. Traditionally, the responsibility for
certain types of investment has been assumed by the public sector because market structures do not enable a private investor to earn a sufficient rate of return, even
though the investment would yield benefits in excess of
costs. The network of urban streets, for example, is of tre-

111

mendous value to local residents and businesses alike but cannot easily yield a stream of revenues to reward a private firm undertaking its construction.

The public sector has also assumed responsibility for certain types of services—and therefore the capital investments they require—for reasons of fairness, or equity. Primary and secondary education, for example, have become a local government responsibility in order to guarantee that all children can learn the basic skills needed in society, regardless of their parents' income and regardless of the admissions policies of local private schools.

Unfortunately, the definition of what constitutes an appropriate public responsibility is vague. Indeed, it changes over time with technological development and evolutions in market structures. It also responds to shifts in public tastes and in public perceptions of problems. Environmental issues became a public responsibility as the costly and hazardous consequences of pollution became apparent. In the past decade, "economic development" has become a public responsibility in some areas because of job loss and persistent high unemployment rates. Public and private responsibilities for capital investments increasingly overlap.[1]

Clarifying public and private roles is a necessary first step in designing a state investment strategy.

It is also necessary to clarify the role of public capital in economic development. Many researchers distinguish between social and economic infrastructure. But this is too narrow a view. A very large share of state and local capital expenditures are for facilities that are concerned primarily with improving the quality of "human capital" which is as vital for economic growth as is physical capital. Education facilities, from primary schools to advanced research centers, are essential to the enhancement of the skill levels of the work force, and most studies have found that investments in these facilities are as important as direct investments in plant and equipment in determining the overall rate of growth of the national economy. Health facilities, from community centers to advanced medical research institutes, have contributed to the steady increase in the health of the work force, another important

112

factor in sustaining economic growth. Human capital investments will prove increasingly necessary as the rate of growth of the work force slows in the next decade and as the technological revolution creates growing demands for highly educated and trained labor. Together, health and education capital expenditures account for nearly half of those public capital investments financed from state and local resources. Although these projects are normally regarded as expenditures—to be cut when the fiscal tide ebbs—they should more properly be regarded as "investments" yielding future benefits in terms of reduced welfare dependency, reduced unemployment insurance expenditures, increased incomes, and more rapid job growth. Infrastructure investments, therefore, refer not only to projects such as roads, bridges, ports, and water supply facilities, but also to the facilities that improve the fitness and skill of the work force.

In spite of the critical importance of state and local capital spending to sustainable economic growth, the economic policy debate in Washington has emphasized private investment incentives almost to the exclusion of public investments, in spite of mounting concern over the condition and level of public investments.[3] In fact, the ability of state and local governments to finance capital investments out of bond revenues has been harmed by recent changes in the federal tax code.

In summary, public capital investments are made to meet public demands for public services. They must be evaluated with the same rigor as private investments, even though the measure of the benefits is not as simple. The services provided through these public facilities are a vital factor in ensuring continued economic growth and are necessary to complement private capital investments.

Current Patterns
of Public Investment

Analyzing public capital investments is not easy.[2] Neither the federal government nor many states maintain compatible and detailed capital budgets from which data on new construction, maintenance, and repair expenditures can be compiled. However, using the data that are

available, we can present an overview of current investment patterns and recent trends. This section reviews
three major aspects of public works investments: (1) the
rate of investment, focusing on the decline during the past
decade; (2) the lack of any clear allocation of fiscal and
management responsibility among federal, state, and local
governments; and (3) changing priorities among different
types of investments.

The Rate of Investment

By almost any measure, the rate of investment in public works is declining. In 1980, federal, state, and local
governments spent $70 billion on nondefense capital proj-
ects—about 2.3 percent of GNP. This is much less than
the 4.8 percent investment rate in 1970, and the peak rate
of over 5 percent in 1965. As a share of total state and local
expenditures, capital investments have declined from 27
percent in 1960 to 15.4 percent in 1980. In constant (1972)
dollars, capital expenditures declined from $53.6 billion
in 1968 to $46.4 billion in 1979 (table 1).

Although the performance over the last decade shows
a sharp decline in the rate of investment, there has been
some recovery in recent years. The lowest rate of investment was reached in 1977, and increased between 1978
and 1980. Peterson and Miller summarize:

> In retrospect, the period 1980–82 may prove to be a water-
> shed for infrastructure financing. Preliminary data point
> to the possibility of a sharp reversal in capital budgets,
> especially in large cities, as the infrastructure problem
> receives more recognition. However, the picture is far from
> clear. . . . The need for infrastructure investment certainly
> has seized public attention, but actual investment growth
> may have been forestalled by high interest rates, federal
> aid reduction, and local budgetary pressures (Peterson and
> Miller, 1981, p. 13).

The ability of state and local governments to sustain
needed capital investment is obviously weakened by the
condition of the economy and by cuts in federal aid. Preliminary data for 1982 indicate a sharp decline in capital
spending in the third quarter. Preliminary data for 1981,

114

Table 1

Government Expenditures for Fixed Capital Investment in Current and Constant Dollars, Selected Years

($ in billions)

	Current Dollar			Constant 1972 Dollar		
		Expenditures			Expenditures	
	Total	Federal*	State & Local	Total	Federal	State & Local
1960	$26.6	$13.1	$13.5	$40.3	$18.5	$21.8
1965	34.2	14.1	20.1	48.4	18.8	29.6
1968	41.5	13.9	27.6	53.6	16.8	36.8
1970	42.8	14.0	28.8	48.2	15.3	32.9
1971	45.6	15.4	30.2	48.1	16.1	32.0
1972	48.9	18.0	30.9	49.3	18.1	31.2
1973	51.5	17.9	33.6	48.8	17.3	31.5
1974	58.4	17.7	40.7	48.0	15.9	32.1
1975	63.0	21.2	41.8	48.3	17.1	31.2
1976	63.3	23.4	39.9	48.5	17.6	28.2
1977	64.2	25.2	39.0	43.6	17.5	26.1
1978	75.7	29.0	46.7	46.2	18.0	28.2
1979	83.7	32.9	50.8	46.4	18.9	27.5

Notes: Includes federal military expenditures.

The data presented are for investments in structures only and are therefore smaller than the investment totals shown in table 3, which include land costs and equipment, as well as maintenance and repair expenditures.

Source: Bureau of Economic Analysis, U.S. Department of Commerce, unpublished data, adapted in Peterson and Miller, 1981.

compiled by the Bureau of Economic Analysis, show sharp cuts in public works spending. Infrastructure maintenance has proved vulnerable when cuts in spending are made (Peterson, 1979; GAO, 1982; Choate and Walter, 1981). Mayor Helen Boosalis of Lincoln, Nebraska, has said that "in the choice between laying off police or maintaining sewers, sewers always lose" (*Newsweek,* 8/2/82, p. 21). Between 1977 and 1979, the city of Raleigh cut capital spending by 60 percent (Wolman and Davis, 1980). In 1978, San Francisco cut investments by 45 percent and St. Petersburg cut capital spending by 43 percent (Ibid). The Joint Economic Committee (1980) conducted a survey of major cities and concluded that neglect of public capital "appears to be the single greatest problem facing our nation's cities."

The Allocation of Responsibility

Although most actual capital spending is done by local governments, a large share of the funding comes from the federal government. During the last decade, federal aid funding increased from 20 percent of state and local capital spending in 1970 to 40 percent in 1980 (table 2). Federal grants have not only increased the level of investment spending by state and local governments, they have also changed investment priorities as localities adjusted their expenditure patterns to capture money from federal agencies. The lack of any clear allocation of responsibility among federal, state, and local governments for capital investments has led to considerable duplication, and costly mandates, regulations, and requirements.

The increase in federal aid arose from two perceptions. The first was that state and local governments were doing a poor job in meeting certain national economic, social, and environmental objectives. The waste water treatment program, financed through the Environmental Protection Agency, was undertaken because local actions were inadequate to protect and restore the nation's lakes, waterways, and oceans. By the late 1970s, the program had surpassed the interstate highway system as the largest federally funded public works program. The expansion of federal funding of mass transit during the decade was intended to reduce the nation's dependence on imported oil. Similarly, the Community Development Block Grant program was an attempt by Congress to ensure that cities met the needs of their poorer communities.

The second perception was that the fiscal position of state and local governments was worsening as a result of the rapid growth in expenditures on social programs, in addition to job and population loss in central cities, and inflation. Although New York City had the most publicized brush with bankruptcy, many major cities and older states did not fare much better. Revenue sharing and categorical grants-in-aid were distributed according to indicators

116

Table 2

Federal Capital Aid Compared to Total State-Local Capital Spending, Selected Years

($ in billions)

Year	Capital Grants	Total State-Local Capital Spending	Federal Capital Aid as a Percent of Total Spending
1970	$ 5.9	$28.8	20.5%
1975	9.0	41.8	21.4
1976	11.4	39.9	28.5
1977	16.4	39.0	42.1
1978	18.0	46.7	38.5
1979	19.8	50.8	39.0
1980	22.3	55.9	40.0

Source: Peterson and Miller, 1981, p. 9

measuring need and fiscal capacity. It is still unclear whether the urban fiscal crises in the mid-1970s were due to a reversible overcommitment to public spending or were due to an irreversible decline in the fiscal base. The economies of Massachusetts and New York have recovered both their economic and fiscal health in a surprisingly short time. However, some cities are still awaiting the first signs of an economic renaissance. Federal fiscal assistance allowed localities to spend more than local resources allowed and to avoid unpopular tax increases. But it also muddled lines of responsibility and accountability.

The federal government is responsible for only a small fraction of *direct* capital spending (if expenditures for national defense and international relations are excluded), a little over $8 billion out of a total of $71 billion. Yet it is responsible for financing nearly half of state and local capital investments (table 3). There are some patterns in the allocation of spending responsibility among the three levels of government. The federal government has the major responsibility for investments in natural resources[4] (the acquisition of land for preservation and recreation), for some pollution control facilities, and for water transportation, ports, and terminals (Army Corps of Engineers projects). State governments are primarily responsible for

117

Table 3

Direct Governmental Capital Outlays in FY 1980, by Function and Level of Government

($ in millions) — Total Capital Outlay

Function	All Governments	Federal Government
All Functions	99,386	36,492
National Defense and International Relations......................	28,161	28,161
Space Research and Technology	239	239
Education	10,834	97
Local Schools	7,362	—
Institutions of Higher Education ...	2,972	—
Other........................	500	97
Highways	19,265	132
Health and Hospitals	3,116	673
Sewerage	6,272	—
Parks and Recreation	2,320	297
Natural Resources	5,098	4,046
Housing and Urban Renewal	2,565	317
Air Transportation	1,542	151
Water Transport and Terminals......	1,626	1,003
Utilities	9,933	—
Water Supply	3,335	—
Electric Power	4,572	—
Transit.......................	1,921	—
Gas Supply	105	—
Other Functions	8,413	1,375

Note: Because of rounding, details may not add to totals. Local government amounts are estimates subject to sampling variations; see—Represents zero or rounds to zero.
See note under table 1 for compatibility of data.

Total Capital Outlay			Construction Outlays	
	State and Local Governments		All	Federal
Total	State	Local	Governments	Government
62,894	23,325	39,568	58,410	6,918
—	—	—	2,038	2,038
—	—	—	138	138
10,737	3,182	7,555	7,460	80
7,362	323	7,039	5,186	—
2,972	2,458	515	1,883	—
403	401	1	391	80
19,133	14,706	4,427	17,327	128
2,443	1,212	1,231	2,238	364
6,272	243	6,028	5,967	—
2,023	488	1,535	1,634	274
1,052	527	526	3,206	2,466
2,248	58	2,190	1,765	—
1,391	235	1,157	1,258	38
623	169	454	1,531	984
9,933	716	9,216	8,631	—
3,335	64	3,270	2,956	—
4,572	345	4,227	4,236	—
1,921	307	614	1,362	—
105	—	105	87	—
7,037	1,787	5,251	5,186	408

Source: U.S. Bureau of the Census, *Survey of Governments 1979–1980* (Washington, D.C., 1981) p. 35.

spending on highways, health facilities, and higher education. The remaining categories are, for the most part, a local responsibility, with local governments outspending state governments by more than $3 to $2. This does not, of course, indicate that states are not paying their share. The state role has increased significantly during the past decade and is likely to increase during the next decade as federal aid shrinks. About 60 percent of state budget expenditures flows to localities or directly to individuals. Local governments—counties, municipalities, and special districts—will remain the primary "spending unit" for public capital investments.

Investment by Type of Project

During the last decade, state and local capital priorities have changed significantly. State and local capital spending on sewers, transit, and water projects have increased more rapidly than other categories (table 4), largely as a result of increases in federal funding for selected programs. The relatively slow growth of expenditures in highways during the 1970s—a category that had grown rapidly in the 1960s—was a result of the nearing completion of the system and the slow growth in trust fund revenues because the federal government had not increased the four-cents-per-gallon gasoline tax since 1962. In addition, some highway construction funds have been diverted to finance transit (table 5). Highway expenditure has also shifted from new construction to a greater emphasis on resurfacing, restoration, and bridge repair:

> During the latter half of the 1970s, federal capital support likewise assumed a geographic purpose. Many of the new programs—Federal Aid Urban (Road) Systems, Community Development Block Grants, Urban Development Action Grants, Mass Transit funding—were especially directed to older cities and their requirements for capital renovation (Peterson and Miller, 1981 p. 51).

These programs, however, are likely to be scaled back and some may be turned back to the states entirely under the president's proposal for a new federalism. Since pat-

120

Table 4

Capital Outlays by State and Local Governments by Type ($ in millions)

Fiscal Year	Local Schools	Highways and Bridges	Sewers	Transit	Water	Total
			Function			
1971	$4,845	$11,888	$1,744	$ 446	$1,247	$33,137
1972	4,759	12,317	2,091	435	1,343	34,237
1973	4,856	11,459	2,428	920	1,435	35,257
1974	5,108	12,152	2,640	926	1,743	38,084
1975	6,532	13,646	3,569	1,203	2,111	44,817
1976	6,547	14,209	3,955	1,339	2,208	46,531
1977	5,982	12,497	4,208	1,573	2,302	44,896
1978	5,709	12,898	4,366	1,407	2,141	44,769
1979	6,370	15,567	5,619	1,618	2,701	53,196
1980	7,362	19,133	6,272	1,921	3,335	62,894
Percentage Growth, 1971–1980	52%	61%	260%	331%	167%	90%

Source: U.S. Department of Commerce, Bureau of the Census, *Governmental Finances,* Fiscal Years 1971–72 through 1979–80.

terms of public capital spending seem to have reflected federal rather than local priorities, the planned withdrawal of Washington will require a radical rethinking of present practices and the reestablishment of local priorities.

The Fiscal Capacity of State and Local Governments

Capital spending by state and local governments must be viewed against the broader background of state and local revenues and expenditures. Revenues provide the resources to finance bond issues and maintain capital projects. In the past decade, state and local governments have sought to diversify their fiscal bases by introducing new taxes and charges, and relying less on traditional tax revenues. Trends in expenditures by category reveal changes in public service priorities which must be considered in making public investment decisions. In general, rapid increases in health and welfare programs have squeezed capital investments.

Recent Trends in Revenues

Overall state and local revenues nearly tripled between 1970 and 1980—with state government revenues growing faster than those of local governments (table 6). Growth was most rapid during the first half of the decade and actually declined in real terms since 1977 as the result of legislative and constitutional limitations on revenue sources, increases in federal aid, and draconian attempts to cut spending. There were, however, pronounced shifts in the relative importance of different revenue sources (table 6):

☐ The dominant revenue source of state governments continued to be the sales tax. However, it accounts for 8 percent less of the share of total revenues in 1980 when compared with 1970. Individual and corporate income taxes increased their share of state revenues from 18.8 percent to 23.7 percent.

☐ Property taxes remained the most important revenue source for local governments but experienced a 13 percent decline in their share of total revenues.

☐ Service charges of local governments experienced a 3 percent increase in share, while the share of charges in state revenues declined.

☐ The most dramatic change has been the tremendous increase in transfers to state and local governments from the federal government, from $21.8 billion in FY 1970 to $83 billion in FY 1980.

☐ State grants to local governments also grew rapidly, from $27 billion in FY 1970 to $81 billion in FY 1980.

From the perspective of financing public works, these shifts are important. Historically, the property tax provided revenues that backed local bond issues, either out of current revenues or out of the incremental revenues attributed to the project. The decline in importance of property taxes has not occurred voluntarily. In many cities and counties, property tax rates have reached constitutional or legislated ceilings, and so local jurisdictions have

122

sought politically more expedient sources. Second, the rapid growth of federal revenues has been reversed and is projected to decline at an annual real rate of 14 percent during the next two years. Third, basic revenues to state governments have failed to grow as rapidly as expenditures. The ACIR summarized the problem: "Without the help of periodic increases in state sales and income taxes, most of our 50 state-local systems cannot generate sufficient automatic revenue growth to keep pace with, much less exceed the rate of growth of the economy" (ACIR, 1981, p. 8). The property tax revenues to local governments have increased more rapidly than the general rate of inflation, in part due to the inflation-induced tax benefits of property ownership. If inflation of property values abates, the reverse will be true—the property tax base will grow much more slowly than the local economy and local government need during the next few years.

Expenditures

State and local expenditures also grew rapidly during the 1970s, although, since 1975, they have declined in real terms—in large part as a result of restrictions on revenues (tables 7 and 8). Summarizing the trends depicted in these tables:

☐ The spending levels of state and local governments nearly tripled between 1970 and 1980. Reflecting their greater ability to raise revenues, state government expenditures grew at a slightly faster rate than localities. State governments rapidly increased their level of spending for public welfare, while decreasing their share of contributions for highway and roads. State matching requirements for federal public assistance and decreases in federal highway aid accounted for most of the state shifts. Education continued to be the largest single expenditure category.

☐ Local governments also continued to spend a major portion of their budgets on education. Outlays for sewers rose sharply in response to the federal funding of 75 percent of costs. Local spending for police protection also grew slightly. Local spending for public welfare, historically considered a local issue, declined

123

Table 5

Outlays for Federal Capital Assistance ($ in millions)

Fiscal Year:	1970	1971	1972	1973	1974	1975	1976	TQ[a]	1977	1978	1979	1980
Interstate Highways	3173	3330	3342	3269	2909	2804	3306	828	2828	2614	3163	3998
Interstate Resurfacing, Restoration & Rehabilitation	—	—	—	—	—	—	—	—	23	94	151	193
Interstate Transfers for Transit	—	—	—	—	51	66	337	216	392	667	700	679
Federal Aid Urban System	—	—	—	11	35	170	342	109	434	472	640	871
Bridge Replacement and Rehabilitation	—	—	3	19	38	46	104	35	131	146	208	548
UMTA Sec. 3 Discretionary Grants	1	285	510	864	870	1197	1092	254	1250	1400	1226	1655
UMTA Sec. 5 Formula Grants	—	—	—	—	—	152	390	55	611	735	1134	1120
Capital Uses of Sec. 5 Grants	—	—	—	—	—	9	25	7	39	N/A	251	431
Waste Water Treatment	—	—	—	680	1560	1940	2429	918	3545	3194	3741	4343
Community Development Block Grants	—	—	—	—	—	38	983	439	2089	2464	3161	3902
Local Public Works	—	—	—	—	—	—	—	—	575	3041	1720	416
Urban Development Action Grants	—	—	—	—	—	—	—	—	—	N/A	N/A	255

Note: 1. Outlays for FY 1965–70; $681 million. a. refers to Third Quarter 1976 when federal fiscal year changed from July to October.

Source: Agency records from the Federal Highway Administration, the Urban Mass Transportation Administration, the Environmental Protection Agency, the Department of Housing and Urban Development, and the Office of Management and Budget, compiled in Peterson and Miller, 1981, p. 51.

Table 6

State and Local Government Revenues by Sources, 1970 and 1980

($ in millions)

Item	State 1970 Amount	Percent	State 1980 Amount	Percent	Local 1970 Amount	Percent	Local 1980 Amount	Percent
General Revenues	57,507	(83.7)	169,266	(79.6)	51,392	(86.2)	130,027	(83.4)
Taxes	47,962	(69.8)	137,075	(64.5)	38,833	(65.2)	86,387	(55.4)
Property	1,092	1.6	2,892	1.4	32,963	55.3	65,607	42.1
Individual Income	9,183	13.4	37,089	17.4	1,630	2.8	4,990	3.2
Corporation Income	3,738	5.4	13,321	6.3	—	—	—	—
Sales & Gross Receipts	27,254	39.7	67,655	31.8	3,068	5.1	12,072	7.7
Other Taxes	6,695	9.7	15,517	7.5	1,173	2.0	3,718	2.4
Current Charges	6,102	8.9	16,545	7.8	8,770	14.7	27,828	17.9
Miscellaneous	3,443	5.0	15,646	7.4	3,788	6.4	15,812	10.1
Utility, Liquor & Insurance	11,185	16.3	43,570	20.4	8,165	13.7	25,845	16.6
TOTAL Own Source Revenue	68,691	100.0	212,636	100.0	59,557	100.0	155,873	100.0
Intergovernmental Transfers	20,248		64,526		29,525		102,425	
From Federal	19,252		51,892		2,605		21,136	
From State	—		—		26,920		81,289	
From Local	995		2,434		—		—	

Notes: Figures in parentheses [( )] are not included in cumulative percent total. (Ed. refers to Intergovernmental transfers can be omitted)

Source: Buckley, Michael Patrick, *Assessing the Issues and Trends in Public Facilities Financing: Planning and Policy Considerations for State and Local Governments in Oregon,* University of Oregon, Masters Thesis, May 1982, various tables.

by nearly 30 percent when compared to its 1970 share of total expenditures.

☐ Both states and localities increased their spending share on debt interest, with the state level undergoing a 50 percent jump, from 3.1 percent in 1970 to 4.7 percent in 1980.

State and Local Fiscal Capacity and Public Investments

During the 1980s, the combination of a weak national economy, high interest rates, and the delegation of greater fiscal and administrative responsibility by the federal government has created serious problems for state and

---

Table 7

State and Local Government Expenditure, as a Percent of Gross National Product, Selected Years 1949–1981

Calendar Year	Total State and Local Expenditures[1]	Federal Aid	State-Local Expenditure From Own Funds	
			State	Local[2]
1949	7.8	0.9	3.4	3.5
1959	9.6	1.4	3.8	4.4
1969	12.6	2.2	5.3	5.1
1974	14.3	3.1	6.0	5.2
1975	14.9	3.5	6.2	5.2
1976	14.7	3.6	6.1	5.0
1977	14.0	3.5	5.7	4.8
1978	13.9	3.6	5.6	4.7
1979	13.5	3.3	5.6	4.6
1980	13.5	3.4	5.6	4.5
1981 est.	12.9	3.0	5.5	4.4

Notes: 1. Derived from National Income and Product Accounts. Numbers include federal aid.

2. The National Income and Product Accounts do not report state and local government data separately. The state-local expenditure totals (National Income Accounts) were allocated between levels of government on the basis of ratios computed from data reported by the U.S. Bureau of the Census in the annual governmental finance series.

Source: Advisory Commission on Intergovernmental Relations, *Significant Features of Fiscal Federalism, 1980–81 Edition,* Washington, D.C., 1981, p. 15.

Table 8

State and Local Government Direct General Expenditure by Function, 1970 and 1980 ($ in millions)

Function	State				Local			
	1970		1980		1970		1980	
	Amount	Percent	Amount	Percent	Amount	Percent	Amount	Percent
Education	13,780	28.2	35,251	24.5	38,938	47.2	97,960	43.8
Transportation	11,395	23.4	21,361	14.9	6,603	8.0	15,942	7.1
Public Welfare	8,203	16.8	33,242	23.1	6,477	7.8	12,310	5.5
Health & Hospitals	4,788	9.8	15,666	10.9	4,880	5.9	16,507	7.4
Police Protection	688	1.4	2,060	1.4	3,806	4.6	11,433	5.1
Sewerage	—	—	334	.2	2,167	2.6	9,558	4.3
Sanitation	—	—	—	—	1,246	1.5	3,322	1.4
Parks & Recreation	—	—	1,274	.9	1,888	2.3	5,247	2.3
Housing & Urban Renewal	23	.0	331	.2	2,115	2.6	5,731	2.6
Governmental Administration	2,060	4.2	6,840	4.8	3,908	4.7	11,595	5.2
Interest on Debt	1,499	3.1	6,763	4.7	2,875	3.5	7,984	3.6
Other	6,313	12.9	20,476	14.2	7,679	9.3	26,132	11.7
TOTAL Expenditure	48,749	100.0	143,718	100.0	82,582	100.0	223,621	100.0

Source: Buckley, Michael Patrick, Assessing the Issues and Trends in Public Facilities Financing: Planning and Policy Considerations for State and Local Governments in Oregon, University of Oregon, Masters Thesis, May 1982, various tables, p. 31–32.

127

local governments, problems that are unlikely to abate in the immediate future. The combined state and local sector faces a negative operating balance in 1982 (figure 1). They have neither carried-over surpluses nor the promise of federal assistance as they did in the recession of 1974–75. Fiscal resources are also undermined by the burgeoning underground economy—estimated to be as much as 15 or 20 percent of GNP (and growing)—which is placing more and more economic activity beyond the reach of state and local tax collectors.[5] In addition, some state and local governments have reduced their tax base by giving tax abatements and exemptions to attract industry without carefully weighing the costs and benefits. Yet deteriorating public capital may deter local industrial development more than tax incentives may encourage it.

The problems created by shrinking tax bases have been made worse by the proliferation of constitutional and legislative constraints on tax increases. Eighteen states now face constitutional or statutory limits—fourteen of these constraints have been enacted since 1978 (table 9). Twenty-nine of them limit states' local property tax rates, and nineteen limit property tax revenues—eleven enacted since 1978. The result is that states and localities have much less flexibility to respond to fiscal problems today then they did in 1975. A recent analysis by Steven Gold (January, 1982) concluded that limitations at the state level have not proved an active constraint on spending levels in large part because of the sharp decline in revenues caused by the recession. With more responsibility delegated from Washington, some states will find constitutional and legislative constraints binding as revenues recover.

These constraints on revenues are not balanced by any real constraints on the expenditure side of the increasingly harder-to-balance equation. School district spending is limited in five states, municipal spending in three, and county spending in two (table 9). Most observers feel, and many state and local government officials have argued, that the sharp recession in 1975 and the growing restlessness of taxpayers during the last five years have sweated much of the fat out of local budgets, reflected in the decline of state and local spending as a percent of GNP, from 15

FIGURE 1

State and Local Operating Balances, 1960–1982

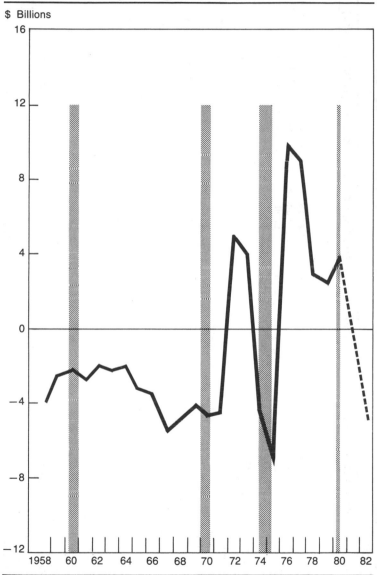

$ Billions

129

Table 9

Restrictions on State and Local Government Tax and Expenditure Powers (June 1, 1981)

States	Overall[1] Property Tax Rate Limit	Specific[1] Property Tax Rate Limit	State Imposed Limits on Local Governments					Limits on State Governments
			Property Tax Levy Limit	General Revenue Limit	General Expenditure Limit	Limit on Assessment Increases	Full Disclosure	
Total	14	29	19	5	6	6	9	18
Alabama	CMS***							
Alaska	CMS**							
Arizona	CMS***	CMS*	CM**		CMS***	CMS***		Const.***
Arkansas		CMS*	CM***					
California	CMS***	CS*	CMS***[2]		CMS***	CMS***		Const.***
Colorado			CM*				CMS***	Stat.**
Connecticut								
Delaware		CS**	C***[2]					Const.***
Dist. of Col.								
Florida		CMS*					CMS**	
Georgia		S*						
Hawaii							C**	Const.***
Idaho	CMS***	CMS*	CMS***					Stat.***
Illinois		CMS*						
Indiana			CMS***					
Iowa		CMS*			S**			
Kansas		CM*	CM**		S*	CMS**		
Kentucky	CMS*							
Louisiana		CMS**	CMS***[2]				CMS***	Stat.***
Maine								
Maryland					CM**	CM**		
Massachusetts	CMS***		CMS***					
Michigan	CS*	M*	CMS***					
Minnesota		CMS**		CM**				Const.**

State						
Mississippi		CMS*			CMS***	Const.***
Missouri		CMS*				
Montana		CMS*	CMS**			Stat.***
Nebraska		CMS*			CMS***, CM**	
Nevada	CMS*					
New Hampshire						
New Jersey		CMS**	CMS**	MS**	C**, CMS***	Stat.**
New Mexico	CMS*	CMS*				
New York		CMS*				
North Carolina		CM**			CMS***, CMS**	
North Dakota	CMS*					
Ohio	CMS*	CMS*				
Oklahoma	CMS*	CMS*	CMS***		CMS*	Stat.***
Oregon		CMS*				
Pennsylvania		CMS*				Stat.**
Rhode Island					(3)	Stat.***
South Carolina						
South Dakota	CMS*					
Tennessee		CMS**	CMS***			Const.***
Texas		CMS*	CMS***			Const.***
Utah		CMS*				Stat.***
Vermont						
Virginia			CM**			
Washington	CMS**	CMS**			S**	
West Virginia	CMS*	CMS*				Stat.***
Wisconsin	CMS*	CMS*		S**		
Wyoming	CMS*					

C—County   M—Municipal   S—School District   *—Enacted before 1970   **—1970 to 1977   ***—1978 and after
Const.—Constitutional   Stat.—Statutory

[1] Overall limits refer to limits on the aggregate tax rate of all local government. Specific rate limits refer to limits on individual types of local governments or limits on narrowly defined services (excluding debt).
[2] Limits follow reassessment
[3] Limit followed transition to a classified property tax.

Source: ACIR staff/C. Richardson based on data from CCH, Steven Gold, IAAO, and state survey.

percent in 1975 to below 13 percent in 1982. Many factors will continue to propel demands for state and local public services upward while fiscal resources will not grow proportionately. A recent report by Merrill Lynch concluded that:

> The planned Reagan Administration cutbacks in federal expenditures bear the greatest challenge to the credit standing of certain state/local governments and the market for their tax-exempt securities since the Great Depression (Herships and Karvelis, 1981, p. 1).

Future Demands for Public Infrastructure[6]

In spite of tight budgets, state and local governments must wrestle not only with how to maintain the current stock of public capital but with how to develop the new infrastructure that will be required by the transformation of the national economy. The most dramatic forces that will influence demands for public investments include:

☐ *Technological Changes.* Scientific advances promise to transform the structure of the national economy and the relationship between where we live and where we work. Coincident advances in data processing and communications technology are dramatically reducing the costs of storing, processing, and transmitting information. The development of new materials will lead to the replacement of structural steel by more durable compounds using silicon and carbon. Biogenetics promises significant breakthroughs in medicine and agriculture. Increased public investments in research facilities and communications systems will be required.

☐ *Demographic Changes.* The population and labor force will grow much more slowly in the 1980s than in the 1970s. By 1985, the labor force growth rate will be half what it was in 1975. The rate of growth of households will exhibit a similarly sharp decline. Housing investments will be less important, while education and training investments will have to be increased. The "graying of America" will propel soar-

ing expenditures on health and social service facilities.
- [ ] *World Trade.* The growing importance of world trade will create rapid declines in employment in import substitute goods and services and a rapid expansion in goods and services for export. There will be severe local economic and fiscal dislocation as a result. Private investments to enhance competitiveness in world markets will have to be complemented by public investments in transportation and distribution systems.
- [ ] *Resource Management.* The 1970s were dominated by rapid increases in oil prices. Conservation and the development of alternative energy sources mean that sharp real increases in oil prices are unlikely during the next decade. However, the consequences of poor management of many resources, including water, topsoil, and the safe disposal of hazardous waste, will require large-scale public investments during the next decade.

Each of these changes will alter the structures of state economies, will shift the relationship between place of work and place of residence, and will change the demand for public infrastructure. States must develop a much-longer-term planning horizon in order to anticipate accurately what types of public investments must be undertaken and where they will be needed. Failure to understand the process of development and its implications for public policies can convert problems into crises. We are still recovering from the urban crisis, the energy crisis, and the reindustrialization crisis. Each could have been ameliorated by analyzing the issues and designing appropriate policies. Public investment policies must be guided by a careful look at the future.

Conclusions

During the next decade, state and local governments must make rapid and fundamental changes in their capital investment strategies. Traditional revenue sources are declining, while the need to increase capital spending is becoming more pressing. State and local governments

133

must recognize and define the limits on public sector responsibility and establish new priorities—priorities that reflect not only the constraints on state and local fiscal capacity, but that also reflect the underlying structural shifts in our economy.

CHAPTER II NOTES

1. The issue of public and private responsibility is discussed in chapter 3, and, in more detail, in volume 1 of this series, *Planning and Managing.*

2. See Holland, 1972 and Abt, 1980. Also, see note 2 in chapter 1.

3. In August 1982, *Newsweek* featured a cover story on the deterioration of the nation's public capital; *U.S. News and World Report* did the same in September 1982; and the *National Journal,* in November 1982.

4. Recently, the U.S. Department of the Interior has begun disinvesting in natural resources, by turning land back to state governments and selling some land to private developers.

5. Estimates are hard to make, see Fiege, 1980.

6. These issues are discussed in more detail in volume 1 of this series, *Planning and Managing.*

CHAPTER III

Guidelines for Financing
Public Capital Investments

DECIDING HOW TO FINANCE public capital investments entails answering three questions. The first is,
Which responsibilities properly belong to the public sector? State and local governments must determine whether
they intend to continue full financial and administrative
responsibility for the services and subsidies they currently
provide. They must also rigorously question new demands
for public activities—convention centers, business development projects, or even new parks.

The second question is, What is the most efficient way
of meeting public sector responsibilities? Economists refer
to this choice as selecting the efficient mix of inputs—land,
labor, energy, and capital. The selection should be based
upon the relative price of the inputs. For example, as energy costs rose during the past decade, local governments
used extra labor and capital to make public buildings more
energy efficient. Now that capital costs have increased—
because of high interest rates—ways must be found to supply public services through capital-efficient techniques.
For example, instead of building a new laboratory for a
community college to teach electrical engineering, a cooperative arrangement could be made with a local manufacturing firm to allow training in the plant.

The third question is, How should required capital expenditures be financed? There are two issues: first, How
should costs be shared between the public sector and private developers? and second, What fiscal resources should

135

be used to pay for the construction and maintenance—debt, general revenues, or fees?

The discussion in the following chapters addresses the last of these three questions. (The first two are discussed in detail in volume 1 of this series, *Planning and Managing*.) This chapter outlines, briefly, how all three questions must be addressed in order to establish a strategic framework for public capital investment policy.

Public and Private Responsibilities

After a century of almost continuous expansion, the last few years have witnessed significant retrenchment of federal, state, and local government activity and employment. In the mid-nineteenth century, state and local governments were responsible for the construction of streets and sidewalks, the provision of police protection, and public education. Other responsibilities were added as a result of public outcry or disaster. Sanitation, fire protection, zoning, and utility regulation expanded municipal control over the social and economic environment. The Great Depression rapidly accelerated the federal government's involvement in direct income distribution and job creation. Since World War II, public sector activity has grown on four fronts: increased services for the poor, including social security, health care, housing, training, education, and day care; regulation of the economy, including environmental policy, worker safety, health, and capital markets; health, mortgage finance, and recreation; and economic development policy, including tax expenditures and private project finance. Economic development policies undertaken during the 1970s most obviously crossed the border that has traditionally divided public and private responsibilities. State and local governments now provide private, for-profit firms with low-interest loans, tax abatements, subsidized production facilities, wage and training subsidies, custom-built transportation links, low-cost water and water treatment, and subsidized energy.

Public services vary among states and localities reflecting historical accident, constitutional and legislative constraints, and local economic conditions. By and large, the gradual transfer of responsibility from private to public hands has been ad hoc with little consideration for the long-run consequences, and with no reference to any guidelines.

Prodded by increasingly tight budgets since 1975, state and local governments have begun the painful process of reconsidering what services and subsidies they can realistically afford to provide. Community centers and libraries are being closed. Developers are asked to build their own streets and sidewalks. Transit fares are raised. Program cuts are being made in the same ad hoc fashion that prevailed during expansion. As governments make these retrenchment decisions, the political strength of constituents is a more important consideration than whether the service is better conducted by the private or public sector. The Reagan administration has accelerated the process by cutting back or terminating many categorical grant programs and by converting others into block grants. "New federalism" would precipitate an even more radical surgery of programs and activities by state and local governments.

Changed circumstances call for a new strategy. States can no longer deal with periodic budget crises by across-the-board cuts in all programs. Further cuts in many programs will seriously jeopardize their usefulness. Nor can states expect, as in the past, to maintain programs by vigorous lobbying in Washington. Instead, state and local governments must determine which services can be turned over to the private sector or terminated. States must redefine their responsibilities if they are to be able to pay for those activities that need direct state government involvement.

Assigning priorities for public spending will require a rigorous questioning of traditional practices. If a convention center is a demonstrable boon to a local economy, why is it not financed privately?[1] Are public subsidies to business activity really necessary? Must a recreation site be developed and operated with public funds? Is public ownership of the water supply system necessary when electricity and gas are privately provided? Does an airport need to be owned by the county? Some economists have pro-

137

posed radical measures such as the outright sale of subway systems and toll bridges to private firms, replacing
public schools with education vouchers, privatizing garbage collection, and selling off state parks. The economics
and politics of these proposals are complex and will require
careful research and analysis by all levels of government.
Little is known about the income distribution implications.
Unfortunately, privatization has become a partisan political issue and therefore has not been discussed objectively
as an integral part of a public investment strategy.

*The basic guideline for state and local officials to
follow in deciding "who does what" is that the public sector should only intervene if market-determined outcomes
are neither efficient nor equitable.* Even if public intervention is required, it does not have to involve spending public
funds or public ownership of facilities. Regulation of private suppliers—of drinking water prices, for example—
can lead to the desired supply of services without full public ownership. The task is by no means easy, but without
cutting back on some public services, there will not be
enough tax revenues to pay for those services that properly
belong in the domain of state and local government.

Efficient Production
of Public Services

Having decided what services to provide, policy
makers will next have to determine the level of services
and how to supply them. These decisions should be made
along the same lines that a for-profit company determines
how to invest—by comparison of costs with benefits. Unfortunately, benefits are much more difficult to measure
for publicly provided services than they are for private investments. Sales revenues provide a private firm with a
rapid check on the profitability of a product or service. In
spite of the difficulties, however, it is possible to measure
the value of public services. There is a growing literature
that shows how to use the revealed preferences of consumers to measure the demand for public services. For example, changes in land property have been used to measure the benefits of highway noise abatement programs and
visit rates can measure the implicit demand for a state

park. (This issue is discussed more fully in *Planning and Managing*.) Comparison of projected benefits with projected costs should be an efficient gauge of whether a public investment should be undertaken. Yet, in planning public investments, many public agencies rely on engineering standards based upon the durability of materials, traffic flow criteria, design and use specifications, or, even inspired guesswork. While these guidelines may indicate where to anticipate structural problems, they do not directly indicate the costs and benefits of specific patterns of maintenance and investments.

If a public facility is fully financed through user fees (or dedicated tax revenues that are equivalent to user fees), planners will have a much clearer measure of the value of the project (chapter 4). Comparison of projected revenues from user fees with projected construction and operating costs indicates whether the project is worth undertaking. User fees have another benefit—they ensure that the service is used efficiently. A pricing system allocates a scarce resource to those who are willing and able to pay for it. Although user fees cannot be used for all public investments, they can be used much more broadly than at present.

Assuming that the appropriate *level* of a public service has been determined, the next decision is how to provide it most efficiently at the lowest possible cost. What is the appropriate input mix? This involves choosing among alternative "production techniques" based upon the relative costs of capital, land, labor, and energy. The pursuit of efficiency would dictate that relative input costs be the only factors considered by local planners, but political reality has often dictated otherwise. For example, capital expenditures on transit rolling stock could be reduced by hiring more maintenance staff and so avoiding the need to replace equipment as frequently. Yet, the Urban Mass Transit Administration was much more generous with capital grants than with operating subsidies. The result, according to several studies, was that many cities spent too little on maintaining and repairing buses and subway cars and too much on the purchase of new equipment. Because of the design of federal subsidies, the "lowest-cost" approach of local government agencies was not the "lowest-cost" solution for society as a whole. Similarly, waste water treatment construction grants subsidized only the construction of facilities, not their operation. Several studies have found that this has led to drastic over-building of plants, reflecting both the availability of free federal construction funds and the desire to minimize operating costs for which the local government is fully responsible.[2]

Within economists' definition of *efficiency*, deferred maintenance of infrastructure is not necessarily inefficient or even short-sighted. If the cost of capital is high relative to other factors, it may be cost-effective to allow roads to deteriorate below established engineering standards and to delay rehabilitating public office buildings. And if public demand for a facility or the service it provides has fallen, disinvestment may be appropriate. We need to develop a framework for analyzing public investment decisions that will lead to more efficient, and, therefore, lower-cost planning and budgeting to meet public service demands.[3]

Principles for Financing Capital Investment

Where grants from a higher level of government are not available, state and local governments must turn to three sources of funds to finance the construction and maintenance of public capital projects. First, they can borrow, and service the debt either from general revenues and the full faith and credit of the issuing jurisdiction (General Obligation bonds, GOBs) or from dedicated tax revenues or user fees (Limited Obligation bonds, LOBs). Second, they can finance the projects directly out of tax revenues or charges and incur no debt. And third, they can require or encourage the private sector to incur at least part of the costs directly.

There is no single efficient or equitable way of funding a public works project, and even if it were possible to identify the most efficient way to finance a project, the legal and institutional capabilities vary greatly among states and among local jursidictions. What may work in one county may be constitutionally prohibited or institutionally impossible in another. This does not preclude us from devising some general principles to guide an effective and equitable financing strategy.

The first principle is that, wherever possible, *those who benefit from a public facility—a road, park, hospital, or port—should pay for its development and operation, and the amount they pay should be related to the level of their use.* In short, those who reap the benefits should bear the costs. However, it is not always possible, through a simple "public pricing" mechanism, to ensure that all those who benefit from a particular project or facility actually pay for it. For example:

☐ Firms and households living downstream from a water treatment plant will enjoy cleaner water as a result of the facility.

☐ Retail stores may experience a boom in business after a nearby bus or rail service is opened.

☐ Commuters on congested highways will be able to get to work more quickly if mass transit services attract other commuters out of their automobiles.

These are examples of what economists refer to as *externalities*—benefits enjoyed by those who are not direct users of the facility. In these cases, revenues from other sources should be used to supplement direct user fees.

There are other reasons for not relying completely on user fees. Direct fees may be very expensive to collect. For example, installing tolls on every street and road to pay for road maintenance and street lighting would be absurd. But even if direct user fees are not possible, taxes can be designed to approximate user fees (see chapter 4).

The second principle is that *the cost of a public capital project should be amortized over the life of the project and the maintenance and operating costs should not be deferred.* This principle naturally follows from the first, since it ensures that there is no intergenerational transfer of net benefits or net fiscal burden. If a long-lived project is financed out of current revenues, then future generations will enjoy the benefits with none of the costs. Conversely, financing a facility with an expected economic life of seven years with twenty-year bonds will shift the cost to future generations and leave the jurisdiction with a future tax burden higher relative to its fiscal and economic base than at present. The failure to pay for adequate maintenance in past decades has transferred a fiscal burden of hundreds of billions of dollars from past generations onto the shoulders of today's taxpayers.

Third, *the operating and maintenance expenses associated with a project—operating a convention center, maintaining a bridge, or repairing and upgrading a resource recovery center, for examples—should be explicitly considered when designing the financing package.* Earmarked revenue sources must be sufficient to cover both debt service and ongoing expenses. Otherwise, unanticipated and often large subsidies from general revenues will be necessary. Too often, project plans contain swollen rhetoric concerning the jobs that will result and the general tax revenues that will be generated if the project is undertaken, but make no provision to ensure that the projected benefits are realized. For example, the operating subsidy for a convention center built from a state or local bond issue could be met from specific revenues identified in advance—such as a hotel room occupancy tax, or a part of the increase in sales tax and local real estate tax revenues. This protects the city or the state from entering into an open-ended, and often rapidly escalating, subsidy out of general revenues. This insulation can be strengthened if the ownership and operation of the facility are in the hands of a public authority—although excessive insulation can reduce public accountability (see *Planning and Managing*). This form of tax limitation can increase accountability and discourage continued public subsidy of a project that never becomes viable.

Fourth, *fiscal and administrative responsibility for a public investment project should be limited to those jurisdictions where most of the impacts are experienced.* For example, a program for maintaining roads and highways should be financed by a statewide tax—on gasoline or vehicle registration, for example. If county governments were individually responsible for their roads, then the transportation network would be a fragmented patchwork of roads that was not in the state's economic interest. On the other hand, a waste disposal facility that serves only one or two

142

counties should be financed and run by those counties. In this instance, the state may serve a regulatory function to ensure compliance with uniform environmental standards. Adhering to this principle reduces the tendency to finance pork-barrel projects at the state level—voting for a state-financed convention center in one city in return for a state-financed industrial park in another.

This principle fails to recognize differences in need and fiscal capacity among jurisdictions. A locality may seek state financing of a facility on the grounds that it has an unemployment rate well above the state average and cannot aford to finance the project without state aid. Rather than helping poor areas by financing specific projects, states might consider less categorical assistance that allows localities to select which capital investments to make. A low-income jurisdiction might be helped more efficiently through revenue-sharing grants from the state rather than project-specific assistance. Most states operate some form of revenue sharing with their component jurisdictions, although few consider need and fiscal capacity when allocating the funds. This approach to local assistance allows localities to determine whether a project is of sufficiently high priority to compete with the other local demands and rely less on ad hoc grantsmanship in the state. If the project is 100 percent state funded, the locality does not have to make that painful decision. If the indirect approach of revenue sharing is not attractive, there are two alternative ways of recognizing local needs. States can engage in negotiating investment strategies with their local areas, or they can provide partial assistance in financing certain categories of investment—with the fraction paid for by state funds increasing according to measures of need and fiscal capacity.[4]

Ideally, all infrastructure financing decisions would be made in adherence to these four principles. In practice, however, decisions are made on political as well as economic grounds. Nevertheless, setting out the broad guidelines through which state aid will be provided is a necessary first step in the development of a long-term public investment strategy. Once the principles are publicly espoused, then the necessary exceptions will be clearly seen as exceptions, and the arguments to justify them will have to be more convincing. Local leaders and state legislators will be more prepared to accept a refusal from the governor to finance a pet project if they know that similar projects will not be financed in neighboring counties and if they can see that the refusal is a result of a consistent policy and does not reflect the governor's view of their political status or of the long-term commitment of the state to the development of the community.

CHAPTER III NOTES

1. Even if the convention center itself is not a viable undertaking, some of the private beneficiaries of convention activity, such as hotels and restaurants, could provide an annual subsidy to the company managing the center.

2. See U.S. Department of Commerce, 1980; American Public Works Association, 1981; U.S. GAO, 1982; Pagano and Moore, 1981.

3. A detailed discussion of cost-benefit evaluation and its use in policy analysis is contained in volume 1 of this series, *Planning and Managing.*

4. Chapter VI describes a framework for negotiating investments between state and local governments over major new projects.

CHAPTER IV

User Fees
for Public Projects

.

A PUBLIC WORKS PROJECT—from a statewide road system to a local library—is a commitment to pay for the construction, operation, and maintenance of the facility. This chapter outlines potential revenue sources to finance these costs in ways that meet the guidelines established in the previous chapter. The analysis emphasizes the imposition of user fees. The term *user fee* is used broadly to include any fee, charge, or dedicated tax that is paid by those benefiting from a facility or the services it provides. For example, user fees would include a gasoline tax where the revenues are dedicated to highway construction and maintenance, tuition charges at state universities, or admission fees to state parks.

How prices for public facilities and services encourage efficiency in both investment and in use is discussed in the first section of this chapter. The second section discusses some of the difficulties of imposing user fees, including how they affect low-income households, influence economic development, and may impede the local budget process. The final section outlines how user fees can be structured for different types of public investments including highways, health and education facilities, ports and terminals, recreation facilities, water supplies, water treatment plants, and waste disposal facilities.

User Fees and Efficiency

User fees should not be regarded as fiscal gimmicks to circumvent local revenue or expenditure limitations.

145

If properly designed, they can serve the same function that freely determined prices serve in private markets for private goods—providing incentives that promote efficiency in both the production and consumption of goods and services. User fees are, in the words of the late Selma Mushkin (1972), "public prices for public goods." Prices set at the correct level by the supplier of the goods or service (that is, at the marginal cost) serve a dual purpose. They encourage consumers to choose efficiently between alternative goods and services, and they signal to the supplier whether to expand, reduce, or maintain the existing level of output. Setting efficient public prices is therefore a valuable component in an effective public investment strategy.

Not all dedicated tax revenues are user fees. For example, Colorado had dedicated 50 percent of the net revenues from its new state lottery for capital projects. While this type of dedicated tax does guarantee a revenue stream for public works, it does not encourage efficiency in use and production that would result from a user fee.

Public policy makers frequently ignore the powerful influence that efficient pricing can have on consumption. When OPEC ended the era of low-cost oil in 1973, many experts claimed that rising prices would not reduce the quantity of oil demanded. A complex set of conservation subsidies and allocative regulations was introduced instead of allowing oil and gas prices to rise. Yet experience over the last nine years has taught us that consumption is very responsive to price changes.

Experience with user fees suggests that they are less likely to encounter as strong opposition as increases in general taxes. Since they are dedicated to specific activities, they are less likely to be diverted to other purposes during periods of fiscal stringency. In Cincinnati, for example, user fees cover 80 percent of the cost of the municipal water supply system. In spite of severe cuts in the city's operating budget during the 1970s, its water system was much better maintained than those in most comparable cities (Humphrey, Peterson, and Wilson, 1979). In general, infrastructure is better maintained in cities that support related services through dedicated user fees than in those that rely on general revenues (Pagano and Moore, 1981; U.S. Department of Commerce, 1980).

State and local governments collected nearly $40 billion through user fees in FY 1977 (table 10). By comparison, they raised about $70 billion through property taxes. Revenues from user charges could be expanded to finance public investments and to allow cuts in property taxes and other general revenue taxes.

The purpose of charging for the use of public facilities is that, if properly designed, user fees ensure efficiency in both production and use because prices send signals to both consumers and suppliers. For example, if consumers of water must pay a price equal to its marginal cost (to the municipality for supplying the water), they will weigh the value of consuming an additional gallon of water—for irrigating crops, washing mined minerals, or for watering lawns—against its price. They may choose to conserve water or consume it, but if they use water, they pay for what they use. Without water metering, artificial "plenty" is introduced, and local users have no incentive to economize on its use. An efficient user fee, therefore, encourages conservation without resorting to cumbersome, and often highly inequitable, tax subsidies of the type passed in many states to encourage energy conservation. Consumers are usually able to judge for themselves whether a particular conservation technique is cost-effective for their residence, factory, or farm. Areas that have installed water meters have experienced sharp declines in per capita water consumption. Consumers may take time to adjust to prices—many homeowners waited several years to determine that oil prices had permanently increased before installing insulation, for example. But we have mounting evidence of the effectiveness of prices in shaping consumer behavior.

User fees will also affect the "fairness" of the distribution of benefits and costs of public services. For example, when water is unmetered, intensive users (who are often high-income homeowners with large gardens) are subsidized by less-intensive users, usually those with lower incomes.

Most discussions of user fees have focused upon the

147

behavior of consumers—the users of public facilities. But prices should also guide agencies managing the facilities. For example, if, at an efficient price for water, the quantity consumed is reaching the capacity of the local system, it may be time to add new wells or reservoirs and treatment plants. Conversely, if revenues from a convention center fail to cover even operating costs, then the local government should seriously consider closing down or selling the facility.

A user fee does not ensure a more efficient use of a public facility unless it is set at a level that reflects the *marginal*, i.e. the incremental, cost of providing the service. Yet, most public officials aim at covering costs when imposing user fees—that is, they select a price equal to the *average* cost (total costs divided by the number of users). In many instances the average cost is not the efficient price. Only if the costs of production are fairly constant over a wide range of output are average and marginal costs equal, and the appropriate price will be the average cost. For example, the costs of accommodating visitors at a state park may rise proportionately with the number of visitors. But if average costs rise with increased output, then the "marginal cost" price will be above the average cost. For example, a waste disposal facility operating near full capacity may be able to handle additional material only by placing its staff on overtime or greatly increasing its per ton energy consumption. If it charges its marginal cost for all the waste it accepts, its total revenues will exceed total costs, which will provide a profit. There is nothing wrong with a public enterprise earning profits. Locally owned natural gas utilities earned an aggregate profit of about $60 million in FY 1976–77 (table 10). However, most publicly owned utilities tend to sell their output at below the market price, often by block discounts to large customers. The result is a subsidy to favored consumers.

Services that require very large capital expenditures and incur only low operating expenses, such as sewer systems or treatment plants, will exhibit marginal costs well below average costs. In these cases, efficiency calls for an operating subsidy paid out of general revenues.

Efficient pricing also requires consideration of the pattern of demand over time. If a public facility is used at a constant rate throughout the year—such as a waste disposal facility—then setting a price is relatively simple. However, most public facilities experience very high use during certain hours of the day or during certain months of the year. Bridges and subway systems are crowed during commuter rush hours and have excess capacity at other times. A park or municipal beach may be heavily used during summer months and deserted at other times. Museums may be full at weekends and much less frequented during the week. Efficient pricing for these facilities requires a two-tier, or even a multi-tier, pricing system. The economies of peak-load pricing are complex. During peak hours, days, or even months, the price should cover both operating and capital costs. During off-peak hours, the price should cover only operating costs. Thus transit fares would be higher in rush hour than during off-peak hours. Admission to campsites would be higher during summer weekends than at other times. Many private enterprises that experience systematic fluctuations in demand use a peak-load pricing system. Theater tickets are more expensive on weekends than during the week Hotels that rely on the week-night business trade often offer discounts for weekend guests. Resort hotels charge a lower price out-of-season.

The economic rationale for the dual price system is that it is peak users that are responsible for the marginal capacity of the system. A transit system must purchase extra buses that are used solely during peak hours. Therefore these users should pay for the cost of that additional capacity. During off-peak hours, there is surplus capacity and users should pay only for the operation and maintenance of the facility or equipment.

The dual price system tends to spread the use of the service or facility more evenly and therefore reduces the overall capacity needs. For example, someone using the transit system for a shopping trip may be persuaded by the lower price to travel during nonpeak hours. A high summer rate on water use may discourage automobile washing during those months.

The benefits of peak-load pricing must be weighed against its costs. Peak-load pricing incurs additional administrative costs—metering and billing, for example—

Table 10

Role of Charges in Local Government Finance, 1976–77

($ in billions)

Category of Local Expenditure	Direct Expenditure	Charges
Education	75.7	3.5
Higher Ed. Institutions	4.8	1.0
School Lunch Sales (gross)	NA	1.6
Other	NA	.9
Highways	9.2	0
Welfare	11.9	0
Health	2.7	0
Hospitals	8.6	6.1
Police	8.8	0
Fire	4.3	0
Parks & Recreation	3.9	.6
Natural Resources	.9	.7
Sanitation & Sewage	8.8	3.1
Housing & Urban Renewal	3.2	.9
Air Transportation	1.1	1.1
Water Terminals Transport	.5	.4
Parking Facilities	.3	.3
Correction	1.6	0
Libraries	1.2	0
Financial Administration	2.2	0
General Control	4.5	0
Interest on Debt	6.3	0
Other & Unallocable	11.7	2.9
Water Supply	6.4	5.0
Electric Power	8.3	6.8
Gas Supply	.8	.9
Transit	5.0	1.7
TOTAL	192.7	37.5

Notes: NA means not available.

a - through a gasoline sales tax.

Charges As a %	Potential for Effective Strategy			
Expenditures	None	Weak	Medium	Strong
5%		x		
21			x	
NA			x	
NA	x			
0				x*
0	x			
0		x		
71				x
0	x			
0			x	
16		x		
18		x		
35			x	
28			x	
100				x
80				x
100				x
0	x			
0		x		
0	x			
0	x			
0	x			
25	NA			
78				x
82				x
108				x
34			x	
19%				

Source: Bureau of the Census, 1977 Census of Governments, Washington, D.C., various tables.

that may outweigh potential benefits. But there are many areas where it can lead to significant capital cost savings. It is regrettable that many municipal utilities price their services perversely. Water is offered at a discount per gallon for major users, even though they consume water during peak hours or weeks. Municipal electric power companies often provide power to commercial firms operating between 9:00 A.M. and 5:00 P.M.—peak hours—at rates below those paid by residential users, even though residential use is more evenly spread throughout the day.

In summary, an efficient user fee system is much more than a source of revenues. It is a way of ensuring that scarce resources are not wasted, that facilities are used efficiently, and that the need for investments in public infrastructure may be reduced. It will also provide an invaluable guide to effective planning and budgeting for public capital investment.

Limits to User Fees

The suggestion of applying user fees to public facilities and services is often strongly opposed. Some of the objections can be justified on economic grounds, others are based on misinformation or upon the politics of user fees. The five most frequent arguments are:

☐ Publicly provided facilities and services bring widespread social benefits for which a price cannot be charged. For example, police and fire protection services cannot easily be charged for when they are used.

☐ The services provided by the local public sector are redistributive—that is, they are provided for those with low incomes who could not otherwise enjoy them —and therefore should be paid for by the entire community.

☐ Public facilities and services are necessary to attract development and therefore should be subsidized from general tax revenues. The fiscal surplus from the ensuing development, it is argued, will pay for the services in the long run.

☐ Dedicating tax revenues for specific purposes reduces the flexibility of the budget-making process to deal

152

with rapidly changing public priorities and needs, and reduces the accountability of local officials.

☐ Dedicated revenues and separate administration of public projects prevent a coordinated approach to public infrastructure development.

There is one barrier to the adoption of user fees that is not based upon economic and political considerations and that states are powerless to influence. It results from a flaw in the federal tax code. Individuals who file itemized federal income tax forms (about one-fifth of all taxpayers—mostly from higher-income households) may deduct state and local taxes from their federally taxable income. This shifts some of the burden of high state and local taxes from high-income state residents to federal taxpayers at large. There is no provision on federal tax forms for itemizing user fees paid to state or local entities. A switch from financing the water supply system out of general property taxes to a quarterly water bill based on meter reading will reduce the homeowners' deductions, therefore raising the cost of water (net of federal taxes) even if the actual amount paid to the municipality remains unchanged. There are changes in the federal tax code that could aid the shift from general revenue financing of facilities to user fees—such as a "supplementary" deduction that would be proportional to the share of state and local revenues that is raised through user fees. It is an issue that should be addressed as part of a national public works investment strategy.

Let us review the five issues listed above.

External Benefits

It is not always easy to identify the beneficiaries of public services. Some public activities provide benefits which are of such widespread benefit and so intangible that user fees would be wholly inappropriate. Police protection is of value to all residents whether or not they are the victims of crime. Fire protection provides a sense of security that is of benefit whether or not one's residence ever catches fire. General revenues are appropriate for these general benefits.

Most publicly provided goods and services provide some external benefits which cannot easily be recovered directly through user charges. Commuters who use mass transit rather than automobiles lessen traffic congestion and reduce air pollution—benefits enjoyed, but not paid for, by automobile commuters. Graduates from the local school system or from local training programs will be less prone to go on welfare or commit crimes—benefits enjoyed by the whole community. Economists argue that those using facilities or services yielding external benefits should be subsidized to encourage increased use. In some instances, these external benefits can be captured—by using a portion of gasoline tax revenues to support mass transit, for example. The existence of external benefits does not always preclude user fees, but it does mean that the type of fees imposed must be based upon a broad study of the benefits of the facility or service.

Income Redistribution

The free provision of public services such as museums, libraries, and garbage collection, and the heavy subsidies to mass transit, are often justified on the ground that the poor could not afford these services if they were not offered below cost. This is a weak argument. Only 13 percent of the urban population is below the poverty level. Although low-income households represent a disproportionate share of mass transit riders (higher-income households tend to use private automobiles) and of public school students (higher-income households are more likely to send their children to private schools), the poor use less than their population share of water, produce less garbage, and are only infrequent visitors to museums and libraries. The subsidy is not only an expensive way to help those in need but also removes the incentives for efficient use.

In some cases, it would be cheaper and more efficient to charge a user fee for these services and facilities coupled with a cash grant to the poor so that they can afford to use them. For example, low income households could be given "museum stamps," or "state park stamps" out of the revenues generated from user fees. The poor may be better helped through specific and targeted income supplements rather than through the mispricing of public facilities. In this way, the efficiency aspects are retained, while the undesired inequity aspects are offset.

If those with low incomes are to receive preferential treatment, then either those with higher incomes may have to pay more than their share, or the subsidy to the poor will have to be paid out of general revenues. Some user fees can be structured so that they are progressive—an ad valorem vehicle registration fee is a good example. Others clearly cannot be—an income-related water rate would be an administrative nightmare. User fees are not necessarily more regressive—that is, they fall disproportionately heavily on the poor—than are general revenues (sales, property, and income taxes). A progressive personal income tax structure can lose a great deal of its progressivity after all the loopholes for home ownership, consumer debt interest, and other preferential activities are included. A sales tax that is levied on food and prescription drugs but not on personal services is regressive. The question of whether the property tax is progressive or regressive has yet to be settled. Increased reliance on user fees, especially if special provisions for low-income households are included, may actually improve the equity of the state and local revenue structure as well as increase its efficiency.

The argument against this change is that either the compensating programs will not be implemented, or, if they are, they will be vulnerable to budget cuts later. Hidden subsidies to the needy, it is argued, are preferable to overt assistance. State and local officials are seen as protectors of the poor against the wishes of taxpayers, and the main protection tactic is deception. Such "protection" may be successful on some occasions but cannot be successful all of the time. Failing to impose user fees leads to deteriorating facilities and services that benefit neither the poor nor those able to afford full-cost pricing.

User Fees
and Economic Development

Many state and local governments construct special freeway linkages, offer low-cost water, or abate taxes in order to attract firms. Whatever user fees the company might owe are partially abated to lower the local business costs in the hope of inducing development. Yet, there is little evidence that these business incentives are effective

(Kieschnick, 1981; Vaughan, 1979). They result in higher taxes or reduced services to other businesses and residents, which may offset any benefits offered to the few fortunate companies. Economic development may be more effectively encouraged by pursuing a prudent fiscal policy and by clearly stating the development policies and priorities. A reliable and equitable system of user fee revenues, guaranteeing the maintenance of highways and roads, a high quality education system, or an adequate water supply, may prove a more compelling inducement to business growth than a policy that mortgages future tax revenues in order to bribe footloose firms. If the relocation of a business is expected to generate increased tax revenues in the future—through increases in property or business tax revenues—then the tax increment should be set aside to finance construction and maintenance of the necessary infrastructure. Tax increment financing is, in principle, a type of user fee.

Flexibility and Accountability

One argument against user fees or dedicated tax revenues is that, by tying up a large share of revenues, the flexibility of the annual budget process is reduced, and the accountability of state and local officials is weakened. Dedicated funds can be cut back or diverted for other purposes—but only by legislative action (at the state level) or council approval at the local level. The decision is therefore made publicly, and after public discussion. From this viewpoint, some loss of flexibility may lead to the development of a planning horizon more compatible with the time horizon of the public investment. One of the major factors that has led to cuts in public spending on infrastructure maintenance and development has been the short-run time horizon of local elected officials and the escalating complexity of state and local budgets. Some balance must be sought between a rigid earmarking of revenues and excessive flexibility that leads to the neglect of long-term investments.

Coordination

Dedicated revenues and fees tend to be channeled through individual departments or even public authorities. Since each agency has less need to negotiate its annual budget, it may be less inclined to cooperate and coordinate with other agencies. This problem can be addressed through the capital budgeting process, through strengthened planning activities, through a stronger cabinet government, or through various ad hoc mechanisms (see *Planning and Managing*).

Some General Principles
For a User Fee System

The preceding discussion suggests some general principles for states seeking tax revenues to finance the capital and operating costs of public projects.

1. Taxes and user fees should be imposed on the major beneficiaries of the project or service.
2. These public prices should be set equal to the marginal, not the average, cost of providing the project or service.
3. Where there are systematic seasonal or hourly fluctuations in use, peak-load prices should be imposed during periods of heavy use and lower prices at other times.
4. Where the shift from general revenue financing to user fees will prove particularly burdensome to low-income households, special provisions should be used to ensure adequate access. This may require higher-income users to pay more than the efficient, marginal-cost price.
5. Revenue sources should be responsive both to inflation and the economic growth rate.

Having discussed some of the general issues associated with user fees, we now turn to an examination of how user fees can be used to finance the capital, operating, and maintenance costs of different types of public investments.

Opportunities
for User Fees

The purpose of a system of user fees is to recapture sufficient benefits that accrue to users and other beneficiaries of public projects and services to cover both capital and operating costs in a way that promotes efficiency in use and production. In many instances, a single tax or fee may be insufficient, and a set of taxes will be necessary. For example, a convention center may bring additional business to local hotels, retail stores, local printing firms, catering companies, and equipment-leasing firms. It may also increase land values in the surrounding areas. Equitable recapture of these different benefits requires taxes on different types of business activity, on property values, and on any external benefits the center may create. Projects that serve broad public purposes may require some subsidy from general revenues.

Earmarking funds to pay for infrastructure capital and maintenance costs can be done within several different administrative frameworks. On the one hand, full fiscal and administrative responsibility for the project can rest with a state or local government agency. On the other, responsibility can be delegated to a special authority. Theoretically, the questions of how to finance and how to administer are separable. In practice, they are not. Many states face constitutional limitations on the taxes they can impose, the extent of earmarking allowed, and the powers that can be granted to local governments or to special authorities. These states must modify their strategies to comply with these constraints.

In this section, eight major categories of capital investment are discussed: road transportation, higher education, transit, water supply, waste water treatment, waste disposal, ports and terminals, and recreation facilities. The section concludes with a brief discussion of tax increment financing and how it can be applied to different types of projects. These do not exhaust the types of public investments made by state and local governments, but the discussions indicate how pricing mechanisms can be applied to public facilities.

Road Transportation

Building and maintaining highways, bridges, streets, street lighting, and traffic systems currently absorb 10 percent of state and local budgets. About one-quarter of the $36 billion in annual expenditures is provided through grants from the federal government. About $16 billion is raised through gasoline and motor vehicle tax revenues (although these revenues are not necessarily dedicated to road transportation programs). Some additional revenues are raised through tolls and miscellaneous charges. In this area, there are many opportunities to increase user fee revenues that can be used to repair and extend the road system. Most of these user fees are best levied statewide in order to minimize collection costs and to reduce the possibility of interjurisdictional tax cut wars. Depending upon how responsibility for road construction and maintenance is shared between state, county, and city agencies, the state can distribute some of the revenues to localities.

Vehicle Registration Fees. Most states charge a fixed annual registration fee for motor vehicles, usually graduated according to the size of the vehicle. These fees must be periodically raised to reflect inflation. An alternative is to make the annual fee proportional to the value of the vehicle. This automatically provides increased revenues during inflationary periods and is more progressive than a flat fee—higher-income households own more valuable automobiles than do low-income households.

Gasoline Tax. The federal government and most states impose a tax denominated in cents per gallon. With the hindsight gained from more than a decade of inflation and a quadrupling of gasoline prices, and ad valorem gasoline tax (which would be equivalent to a sales tax) would have yielded much greater revenues. The American Highway Association magazine reported in 1981 that forty states had increased or were contemplating an increase in gasoline taxes. Unfortunately those that converted from a flat tax to an ad valorem tax recently suffered both from the slow rate of growth of gasoline sales and the decline in gas prices. These declines are unlikely to persist, and, in the long run, conversion should produce a strong revenue flow. We have argued that a strong case can be made for using some of the revenues to subsidize mass transit.

Other Sales Taxes. The Federal Interstate Highway Trust Fund collects taxes on the sale of batteries, tires, and lubricating oil as well as gasoline. Most states impose general sales taxes on these items and could impose an additional tax, dedicated for road repair. It would be administratively simple. Other possible revenue sources could in-

159

clude a vehicle transfer tax and increases in fines for traffic violations.

Private Construction. Some highway spurs and even roads and highways are constructed for the benefit of a single private developer—a new factory or a large resource development project. Too often, state governments have been prepared to underwrite the full cost of the construction as part of an incentive package to lure the corporation. Where a single, primary beneficiary can be identified, that beneficiary should finance at least part of the costs (chapter 6 discusses these types of arrangements in more detail).

Bridge and Highway Tolls. Before the advent of the Federal Interstate Highway Trust Fund, many intercity highways and major road bridges in the Northeast and Midwest were developed using tolls to back bond issues and to pay for maintenance, usually administered through a public authority. The Federal Highway Program, which paid 90 percent of the construction costs, explicitly prohibits tolls on highways. Existing tolls on designated interstate highways that have accepted federal funds are scheduled to be phased out when bonds are retired. Yet, tolls are an efficient, if unpopular, user fee and have the advantage that they can be varied by time of day to discourage rush hour travel.

Consideration should be given to expanding highway tolls—including tolls on federally financed portions of the highway—and to developing peak-hour pricing on toll systems. Other innovations worth considering include commuter licenses displayed in automobile windshields allowing the licensee to use express lanes on highways or allowing access to specific highway segments during rush hour; highway-use meters installed in motor vehicles which would allow authorities to record time and use of highways of individual vehicles; and a sales tax surcharge on parking lots in designated areas during prescribed hours. Appropriate pricing for commuter access to the road system would encourage increased use of transit systems, reduce the rate of highway deterioration, and provide the revenues necessary to improve the quality and safety of road transportation.

160

There are other aspects of road transportation management that should be fully self-financed—from motor vehicle inspection and drivers licenses to highway patrol and traffic courts. The budgets of these administering agencies need not be supplemented by any general revenues, and charges could be adjusted automatically to cover operating expenses.

Institutions of Research and Higher Education

Universities, colleges, community colleges, and medical research facilities are a major state capital expense, and, increasingly, a central factor in shaping economic development. The rapid rate of technological change will require major public investments in new facilities and equipment if graduates are to learn the skills desired by industry. The growing demand for engineers, technicians, and physical scientists will be met only if the capacity of higher education institutions is expanded.

Nationwide, approximately one-third of the $40 billion spent annually by state and local governments on higher education are met through user fees, mostly tuition fees, which have been sharply raised in almost all states. Yet increased capital investments will only be possible if more revenues are raised to cover operating expenses. Tuition increases obviously impose special problems for the poor, especially in view of substantial reductions in federal grants and loan programs for higher education. Increases in state tuition costs should be accompanied by the introduction or expansion of state programs to assist low-income students.

In addition to tuition assistance, there are other innovative sources of revenue that can be used to finance public investments, higher education, and research facilities.

Currently less than 2 percent of university research is funded by private industry, while about 50 percent is funded by federal agencies. The remainder is financed by private foundations, state agencies, university endowments, and operating funds. Increased involvement by private corporations can help finance the construction of new facilities and the acquisition of modern equipment, as well

161

as spur increased research efforts in areas that have the potential for commercial and industrial development.

State Matching Grants For R and D. The state of California has instituted the MICRO program that provides a proportional grant to universities that receive a grant from private firms to undertake research in the micro-processing field. The state of Pennsylvania has begun the Ben Franklin partnership which also matches private sector contributions. These programs do not necessarily require an increase in state spending, but, rather, they redesign the criteria through which funds are allocated and share the costs with private firms.

Patent Policy. In most states, patent royalties are simply regarded as general revenues to the state. Yet royalty revenues can be increased and earmarked for the expansion of R and D facilities. A more aggressive patent policy would have three elements. First, a substantial share of royalties should go to the inventor; second, the institution should be allowed to keep some of the revenues, perhaps to purchase research equipment and to encourage a more entrepreneurial approach to research funding. Finally, the remaining revenues could be earmarked to fund basic research.

Tax Policy. Some states provide tax incentives for corporate donations of equipment to educational institutions—following the federal tax incentive provided in the National Economic Recovery Tax Act. Universities should also be made aware of the advantages of leasing or contracting the services of equipment and facilities from private, for-profit corporations. These arrangements pass on to the institution the tax benefits of rapid depreciation and tax credits (see chapter 7). These measures can reduce the cost of equipment for research and higher education.

Cooperative Arrangements. The cost of R and D infrastructure can be reduced by cooperative arrangements with private corporations in which the firm offers research grants, equipment, and even the use of its own facilities in return for long-term research in specified areas conducted by the university's faculty and graduate students. State administrative procedures and university charters

162

can discourage these arrangements. While there are legitimate concerns about academic freedom and about the rivalry between teaching and corporate research, a more aggressive state role can be negotiated that harnesses private resources to help finance public facilities.

Transit

The average, publicly owned, transit system covers less than 30 percent of its capital and operating expenses from farebox revenues. About half the gap is filled with federal capital and operating grants, and the remainder is met from state and local tax revenues. Supporters of transit subsidies argue that public transportation (1) is a necessary service for the poor—an argument that does not require such extensive subsidies, as we have seen; (2) is an important step in reducing our dependence on foreign oil—but high gasoline prices have proved a far more effective incentive; and (3) helps reduce traffic congestion. Some subsidies from federal, state, and local general revenues are appropriate but no empirical studies have concluded that they should be as large as present levels.

Mass transit systems do allow for a denser land use in urban areas and therefore increase the value of commercial and even residential land downtown. Therefore some case can be made for some subsidy financed from local property taxes. Overall, there is a strong argument for increasing transit fares—a move that has been made, amidst great publicity, in Chicago, New York, Boston, and other large cities. In no instance were special provisions made to assist poor households (although some systems do offer discounts to senior citizens).

To some extent, the problem of excessive subsidies for transit has arisen as a result of federal policies. When UMTA operating subsidies were first offered, only public systems that ran deficits were eligible. A local subsidy from general revenues could leverage increased federal funds while a hike in fares would reduce federal aid. Federal capital grants encouraged over-buying of buses and rolling stock and the construction of projects such as the Buffalo, New York, system that will not be able to cover more than a fraction of its operating expenses whatever fare is charged. However, cuts in federal aid are inevitable, and cities will now have to live with the expensive systems they lobbied so hard to win.

Unpopular though it may be, the efficient long-run solution to financing urban transit needs will require four steps. The first, which we have already discussed, is to increase fares. The second, no less difficult, is to cut back on public services. Some deficit-ridden routes and services might have to be abandoned. The third step is to encourage the growth of what have been called para-transit systems. These are new, low-cost, ways of providing transportation services. They may include jitney services—a hybrid between a bus and a taxicab—or community-owned, not-for-profit buses or dial-a-ride systems. Para-transit services will, in some areas, cushion the blow of the withdrawal of public transit services. Jitney routes would tend to develop in low-income neighborhoods where gypsy or pirate cabs now operate, often illegally. The fourth step is to remove or reduce the subsidies to automobile commuting such as toll-free bridges and under-priced downtown parking. If drivers had to pay the true cost of getting to work, more would become riders, and the escalating needs to expand highway capacity would abate. Innovation in service delivery and pricing can reduce the level of public capital investments needed.

Water Supply Systems

In *America in Ruins,* Pat Choate and Susan Walter estimate that refurbishing municipal water supply systems will require between $75 billion and $110 billion over the next twenty years, a level of expenditure that is more than four times the current level. Yet, less than half the water used by residential, commercial, and industrial customers is metered. Even where water is metered, the rates charged often do not reflect the marginal cost of supplying the water. Nonmetered users pay either through a flat assessment to a local special district or through general property and sales taxes to the local municipality.

In addition, fees and charges for hooking up a new user to the distribution system are often below the cost of the actual construction involved. The result is often waste in water use and implicit subsidies to new sprawling development. The massive subsidies for utility hook-ups are not restricted to water systems alone but apply to electricity, gas, and sewage systems. Until it raised charges in the late 1970s, the state of Vermont charged less than $20 for a new link to the electricity network, although the actual cost averaged more than $1,300. After the passage of Proposition 13 in California, the city of Petaluma imposed an impact fee of $3,000 per acre to developers in order to finance utility hook-ups. Other jurisdictions have imposed development fees as high as $4,000 per bedroom to cover utility system costs for new residential subdivisions (Peterson and Miller, 1981). There is no reason why the cost of water and other utility linkages should not be fully paid by those needing them. It has mistakenly been argued that development fees of this sort will raise the cost of new residential and commercial property and will therefore slow growth. But this is not true. The cost of housing is determined by demand and supply in a very broad metropolitan market in which any new construction is a tiny fraction of increased supply. Housing prices will, therefore, remain unchanged while the value of unimproved land will decline. Fees would therefore depress the value of land for residential uses, which may reduce land speculation at the urban fringe.

Areas not metering water should seriously consider installing meters. Where there is substantial excess supply capacity and very little seasonal fluctuation in demand (in urban areas in the Northeast), the costs may outweigh the benefits. In other areas, where water is scarce, metering may help reduce the need to expand capacity. The issue is often complex. In some area, municipalities, farmers, and mining interests compete for the same artesian water, and ownership rights are not clearly defined. In the long run, however, meeting growing demands for water will be possible only through a system of prices. State governments will, necessarily, play a larger role over time, assisting local governments in developing fee systems, financing water projects, and regulating private suppliers. For many states, these are unfamiliar functions, but functions that will be needed as part of an overall capital investment strategy.

165

Waste Water Treatment

Capital and operating costs for waste water treatment plants will grow rapidly during the next decade as local governments seek to comply with federally mandated water standards. In the past five years, the federal government has provided over $20 billion in grants to state and local governments for the construction of facilities, although these grants are now being scaled back (chapter 2). Localities are required to operate these plants through the imposition of user fees, although relatively little attention has been given to the structure of these charges.

While household waste water cannot easily be metered, the volume and concentration of industrial, commercial, and agricultural waste water can be measured. Many European countries already use fairly sophisticated waste water charges—with the rates set according to both the volume and type of pollutants. The topic is complex and will require extensive research and experimentation. State governments will be called upon to work with local governments and sanitary districts in developing consistent and realistic fees to finance waste water treatment.

Hazardous Waste Disposal

The consequences of unplanned and unregulated disposal of hazardous wastes are only just being understood. Love Canal has become a national symbol for the problem. Congress has appropriated money to a superfund to finance the clean-up of a growing list of waste dumps that threaten public health and safety. There is still no viable solution to the disposal of either high- or low-level nuclear waste.

Some of the problems have been caused by illegal dumping. Others have arisen from accidental spills. But many have arisen because, when the waste was dumped, the full environmental and health implications were not known. There are probably many more chemical and biological time bombs as yet undiscovered in landfills, lakes, rivers, and oceans.

It is the potential for as-yet-undiscovered hazard that makes it impossible to develop a private-sector solution to the waste disposal problem. No private firm wishing to set up a waste disposal site could obtain adequate insurance to cover potential health damages to employees or nearby residents. Anyone who would be harmed would have to establish negligence on the part of the company, which may be difficult and costly. These unusual risks will make it necessary for state and local governments to provide the facility and to guarantee residents compensation for any potential damages, regardless of whether the facility was operated negligently. The facility may be run by a private company under contract, but site selection, preparation, and regulation will have to be a state government responsibility.

For many industries—especially those developing new technologies—a modern disposal site for hazardous waste, operated under the auspices of the state government, will be a strong location incentive. Waste disposal will be an economic development inducement.

The cost of developing these sites need not fall on local taxpayers. Waste disposal facilities can be totally self-financing, with users paying for each ton or gallon of waste they bring to the site—a disposal fee usually less costly to a firm than the possibility of protracted lawsuits. The fee should not be viewed as a license to pollute. It could vary by type of waste and reflect the full cost of treating or storing the substance. It would, in fact, encourage companies to minimize waste production through using less-toxic materials, recycling, or treating the waste at their own plant.

Ports and Terminals

Marine ports, airports, and even trucking terminals are often publicly owned—usually administered through special public authorities. Most of their costs are covered through direct user fees. Some large ports, however, do not fully cover their operating costs and are subsidized from general revenues from city and state governments. Based upon general trends in transportation, these subsidies would seem geared more to preserving the historic past and favoring established interests than to investing in the future of an industry. The subsidies have been provided to protect or generate jobs, but the evidence of their effectiveness is no more than that for tax incentives or sub-

167

sidies of industrial parks. Some profitable transportation facilities could be turned over to private ownership, particularly if substantial new investment or rehabilitiation is required, to take advantage of the tax benefits (see chapter 7). There are some opportunities to increase user fee revenues. For example, general aviation is subsidized by commercial airlines and by the federal and local governments. An aviation fuel tax could be imposed to finance that fraction of airport costs attributable to serving private planes.

Recreation Facilities

There are numerous potential revenue sources to finance recreation facilities that have been poorly exploited. From docking fees at municipal marinas to charges at state-run campsites, revenues rarely pay for the full cost of the facility. Public golf courses charge much less than comparable private courses and must rely on queuing to allocate access to the course. Fees for concessions are often left unadjusted for years, when an annual auction would be more efficient and yield more revenues. Yet these are all types of user fees that can be expanded.

Admission fees are not always feasible for parks, but there are alternative user fees. The development and maintenance costs of an urban park could be financed, in part, by a special assessment on nearby residents. Tax increment financing is particularly suitable as a source of revenues for new urban recreation projects—from parks to pedestrian malls—because these projects enhance property values (commercial and residential) within a limited and identifiable location. The technique does not have to be limited to property taxes. A successful downtown plaza will draw additional trade to retail establishments, generating additional sales tax revenues that can be earmarked to maintain the area.

Many studies have documented the serious under-investment in recreational open space, yet, with so many pressing and mandated demands on the municipal budget, recreation programs are invariably cut. Increased revenues paid by beneficiaries would ensure more adequate funding.

Tax Increment Financing

One mechanism for capturing the benefits of a public project is the earmarking of increases in general revenue taxes—tax increment financing. A new park will increase the property values of adjacent residences. A new convention center will increase hotel occupancy rates and the volume of business for service firms. A new or improved transit service will increase the values of nearby commercial and residential property. These increases in sales or property values lead to increases in sales, business income, and for the local and state government, property tax revenues—revenues that could pay for the maintenance of the facility or to service the debt incurred in its construction.

But not all tax revenue increments represent a fiscal bonus to jurisdictions. A large part will reflect increased demands for public services. For example, a new state park or transit route that leads to new residential development on land that was previously agricultural will certainly increase tax revenues but will also require additional public facilities and services. Very little of the tax increment should be used to pay for the original capital investment. At the other extreme, a public project in an already developed area—the conversion of abandoned inner city industrial space into a park or commercial center—may have very little effect on the demand for public services, and therefore most of the tax increment can be dedicated to meeting project costs.

There are many instances of tax increment financing—almost all have used increments in property tax revenues. In California, after Proposition 13, many towns and counties have used the technique to pay for infrastructure for new residential development. However, most of these financings have set aside the full increment in tax revenues to back bond issues and have made no provision for increased expenditures on public expenditures. In Buffalo, an improvement district has been proposed to pay for the maintenance of a commercial mall developed in conjunction with the new subway system. The district will impose a special tax on adjacent commercial properties.

Conclusions

This chapter has only touched upon the possibilities of funding the construction and maintenance of public facilities through the imposition of user fees. Many regulatory agencies can be financed through license application fees, charges for rate hearings, and other similar policies. Grazing rights on state lands can be determined by competitive bidding and the revenues used to pay for the preservation of wilderness areas.

User fees could provide an additional $30 billion for state and local governments—about a quarter of this would come from increased gasoline taxes and motor vehicle registration fees, a quarter from utility hook-up fees and water rates, and the rest from other sources. A part of these revenues could be used to finance the maintenance and development of public facilities. Part could be used to provide the resources to make up for reduced federal aid. The remainder could be used to reduce other taxes, or, more realistically, to reduce increases in other taxes.

The state's role will extend beyond that of managing its own fiscal problems. It must work with local governments to tackle the complex technical issues in setting and administering public pricing systems. It may also have to use both carrot and stick to ensure that localities do not try to compete for industry through cutting public prices and to ensure the consistency of local actions with broad state goals.

User fees cannot be applied to all public services and facilities. Many services should be paid for out of general revenues. But many public activities can be more efficiently paid for by the beneficiaries. User fees encourage efficient capital budgeting and efficient facility use. Dedicating revenues does reduce budgetary freedom. But this freedom, exercised within the short time-horizon of local elected officials, has led to the neglect of public capital and to fiscally imprudent financing decisions. The environment necessary for sustained residential, social, and economic development is not created by investment decisions that are reversed, altered, or abandoned every few years.

Decisions will be more carefully considered if they involve the long-run commitment of public revenues for a clearly specified purpose.

CHAPTER V

Improving the Operation
of the Bond Market

ABOUT ONE-THIRD of state and local capital investments are financed through issuing tax-exempt bonds.[1] In recent years, the cost of debt financing has risen, both in absolute terms and relative to federal and corporate debt. Some jurisdictions have been driven out of the bond market altogether. While many of the factors that have escalated the cost and the difficulty of public debt finance are beyond the control of state governments, there are state actions that could reduce the costs of issuing bonds and ensure a more orderly market. This chapter examines these actions including finance and budgeting assistance, state bond-banks, state guarantees for local issues, and limits on the use of tax-exempt debt.

The first section of this chapter provides a brief overview of the use of debt by state and local governments. The second section describes the market for tax-exempt securities and why the market has deteriorated. The final section describes steps that states can take to improve the operation of the bond market. It must be emphasized that these are incremental changes. And, while they may assist small, distressed communities, they will do little to improve the overall operation of the bond market. In the face of high rates and a narrow market, state and local governments will have to be much more rigorous in determining what types of investment merit tax-exempt financing.

State and Local Debt

During the last decade, state and local indebtedness has grown but not as rapidly as GNP. State debt has grown more rapidly than local debt, although state debt is less than one-fifth of total exempt debt issued. The interest costs of state debt have tripled as a share of GNP since 1964, while they have remained a constant share of GNP for localities. There are wide variations among states in the level of indebtedness, largely as a result of constitutional limitations. Among new issues, revenue bonds are now nearly triple general obligation bonds, and most of the growth has come from issues by statutory authorities rather than state or local governments. High interest rates and lender uncertainty about future interest rates have forced state and local governments into short-term financing.

Overall Levels of Debt

In 1981, total state and local debt outstanding reached $370 billion (table 11), about 13.3 percent of GNP, and about 10 percent of all medium- and long-term securities outstanding. Revenues from bond sales financed about 30 percent of state and local capital expenditures in 1980, a decline from 50 percent in 1970. Most of the decline in bond financing was a result of the sharp increase in federal grants, which, by 1980, had become the single largest funding source (table 12). State and local debt as a share of GNP has actually declined since 1964, as has gross federal debt—in part a reflection of reduced investment in public infrastructure, but also reflecting how rapid inflation has reduced the value of long-term indebtedness. State participation in the bond market has grown relative to municipalities. During the past fifty years, state debt has grown from only 16 percent of the level of local debt in 1929 to about 60 percent of that level today. By comparison, state debt grew by 180 percent during the 1970s, federal debt by 144 percent, consumer debt by 176 percent, and residential mortgage debt by 202 percent. The volume of new debt issued by state and local governments has increased much more rapidly than private sector debt and equity. In 1970, new corporate debt and equity issued

173

Table 11

Federal, State, and Local Debt, Selected Years 1929–1981

($ in billions)

Fiscal Year	Gross Federal Debt	Total State Debt	Total Local Debt	Gross Federal Debt	Total State Debt	Total Local Debt
	Amount			As a Percent of GNP		
1929	$ 16.9	$ 2.3	$ 14.2	16.9	2.3	14.2
1939	40.4	3.5	16.6	46.1	4.0	18.9
1949	252.8	4.0	16.9	96.6	1.5	6.5
1954	270.8	9.6	29.3	74.5	2.6	8.1
1959	284.7	16.9	47.2	60.4	3.6	10.0
1964	316.8	25.0	67.2	51.4	4.1	10.9
1969	367.1[1]	39.6	94.0	40.6	4.4	10.4
1970	382.6	42.0	101.6	39.8	4.4	10.6
1971	409.5	47.8	111.0	40.2	4.7	10.9
1972	437.3	54.5	120.7	39.3	4.9	10.9
1973	468.4[2]	59.4	129.1	37.8	4.8	10.4
1974	486.2	65.3	141.3	35.8	4.8	10.4
1975	544.1	72.1	149.1	37.5	5.0	10.3
1976	631.9	84.4	155.7	38.9	5.2	9.6
1977	709.1	90.2	167.3	38.0	5.1	9.4
1978	780.4	102.6	177.9	37.4	5.1	8.8
1979	833.8	111.7	192.4	35.4	4.9	8.4
1980	914.3	122.0	213.6	35.6	4.8	8.5
1981 Est.[4]	995.1	135.5	235.0	34.9	4.8	8.5
	Percent Distribution			Annual Percent Change[3]		
1929	50.6	6.9	42.5	—	—	—

Year						
1939	66.8	5.8	27.4	9.1	4.3	1.6
1949	92.4	1.5	5.2	20.1	1.3	0.2
1954	87.4	3.1	3.5	1.4	19.1	11.6
1959	81.6	4.8	13.5	1.0	11.9	10.0
1964	77.5	6.1	15.4	2.2	8.1	7.3
1969	73.3	7.9	13.8	3.0	9.6	6.9
1970	72.7	8.0	13.3	4.2	6.1	8.1
1971	72.1	8.4	13.5	7.0	13.8	9.3
1972	71.4	8.9	13.7	6.8	14.0	8.7
1973	71.3	9.0	13.7	7.1	9.0	7.0
1974	70.2	9.4	20.4	3.8	9.9	9.5
1975	71.1	9.4	13.5	11.9	10.4	5.5
1976	72.5	9.7	17.9	16.1	17.1	4.4
1977	73.4	9.3	17.3	12.3	6.9	7.5
1978	73.6	9.7	15.8	10.1	13.7	6.3
1979	73.3	9.8	15.9	6.8	8.9	8.2
1980	73.1	9.8	17.1	9.7	9.2	11.0
1981 Est.4	73.0	9.8	17.2	8.8	9.4	10.0

Notes: 1. During 1969, three government-sponsored enterprises became completely privately owned, and their debt was removed from the totals for the federal government. At the dates of their conversion, gross federal debt was reduced by $10.7 billion.

2. A procedural change in the recording of trust fund holdings of Treasury debt at the end of the month increased gross federal debt by about $4.5 billion.

3. The percent changes indicated for years prior to 1970 are annual average changes since the previous year shown.

4. Estimated.

Source: ACIR staff compilation based on U.S. Bureau of the Census, *Governmental Finances*, various years; Office of Management and Budget, *Special Analysis, Budget of the United States Government. 1982*; United States Treasury Department, *Treasury Bulletin*, July, 1981; and ACIR staff estimates.

totalled $38.5 billion, while new municipal bond issues were only $18.1 billion. In 1979, $43.3 billion of new state and local debt was issued, while new corporate issues were only $42.2 billion.

Although public debt as a share of GNP has declined, annual interest payments as a share of GNP have grown since 1964 (table 13). State governments have been especially harmed by rising interest costs, primarily because a much higher share of their debt has been issued more recently and is in shorter-term maturities. In 1981, the

---

Table 12

Sources of Financing for State and Local Capital Expenditures

Item	1960	1965	1970	1973	1977
Federal Aid	20.0%	22.0%	22.0%	25.2%	43.3%
Long-Term Bonds	37.1	35.0	51.0	45.0	32.1
Other Local Resources	42.9	43.0	37.0	29.8	24.5
Ratio of Annual Tax-exempt Bond Issues to Annual Capital Outlays	50.2%	51.8%	59.5%	67.5%	118.7%

Source: George E. Peterson, "Capital Spending and Capital Obsolescence: Outlook for Cities," in The Fiscal Outlook for Cities, edited by Roy Bahl (Syracuse: Syracuse University Press, 1978), p. 53.

Table 13

Interest Payments on Government Debt, Selected Years 1929–1981

($ in billions)

Fiscal Year	Federal[1]	State[2]	Local[2]	Federal	State	Local
		Amount			As a Percent of GNP	
1929	$ 678	$ 95	$ 550	0.7	0.1	0.5
1939	941	129	534	1.1	0.1	0.6
1949	5,339	97	330	2.0	*	0.1
1954	6,382	193	525	1.8	0.1	0.1
1959	7,593	453	963	1.6	0.1	0.2
1964	10,666	765	1,590	1.7	0.1	0.3
1969	16,588	1,275	2,457	1.8	0.1	0.3

Fiscal Year	Federal[1]	State[2]	Local[2]	Federal	State	Local
		Amount		As a Percent of GNP		
1970	19,304	1,499	2,875	2.0	0.2	0.3
1971	20,959	1,761	3,328	2.1	0.2	0.3
1972	21,849	2,135	3,894	2.0	0.2	0.4
1973	24,167	2,434	4,351	2.0	0.2	0.4
1974	29,319	2,863	4,803	2.2	0.2	0.4
1975	32,665	3,272	5,511	2.2	0.2	0.4
1976	37,063	4,140	6,129	2.3	0.3	0.4
1977	41,900	5,136	6,257	2.3	0.3	0.3
1978	48,695	5,268	6,714	2.4	0.3	0.3
1979	59,837	5,790	7,197	2.5	0.3	0.3
1980	74,860	6,763	7,984	2.9	0.3	0.3
1981 Est.	90,600	7,700	8,800	3.2	0.3	0.3
		% Distribution		As a Percent of General Revenue[3]		
1929	51.2	7.2	41.6	19.2	4.8	10.9
1939	58.7	8.0	33.3	20.9	3.6	10.7
1949	92.6	1.7	5.7	13.2	1.6	3.7
1954	90.0	2.7	7.4	9.1	1.6	3.9
1959	84.3	5.0	10.7	10.0	2.5	4.6
1964	81.9	5.9	12.2	10.4	2.7	5.3
1969	81.6	6.3	12.1	10.2	2.6	5.4
1970	81.5	6.3	12.1	11.8	2.6	5.6
1971	80.5	6.8	12.8	13.2	2.9	5.8
1972	78.4	7.7	14.0	12.5	3.0	5.9
1973	78.1	7.9	14.1	12.4	3.0	6.2
1974	79.3	7.7	13.0	13.5	3.2	6.3
1975	78.8	7.9	13.3	14.7	3.4	6.5
1976	78.3	8.7	12.9	15.6	3.9	6.6
1977	78.6	9.6	11.7	14.8	4.2	6.1
1978	80.3	8.7	11.1	15.3	3.9	6.1
1979	82.2	8.0	9.9	16.1	3.8	6.1
1980	83.5	7.5	8.9	17.9	4.0	6.1
1981 Est.	84.6	7.2	8.2	18.8	**	**

Notes: *Less than .05 percent.   **Data not available.

1. Interest on the public debt. Data for 1929–1949 are administrative budget figures; for 1964–1981, unified budget figures.
2. Interest on general debt.
3. General revenue from own sources (before intergovernmental transfers).

Source: ACIR staff compilation based on U.S. Bureau of the Census, *Governmental Finances,* various years; Office of Management and Budget, *Special Analysis, Budget of the United States Government. 1982;* U.S. Treasury Department, *Treasury Bulletin,* various issues; and ACIR staff estimates.

level of state debt was about 60 percent of the level of local debt, yet annual interest paid by state governments was about 85 percent of the interest paid by local governments. Interest costs on debt represented 4 percent of total state spending in 1981 compared with just over 1 percent in 1964.

However, these aggregate data mask considerable interstate variations (table 14). Eleven states have combined state and local debt in excess of $2,000 per capita.[2] Nine states have per-capita indebtedness below $1,000.[3] Care should be taken in interpreting these data. High indebtedness is not necessarily a sign of fiscal imprudence or impending fiscal collapse any more than low indebtedness is a good sign. Generally, a high level of indebtedness reflects past investments in public capital—although the relationship is not straightforward because there are great differences among states in the amount of public invest-

Table 14

State and Local Debt Levels in the 50 States: FY 1980

	Debt Per Capita	Debt as Percentage of Own Source Revenues	Debt Interest as % of State Expenses	Debt Per $1,000 of Per Capita Income
Alabama	1,049.14	93.9	3.3	151
Alaska	10,098.03	77.6	8.6	900
Arizona	1,748.42	74.9	2.9	208
Arkansas	882.79	102.2	2.4	127
California	1,022.83	151.1	2.1	102
Colorado	1,315.76	107.0	2.7	144
Connecticut	1,862.07	70.3	5.9	184
Delaware	2,725.79	54.8	5.9	292
Florida	1,075.34	100.0	3.4	126
Georgia	1,135.58	98.3	2.8	149
Hawaii	2,260.25	72.1	6.0	245
Idaho	712.33	151.0	2.2	94
Illinois	1,338.49	100.2	4.1	137
Indiana	714.90	144.3	3.0	83
Iowa	787.82	166.9	1.7	90
Kansas	1,386.64	91.6	3.1	150
Kentucky	2,027.27	49.6	6.6	274

	Debt Per Capita	Debt as Percentage of Own Source Revenues	Debt Interest as % of State Expenses	Debt Per $1,000 of Per Capita Income
Louisiana	1,686.22	75.6	4.7	222
Maine	1,190.43	89.2	4.0	169
Maryland	1,779.07	83.4	4.2	191
Massachusetts	1,784.41	82.8	4.8	201
Michigan	1,200.87	122.2	3.3	127
Minnesota	2,129.13	74.3	4.1	240
Mississippi	845.24	112.1	2.9	137
Missouri	860.17	116.6	2.6	104
Montana	1,083.49	125.1	3.2	141
Nebraska	2,932.67	46.8	2.1	338
Nevada	1,645.41	87.2	3.8	156
New Hampshire	1,405.80	70.2	5.7	168
New Jersey	1,713.39	82.5	4.8	176
New Mexico	1,455.80	103.6	3.9	193
New York	2,648.31	69.6	6.7	291
North Carolina	751.94	130.7	2.4	102
North Dakota	1,264.62	117.5	3.0	154
Ohio	970.77	113.3	3.3	111
Oklahoma	1,115.42	105.3	2.8	131
Oregon	2,668.45	54.7	6.3	299
Pennsylvania	1,718.43	71.7	6.1	201
Rhode Island	2,142.49	62.4	6.6	252
South Carolina	1,073.32	91.2	2.4	152
South Dakota	1,642.95	69.8	3.6	220
Tennessee	1,315.59	71.2	3.9	179
Texas	1,452.07	79.9	3.6	165
Utah	968.12	120.4	2.7	135
Vermont	1,543.84	77.3	5.0	211
Virginia	1,096.77	103.7	3.7	128
Washington	2,814.70	50.8	3.1	294
West Virginia	1,665.18	64.5	5.1	226
Wisconsin	1,205.79	118.6	3.1	142
Wyoming	2,476.76	85.9	5.2	250
District of Columbia	4,165.98	41.4	5.1	394
U.S. Average	1,481.66	89.2	4.0	16.9

Source: Calculated from Bureau of the Census, *Survey of Governmental Finances, 1981,* Washington, D.C., 1981, various tables.

ment that was federally financed. In the case of New York, some of the debt was incurred financing operating expenses before the city's fiscal crisis led to a return to Generally Accepted Accounting Principles (GAAP). In other states, infrastructure has been paid for out of general revenues. What really matters, from the perspective of the long-term economic and fiscal health of a state, is whether the accumulated investments were made wisely, whether they have been adequately maintained, and whether voters, legislators, and officials are prepared to take any action necessary to protect the integrity of their past investments.

Type of Public Debt

Long-term debt can be divided into two types.

☐ *Full faith and credit*—sometimes known as general obligation bonds (GOBs). This debt is unconditionally backed by the credit of the issuing government, implying its ability to tax. It includes debt whose interest and amortization is financed from specific tax and nontax sources, but which represents a liability payable from any other available resources if the pledged sources are insufficient. Most GOB issues require voter approval.

☐ *Nonguaranteed debt*—sometimes known as limited obligation bonds (LOBs). This consists of debt payable solely from earnings of revenue producing activities, from special assessments, or from specific nonproperty taxes. LOB issues do not usually require voter approval. Industrial Development Bonds (IDBs) are an example of LOBs.

Nationally, nearly 55 percent of state debt was nonguaranteed in 1980, 37 percent was in the form of general obligation bonds, 6.2 percent was full faith and credit payable from specified nontax revenues, and 2.1 percent was short-term (Gold, 1981).

There are substantial variations among states. In only thirteen states—mostly those with high per-capita debt levels—did general obligation bonds account for more than half of total debt in 1981.[4] Nine states have no general obligation debt because of constitutional constraints.[5] Table 15 describes the constitutional limitations on state borrowing.

At the county and municipal level, growth of general obligation debt has been more constrained. Table 16 describes the constitutional and statutory limitations on local borrowing. Limited obligation debt has therefore been a more important part of debt expansion during the past decade. Partly because of defaults on municipal GOBs in the 1873–79 depression and during the 1930s, 80 percent of the states have local debt limits on GOBs, usually expressed as a percentage of assessed property values, and about the same number require a community to hold a referendum before issuing GOBs (Shaul, 1980). About 65 percent of states and localities have reached these self-imposed debt ceilings. LOBs (excluding IDBs) have grown from 16 percent of new issues in 1952 to nearly 40 percent today. Among all new tax-exempt issues, revenue bonds are now nearly three times the volume of general obligation bonds, while they were only half the volume in 1970 (Public Securities Association, 1981). Because of the ease with which LOBs can be issued and the very large number of political entities that can issue LOBs, their rapid growth contributed to the growing disorder and high-risk premiums in the tax-exempt market.

The Term Structure of Public Debt

Between 1975 and 1980, most state and local borrowing was long-term (over twenty-four months). Since 1980, the trend has reversed. In 1981, the volume of new long-term debt declined while the volume of short-term increased by 36 percent. This was a result of high interest rates and uncertainty concerning future interest rates. Lenders are unwilling to purchase long-term fixed rate assets—in the late 1970s, many had been caught by the sudden upsurge of inflation holding assets that yielded a negative rate of interest. Borrowers have been reluctant to commit themselves to long-term obligations in the hope that rates will have fallen when they have to roll over the debt. The increasing share of short-term debt makes budgeting less certain. (See figure 2.)

Table 15

State Constitutional Limitations on State Borrowing, 1976

	Legislative Borrowing Power Limits				Exceptions to Limits			
State	No Limitations	For Casual Deficits or Extraordinary Expenses Only	For Any Other Purpose	Referendum Required To Create Debt	Referendum Required To Exceed Limit	For Refunding	Limit May Be Exceeded: For Defense of State or Nation	For Other Purpose
Alabama		$3,000,000	(1)	(1)		x	x	
Alaska	x		(3)	x		x	x	
Arizona		350,000					x	
Arkansas				x		x		
California			$300,000		x		x	
Colorado		100,000	50,000 (7)		x		x	x
Connecticut	x							
Delaware	x					x	x	
Florida			(9)	x		x		
Georgia		(10)	(10)	(10)		x		
Hawaii			(11)			x	x	
Idaho			2,000,000	x			x	
Illinois	x	(13)						
Indiana		(15)			x			
Iowa		250,000			x		x	
Kansas			1,000,000		x		x	
Kentucky		500,000			x	x	x	
Louisiana	x					x	x	
Maine		(16)	2,000,000		x			
Maryland	x						x	x
Massachusetts	x						x	x
Michigan		(19)		x			x	x

State							
Minnesota	x						
Mississippi		$1,000,000	(20)				x
Missouri	x			x			x
Montana	x						
Nebraska	x	100,000	(21)				x
Nevada							x
New Hampshire		200,000	(22)	x	x		x
New Jersey			(21)	x	x		x
New Mexico					x		x
New York						x	x
North Carolina		(15)	(23)	x	x		x
North Dakota		2,000,000			x		x
Ohio		750,000			x		
Oklahoma		500,000		x	x		x
Oregon		50,000		x	x x x		x
Pennsylvania				x			
Rhode Island		50,000			x		x
South Carolina		(15)		x			
South Dakota		100,000	21, 1		x		x
Tennessee	x						
Texas		200,000			x		x
Utah	x		(21)				x
Vermont	x						
Virginia		(28)	(28)	x	x		x
Washington		(15)	(29, 12)	x			x
West Virginia		(15)		x	x		
Wisconsin			(21)				x
Wyoming			(21)	x			x

Source: Advisory Commission for Intergovernmental Relations, *Significant Features of Fiscal Federalism, 1976–77* (Washington, D.C., 1977), p. 94–95.

183

Table 16
State Constitutional and Statutory Referendum Requirements for Local Government Issuance of General Obligation Long-Term Debt, 1976

State	Citation[1]	Referendum Required	Approval[2]	Remarks
Alabama	C	X	M	
Alaska	C	X	M	
Arizona	C	X	M	Only for debt in excess of the 4 percent limit.
Arkansas	C	X	M	
California	C-S	X	M	
Colorado	C-S	X	M	
Connecticut	.....	None required	.....	
Delaware	S	X	M	
Florida	C-S	X	M	
Georgia	C	X	M	
Hawaii	.....	None required	.....	
Idaho	C-S	X	2/3	
Illinois	S	X	M	
Indiana	.....	None required	.....	
Iowa	S	X	2/3	
Kansas	S	X	M	
Kentucky	C-S	X	2/3	
Louisiana	C-S	X	M	
Maine	S	X	M	Applies to municipalities only.
Maryland	C-S	X	M	Constitutional requirement applies to municipalities, statutory requirement applies to charter counties.
Massachusetts	.....	None required	.....	Except for debt issued by regional school districts in which case a referendum may be called by the towns comprising the district; in this event, simple majority approval is required.

State		Referendum required	Majority	Notes
Michigan	S	X	M	Not applicable to school districts. Numerous statutory exemptions as to when applicable.
Minnesota	S	X	M	Does not apply to Minneapolis, St. Paul, and Duluth.
Mississippi	S	X	3/5	Only on petition of 20 percent of the electors for county bonds; 10 percent or 1,500, whichever is less, for municipal bonds.
Missouri	C	X	2/3	
Montana	S	X	M	If turnout is less than 40 percent of the electorate (30 percent for schools), the bond issue fails. If turnout for school bond issue is between 30 and 40 percent, 60 percent majority is required.
Nebraska	C-S	X	M	Fifty-five percent for school districts.
Nevada	S	X	M	
New Hamshire	S	X	2/3	Not applicable to cities or counties.
New Jersey	S	None required	......	Except for debt issued by certain classes of school districts (simple majority).
New Mexico	C	X	M	Except for debt issued by certain classes of school districts (simple majority). Permissive referendum for most town and village issues.
New York	S	None required	......	
North Carolina	C	X	M	Referendum is not required if the amount of issue does not exceed 2/3 of the net debt reduction for the preceding fiscal year.
North Dakota	C-S	X	2/3	Simple majority for county bonds; 60 percent for municipalities and school districts with over 5,000 population.
Ohio	S	X	M	
Oklahoma	S	X	3/5	Except that in the case of county hospital bonds a referendum is required on petition only (20 percent of the electors).

(Table 16 continued on next page.)

185

Table 16 *(continued)*

State	Citation[1]	Referendum Required	Approval[2]	Remarks
Oregon	S	X	M	Applies only to debt in excess of statutory limit up to specified maximum.
Pennsylvania	S	X	M	
Rhode Island	S	X	M	Optional.
South Carolina	C	X	M	Applies only to debt issued by cities and towns.
Tennessee	....	None required	....	Except that a 3/4 majority vote is required for issuance of general obligation industrial development bonds.
Texas	S	X	M	Applies to county debt only. No referendum required in counties that elect to be treated as cities.
Utah	S	X	M	
Vermont	S	X	M	
Virginia	S	X	M	
Washington	C	None required	....	Except for township debt (2/3 majority) and debt issued in excess of constitutional limits (3/5 majority).
West Virginia	C-S	X	3/5	Applies only to school districts and townships. No referendum required for county or municipal bond issues.
Wisconsin	S	X	M	
Wyoming	C-S	X	M	

Notes: 1. The citation is either the state's constitution (C), statutes (S), or both (C-S).
2. A simple majority (a favorable majority of 50 percent plus 1 of all votes subject to counting on the question) is indicated by "M"; where more than a simple favorable majority is required, the required percentage is entered.

This table deals only with referendum requirements that apply generally to general obligation debt issued by cities, counties, and school districts in each state. As in the case of debt limits, there are numerous exceptions and special provisions, particularly regarding debt issued by special districts and for specific purposes. No attempt has been made to treat those special provisions in this tabulation.

Source: ACIR staff with the help of state attorneys general or other state officials.

Figure 2
State and Local Borrowing Volume 1971–1981 (in billions)

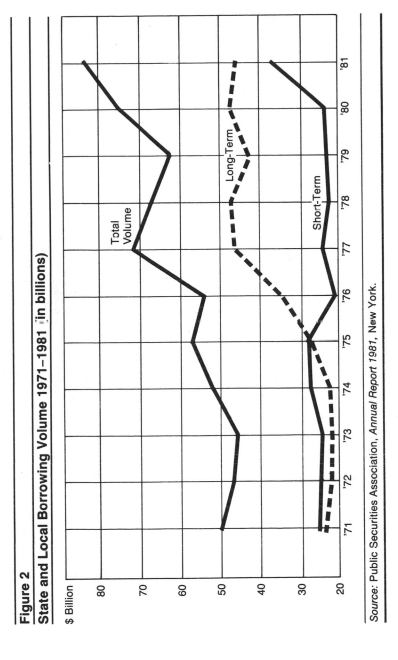

Source: Public Securities Association, *Annual Report 1981*, New York.

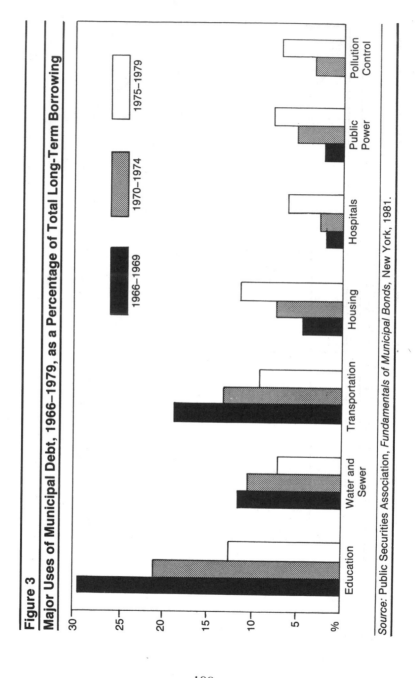

Figure 3

Major Uses of Municipal Debt, 1966–1979, as a Percentage of Total Long-Term Borrowing

1975–1979

1970–1974

1966–1969

30   25   20   15   10   5   %

Education   Water and Sewer   Transportation   Housing   Hospitals   Public Power   Pollution Control

Source: Public Securities Association, *Fundamentals of Municipal Bonds*, New York, 1981.

Table 17

Volume of Tax-Exempt Borrowing by Purpose
($ in billions)

Purpose of Issue	1970	1971	1972	1973	1974	1975	1976	1977	1978	1979	1980	1981[1]
Education	5.0	5.3	2.9	2.3	3.7	4.7	5.3	5.1	5.0	5.1	4.6	4.5
Transportation	3.2	4.3	1.7	1.6	1.5	2.2	3.4	2.9	3.5	2.4	2.6	3.5
Water & Sewer	2.4	3.2	1.3	1.9	2.0	2.3	3.0	3.3	3.2	3.1	2.9	2.9
Public Power	1.1	1.3	1.2	1.4	0.9	2.7	2.7	4.8	5.8	5.4	5.1	6.3
Pollution Control	NA	0.9	0.4	1.5	1.5	2.2	1.9	2.6	2.7	2.1	2.3	4.4
Hospital	NA	0.4	0.6	0.7	0.8	2.0	2.3	3.3	2.3	3.4	3.6	5.4
Indus. Revenue Bonds	NA	NA	NA	NA	NA	1.3	1.5	2.3	3.5	7.1	8.4	10.1
Housing	0.2	1.9	0.9	1.1	1.0	0.6	3.1	3.7	5.8	9.7	16.6	5.9
Total Long-Term**	18.1	24.9	23.7	23.8	23.6	30.7	35.4	46.7	48.1	48.7	58.3	47.7*
Short-Term Volume	17.9	26.3	25.2	24.7	29.4	29.0	21.9	24.8	21.4	21.7	27.7	—
TOTAL VOLUME	36.0	51.2	48.9	48.5	53.0	59.7	57.3	71.5	69.5	70.4	86.0	—

Notes: NA indicates figures not available
    1 Indicates totals for first 6 months
    * PSA Estimate
    ** Totals include Recreation, miscellaneous, and Refunding not broken out

Source: Francis Viscount, *Municipal Bonds: The Need to Regulate* (Washington, D.C.: National League of Cities), p. 9, from data in the *Daily Bond Buyer*, and in Public Securities Association annual reports.

189

Purpose of Debt Issues

The investment categories financed by debt have changed over the last decade (figure 3 and table 17). Of traditional public infrastructure purposes, education, transportation, and water and sewers halved their share of new issue revenues between 1966–69 and 1975–79, while housing, hospitals, public power, and pollution control investments (by private firms) doubled their share. Most of the increase in LOBs has been for investments that are not traditionally a public responsibility—mortgage subsidies, industrial revenue bonds, and pollution control. In 1980, Congress severely limited mortgage revenue bonds that had absorbed more than one-quarter of all the revenues from tax-exempt bond sales in 1980 (table 18). Those restrictions have been eased in the 1982 tax act and issues are again increasing. Industrial revenue bonds grew from only $1 billion in 1975 to over $10 billion in 1981 (table 17), prompting federal legislation to limit them somewhat in 1982, after a fierce and protracted battle with powerful lobbying groups.

Issuers of Tax-Exempt Debt

States play a small direct role in the issuing of tax-exempt debt. Only 10 percent of new issues in 1979 were by state governments, less than half their share a decade earlier (table 18). The share of counties in the total has remained fairly constant. The sharp decline in municipalities' share reflects the fiscal constraints and constitutional limits.

But states have been responsible for setting up the statutory authorities—from public utilities to port authorities—that now issue more than half of all new long-term tax-exempt debt. Unless the investments of these authorities are carefully coordinated, they may crowd out more traditional state and local capital investments.

The Tax-Exempt Bond Market

Interest rates on tax-exempt bonds have risen alarmingly since 1979, both in absolute terms and relative to

Table 18

**Municipal Borrowing by Type of Issuer,
Selected Years, 1966–1981**

	1966	1970	1974	1978	1980–81
States	21.0%	22.0%	15.9%	10.0%	11.0%
Counties	6.6	9.1	8.7	10.3	10.3
Municipalities	20.9	26.3	27.0	20.3	18.0
School Districts	14.2	11.8	9.2	5.4	4.0
Special Districts	6.9	6.4	5.3	2.3	3.1
Statutory Authorities	30.4	24.4	33.9	51.7	53.6

Source: Public Securities Association, *Fundamentals of Municipal Bonds* (New York, 1981), p. 51.

taxable bonds. Many issuing agencies have suffered lower credit ratings, and others have been scared away from issuing new debt. The problems have arisen from the increased volume of tax-exempt paper for sale, from reduced demand for tax-exempt securities because of changes in federal policies, and from the growing confusion in the operation of the market itself.

Tax Exemption
of State and Local Debt

With one minor exception, all interest payments on bonds issued by state and local governments are exempt from federal income taxes and often from state and city income taxes as well.[6] This characteristic has established a somewhat separate capital market for state and local debt, set apart from federal and corporate long-term debt. Because investors are willing to accept lower yields to obtain tax-free income, this exemption lowers the borrowing costs of state and local governments—a subsidy paid by the U.S. Treasury. Before World War II, when personal and corporate income tax rates were low, this exemption led to a relatively small differential between taxable and tax-exempt bond rates. The interest on municipal bonds averages about 95 percent of the rate on taxable bonds. By the 1970s, however, dramatic increases in income tax rates—which increased the advantages of investing in tax-exempt bonds—had widened the differential from 5 per-

191

cent to about 30 percent, a spread that had, in part, cushioned state and local governments from the full effect of rising interest rates (Peterson, 1982). In fact, if inflation is taken into account, state and local governments were able to borrow at *negative real* interest rates for most of the second half of the 1970s.[7] However, because of the increased volume of bonds and reduced demand, that trend has been reversed and the differential has narrowed from 35 percent in 1979 to below 20 percent in the first half of 1982 (Peterson, 1982).

Although tax exemption for public bonds does reduce the cost of public borrowing below the private sector rate, it only does so on a "before-tax" basis.

> Because private investors can deduct interest payments, the private before-tax borrowing rate is reduced by a percentage equal to the applicable marginal tax rate of the private borrower. Most private capital formation is carried out by the corporate sector, and since the corporate tax rate exceeds the implicit tax rate on tax-exempt bonds, the after-tax borrowing rate of these corporations is considerably below that of state and local governments. Furthermore, private investors receive additional subsidies through such mechanisms as the investment tax credit and accelerated depreciation, although the effect of these subsidies is somewhat offset by the fact that private net revenues from investment projects are subject to tax, while state and local revenues are not (Kopcke and Kimball, 1979, p. 21).

The result is that, even with the tax-exempt provision, the public sector must pay more to finance an investment than the private sector. This has led to recommendations to provide a more direct and deeper subsidy for state and local government borrowing—measures that are discussed in chapter 8.

Reduced Demand for Municipal Debt

Higher relative interest rates on tax-exempt securities have been necessary to attract investors in the face of declines in demand (or, more properly, a slower rate of growth of demand) that have resulted from:

☐   Changes in tax laws, including the reduction in the

maximum tax rate from 70 percent to 50 percent, the creation of tax-exempt All Savers Certificates, and the expansion of tax-deferred Individual Retirement Accounts, that have created competitive alternatives to tax-exempt bonds.

☐ Changes in behavior by institutional investors, especially the growth of leasing by commercial banks, that have reduced their demand for tax-exempt bonds. The recently enacted corporate minimum tax is estimated to raise the interest rate on municipal bonds by 60 basis points (Trent, 1982).

☐ Reduced confidence in the fiscal strength of many states and local governments, following the well-published brushes with bankruptcy of New York City, Cleveland, and other cities, and revenue and tax rate limitations that weaken a state or local government's ability to repay.

☐ The rapid expansion of tax-exempt issues for nontraditional purposes such as industrial development, pollution control, and residential mortgages.

☐ Massive increases in new federal borrowing as a share of net annual savings.

The combination of sharply reduced demand for tax-exempt bonds and a rapid expansion in the volume of these bonds has driven up their interest rates relative to taxable issues and squeezed many weaker jurisdictions out of the bond market altogether.[8]

To an unknown extent, some of these measures will encourage an increase in household savings, now running at an annual rate of about $200 billion or about 5 percent of GNP. Yet they will also divert savings from traditional investments such as savings accounts and municipal bonds. Household savings will be the primary source of revenues for municipal bond sales because institutional investors have cut back on the purchase of new tax-exempt issues. Commercial banks and casualty insurance companies have traditionally purchased three-quarters of new state and local issues. However, changes in the corporate tax code have led to a sharp decline in the amount of income that these corporations need to shelter by buying tax-exempt securities. Expansion of leasing activities

193

and high rates of interest have reduced the attraction of municipal bonds. In 1981, commercial banks purchased only 18 percent of net new municipal issues, and casualty insurance companies only 7 percent. Some of this decline is a cyclical pattern, but much of it represents a permanent change (Trent, 1982; Viscount, 1982; Peterson, 1982).

However, state and local governments will have to compete with the federal government for households' investments. Although the two types of securities are not strictly competing—the interest on federal securities is taxable—the huge increase in federal demands for funds will crowd out all other types of debt instruments and drive up interest rates. In 1970, federal securities absorbed less than 10 percent of the new loanable funds available. In 1979, the federal government required only 18 percent of the capital markets' new resources. In 1982, that requirement will have more than doubled. For the first time in peacetime, net federal borrowing is now greater than the net increase in household savings. Deficits are projected to increase significantly during the next three years, and the total federal debt is projected to grow by 50 percent between 1981 and 1985. State and local debt rose by a third of the total increase in Treasury and federal agency debt in 1981. The tax cuts are intended to encourage increased economic growth in the long run, but in the short run the resulting deficit is driving up interest rates. In competing with the federal government to sell securities, Henry Kaufman of Solomon Brothers has said, "state and local governments cannot win."

One of the reasons that they cannot win is that the fiscal crises experienced by New York City, in 1975, and by several other cities since have shaken investor confidence. City governments and statutory agencies demonstrated that they were not always willing to use revenues to pay off bond holders before meeting other obligations. Credit ratings have been downgraded by Moody's and Standard and Poors, and, by some estimates, all municipal bonds must now pay a risk premium in the form of higher rates.[9] Reduced rating can raise borrowing costs by as much as two percentage points. In the past two years, six states have lost their favored AAA status.

Confusion in the Bond Market

There are more than 1.5 million different tax-exempt issues outstanding—sold by state and local governments, special districts, public authorities, and industrial development agencies. Some issues were for billions of dollars, others for less than one million. The issues are purchased by individuals (either directly or through pooled funds), by banks, insurance companies, and even by nonfinancial corporations. Some issues are in the hands of a single investor. Others are held by hundreds of investors.

The growing complexity of municipal bond issues and the proliferation of special authorities with bonding power have also clearly worried investors who are unfamiliar with the type of issue or with the issuing agency. A single bond issue might have thirty different maturities with twelve coupon interest rates. More than 50,000 political entities have debt outstanding. There are no organized exchanges for municipal securities as there are for corporate securities. States and localities do not have to conform to disclosure requirements required by federal law for corporate securities. They use private bond-rating agencies to assess the quality of bonds on behalf of investors—Moody's, Standard and Poors, and Fitch's.[10] Sixty percent (by dollar volume) of municipal debt is rated, but only 30 percent of all issues (Ingram and Copeland, 1982). The "chaotic" municipal security market, as it was labeled by the Joint Economic Committee (1981), increases the costs of public finance.

These changes in the tax-exempt market will not be reversed as inflation abates or when the economy recovers. The structure of the market has been permanently changed (Peterson, 1982) and could only be reversed if the massive tax reforms of 1981 were undone—if personal income taxes were raised, and if other tax-exempt instruments were abolished—events that are highly unlikely. The public sector will continue to face a hostile bond market in the foreseeable future, and must design its capital investment strategy accordingly. Some of the proposed federal initiatives, such as direct interest subsidy payments for a "taxable" public bond, that could reduce public borrowing costs are discussed in chapter 8.

Reducing the Cost
of Debt Finance

The ability of state governments to affect the cost of borrowing is very limited. The major factors that have driven up the cost of interest are beyond the control of state governments, and are, in major part, the result of federal actions. Significant changes in federal tax law, in the level of federal deficits, and in monetary policy would be necessary to reduce the cost of long-term state and local debt.

Even where state actions have contributed to the problem—such as through the proliferation of tax-exempt issues for purposes that are not clearly public—it is difficult for any single state to have any real effect on the tax-exempt bond market. It would also earn a reputation for being anti-business or anti-development. A state that abolished its industrial development agencies would have little impact on the overall volume of IDBs flooding the market and would arouse the ire of its business community and many local officials. Again, federal action would be required.

Perhaps the most significant step that a state government can take is to carefully review the purposes for which it is issuing debt. Is the investment one that really requires public funds, or is it more properly the responsibility of a private firm? Is the investment necessary, or are there cheaper and more efficient ways of meeting public service needs? By cutting back on the public debt for industrial subsidies, not-for-profit private health care facilities or private pollution control projects, a state could use its debt for vitally needed *public* investment projects. States (and localities) should also review their use of business tax incentives. Although no accurate data are available—only a handful of states keep records of tax expenditures—evidence suggests that more than $1 billion in potential annual tax revenues is not collected because of abatements, exemptions, and tax credits (Kieschnick, 1981). These potential revenues could be used to finance direct public capital investments.

The next significant step is for the state to provide for adequate revenue sources to back the bond issue and to cover the operation and maintenance of the facility, an issue discussed in detail in chapter 3. The selection of appropriate revenue sources will enable the state to protect its fiscal integrity and so guarantee a high quality bond rating. It is also important for states to provide local governments with the taxing powers necessary to back limited obligation and even general obligation bonds. Sales and property tax increment financing could be a valuable mechanism to ensure that those benefiting from a project pay for it and that the facility will be adequately maintained. Taxes levied by special assessment districts can provide a way of recapturing local benefits from projects. As states develop capital investment strategies in conjunction with their localities, some will have to delegate increased taxing and spending powers to ensure a full and cooperative relationship.

The most important actions states can take to assist local governments to issue debt, is to provide fiscal assistance. Intra-state revenue-sharing programs, categorical grants, and state assumption of program responsibilities will probably have to be increased. However, there are ways in which the state can reduce the costs of local government borrowing that do not involve direct financial assistance but which are based on improving the way the market for tax-exempt issues operates. Forbes and Peterson (1978) classified these mechanisms under four headings:

☐   state supervision and technical assistance;
☐   financial intermediation;
☐   grants for local debt service costs;
☐   guarantee of local debt.

There are both advantages and disadvantages of increased state intervention in local bond issues. It provides the state with the power to coordinate state and local infrastructure planning, enforce state policies (such as the imposition of user fees), reduce the probability of a local default (which might weaken the state's own rating), and reduce interest costs. However, this power incurs responsibilities. The exercise of power will necessitate refusing certain bond issues or demanding locally unpopular changes in plans and in local policies. It will, inevitably, cause some local resentment at the intrusion of the state, a problem with obvious political implications. But in most states, increased state involvement in local affairs will be the inevitable result of reduced federal involvement and the expansion of state-run block grants. Some of the promising policies in each of the four areas are described below.

Supervision and Technical Assistance

A study by the National Conference of State Legislatures summarizes the activities in specific states:

> North Carolina and New Jersey provide the most extensive service. The North Carolina Local Government Commission provides... "assistance in setting up new budgeting and accounting procedures as well as training sessions to help local officials manage their city's financial affairs." The Commission also has ultimate responsibility for marketing of local debt issues....
>
> In New Jersey the Local Finance Board exercises extensive regulatory power over local finance. The state has established comprehensive budgeting, accounting and financial reporting standards. For example, local governments must be audited annually and must have their operating and capital budgets approved by the state.
>
> But the state also provides extensive technical assistance and training effort through Rutgers University and the Bureau of Financial Management Services (Watson, 1982, p. 12).

The number of states providing the types of supervision and assistance are shown in table 19.

Financial Intermediation

The myriad of small issues sold by local governments and special districts is an expensive way to raise funds. The transaction costs are high, and investors who are unfamiliar with the issuing agency may require a risk premium, which drives up interest rates. These costs can be reduced through a state agency or authority acting as an intermediary between local governments and the credit market. There are two ways in which this intermediation can occur. The state can issue bonds and use the proceeds either to purchase local government obligations (bond

Table 19

How States Supervise and Assist Local Debt Management

Activity	Number States
State supervises or collects data on local government debt issues	41
— Collects and disseminates data	24
— Maintains data file	22
— Prescribes contents of official statements	14
— Reviews local bond issue	19
— Approves local bond issue	9
— Helps market local bond issue	9
— Other	12
State provides technical assistance to local government in debt management	32
— Helps with official statements	14
— Provides data to	
Issuers for use in official statements	14
Bond rating agencies	16
Underwriters and dealers	18
Prospective investors	11
— Helps evaluate bids	7
— Issues bulletins, pamphlets, manuals	12
— Conducts seminars and conferences	12
— Other	7

Source: National Conference of State Legislatures and Municipal Finance Officers Association, *Watching and Counting,* October, 1977, p. 9.

banks) or make loans directly for specified programs (loan programs).

Bond Banks. Six states have set up bond banks— Maine, New Hampshire, Vermont, Puerto Rico, Alaska, and North Dakota. Only in North Dakota does the state place its full faith and credit behind the bonds it issues to purchase local debt. In the others, the state bonds are, essentially, backed by the credit worthiness of the local governments whose issues are purchased. In Maine, the state issues are also backed by a lien on state grants-in-aid, and, as a last resort, the state's moral obligation. The NCSL study describes the advantages of the Maine bond bank:

Savings are realized on underwriting and marketing costs because of the larger issues and better credit rating of the

bond bank. . . . Katzman (1980) estimates that transactions
(costs) savings amount to 1.4 percent of the locality's bond
issue. . . . The most significant savings realized by the bond
bank is from the improved credit rating and thereby
lowered interest payments. The bank has a credit rating
of Aa, just one step lower than the Aaa rating for the state's
own general obligation bonds. The majority of localities selling to the bank have Baa ratings or no ratings at all. . . .
To date the Maine Bond Bank has issued $300,000,000 in
bonds. It purchases 90 percent of all local government
issues in the state (Watson, 1982, p. 20).

Opposition to bond banks typically comes from investment bankers and bond counselors who fear loss of business. Bond banks would not be effective in all states. Empirical research (Jarrett and Hicks, 1977; Katzman, 1979
and 1980) suggests that it is a program that can be successful in reducing costs where:

☐ there are many small localities and special districts
   with bonding power; and
☐ the credit rating of many of these local jurisdictions
   is weak; and
☐ the state's credit rating is Aa or Aaa.

Loan Programs. Several states have loan programs
that provide local governments with low-cost loans for
specified purposes. The programs are usually financed
through the issue of state general obligation bonds, but
some western and mountain states provide loans to energy
boom-town communities from funds built up from severance tax revenues (discussed in detail in chapter 6). In thirteen states, loan programs have been set up to lend money
to localities for sewer and water projects. Most of the loans
were for the 25 percent match on federally funded sewer
and water projects (recent federal budget cuts have reduced the federal share to 55 percent [from 75 percent],
which will probably lead to increases in the share that
localities can borrow from the states).

An interesting example is provided by the Texas
Water Development Fund that lends to localities to build
water supply facilities (but not distribution systems). The

200

rate at which a municipality can borrow is one-half of a percentage point above the weighted average of the past three issues of the fund—but with a constitutional upper limit of 6 percent, a constraint that is currently precluding any lending. The upper bonding limit of the fund is $600 million.

Colorado has lent nearly $60 million to localities at 5 percent to finance 50 percent of the construction costs of new water supply facilities. Pennsylvania was recently authorized by the voters to issue $220 million in state bonds for the repair and construction of water supply systems. The interest rate will be equal to the rate paid on state bonds.

Grants for Debt Service

These programs earmark state grants to localities for debt service—in some cases, state monies are sent directly to bondholders. This earmarking of grants is intended to reduce the risk of the bond issue and so reduce the interest rate at which it can be marketed. The most successful example is the New Jersey Qualified Bond Program (Peterson and Miller, 1981; Watson, 1982). This program combines strict supervision of bond issues with direct payments to bondholders. For example, Newark agreed to raise its water rates by 50 percent to receive the board's approval for a water system bond issue. Under this program, localities can earmark state urban aid grants or grants from the state's Property Tax Replacement Program as a guarantee of repayment to the bondholder, without passing through the local budget process. "Purchasers of debt issues are thus guaranteed first access to the locality's most stable revenue source, greatly reducing the risk of default" (Peterson and Miller, 1981, p. 63). The localities must agree to replace these earmarked revenues from local revenues to ensure "maintenance of effort" in meeting local public service demands. The program has allowed Newark and Jersey City to improve their rating on qualified issues from Baa to A, a saving of nearly 200 basis points on each issue. This type of program is particularly effective where a state has a much stronger rating than many of its major cities and if it has an intra-state grant-in-aid program.

201

State Guarantees of Local Debt

There are various approaches to using the credit worthiness of the state to guarantee local bond issues so that they can enjoy lower interest rates. New Hampshire places it full faith and credit behind local bond issues for school construction and pollution control projects. Michigan guarantees school bonds not with its full faith and credit but with an agreement to sell general obligation bonds to pay interest and principal on local bonds nearing default. Minnesota has a similar program. However, if used excessively, these programs can jeopardize the state's own credit rating.

Conclusions

What all the programs discussed in this final section rest on is the ability of a state government to regulate local bond issues and fiscal practices more efficiently than would be done by local governments acting individually. If the state acts only as a rubber stamp on local issues, then it will lower its own bond rating and lose the ability to cut the cost of local borrowing. The examples briefly discussed here suggest that state and local governments can act together to the mutual benefit of both. But it is not a partnership that is achieved without cost.

Many of the programs also involve states issuing more debt. Although voter approval of bond issues has now climbed back over 50 percent (from only 33 percent in 1975), selling a bond issue is not an easy task. Political leaders must explain the consequences of cutting capital spending. In 1982, in spite of a worsening economic and fiscal environment, Missouri voters broke with tradition and approved a $600 million general obligation bond issue for an array of capital projects including soil conservation, road repair, state university facilities, and the rehabilitation of state office buildings. Governor Bond led a strong campaign to depict the consequences of continued underinvestment in public works. Bond issues cannot be sold as a free good. Taxes will have to be raised to service the debt, and trying to shield this from voters allows opponents an easy way to undermine the education process.

Unfortunately, there is little hard evidence to prove that an investment in infrastructure may be a more powerful inducement for economic development than a business tax cut. But the link can be drawn, and, in several states, the business community has been a powerful advocate for bond issues for public capital investment.

CHAPTER V NOTES

1. The U.S. Census Bureau defines public debt as "long-term credit obligations of the government and its agencies, and all interest-bearing, short-term (i.e., repayable within one year) credit obligations" (cited in Gold, 1981, p. 12). These include "judgments, mortgages, and revenue bonds as well as general obligation bonds, notes and interest-bearing warrants. On the other hand, non-interest-bearing, short-term obligations, interfund obligations, amounts owed in a trust or agency capacity, advances and contingent loans from other governments, and rights of individuals to benefits from employee-retirement funds are not included" (cited in Gold, 1981, p. 12). Short-term debt instruments such as tax anticipation notes are designed to bridge gaps between inflows of revenues—which may be received quarterly or even at the end of the fiscal year—and necessary expenditures. However, for the purpose of discussing the finance of long-term public investment, we can exclude short-term debt.

2. Alaska, Delaware, Hawaii, Kentucky, Minnesota, Nebraska, New York, Oregon, Rhode Island, Washington, and Wyoming.

3. Arkansas, Idaho, Indiana, Iowa, Mississippi, Missouri, North Carolina, Ohio, and Utah.

4. Connecticut, Hawaii, Louisiana, Maryland, Massachusetts, Michigan, North Carolina, Oregon, Pennsylvania, Tennessee, Washington, Wisconsin, and West Virginia.

5. Arkansas, Arizona, Colorado, Indiana, Iowa, Kansas, Nebraska, South Dakota, and Wyoming.

6. The single exception is the arbitrage bond issue solely for the purpose of investing in higher yielding taxable securities.

7. The real interest rate is the difference between market rates and the rate of inflation.

8. For a concise summary of these changes, see Herships and Karvelis, 1981.

9. Municipal investors are concerned with four types of risk: default,

203

marketability, maturity, and business cycle risk. Default risk measures the probability that principal and/or interest will not be paid when due. Marketability risk concerns the ability to convert securities into cash before maturity. Maturity risk relates to the expected rate of interest prevailing at the maturity date, and business cycle risk concerns changes in the overall level of yields from general economic fluctuation (see Ingram and Copeland, 1982).

10. Municipalities must pay for this service, and provide the rating agencies with information on their fiscal position that is not necessarily available to the public (see John Petersen, *The Rating Game*, The Twentieth Century Fund, New York, 1974).

CHAPTER VI

Financing Large-Scale Resource Development Projects

BETWEEN 1967 AND 1970, the population of the city of Gillette, Wyoming, doubled as a result of intensive oil and gas exploration in surrounding areas. During the past decade, the population tripled, this time as a result of coal development (Leistritz and Maki, 1981). Very rapid development in small communities can place extreme demands for the rapid expansion of infrastructure and public services, often beyond the fiscal or institutional capacity of the local community and even the state. Boom towns usually grow as the result of massive private investments in the development of natural resources, such as Rock Springs, Wyoming, and Parachute, Colorado. But they may also arise because of the construction of port facilities, such as Valdez in Alaska, or from the building of military facilities.

Without a carefully designed strategy to deal with boom towns, severe problems can occur. A major study by the Massachusetts Institute of Technology of the impacts of large-scale energy developments in western and mountain states identified eight types of problems (see table 20), including social disruption, shortages of goods, poor quality public services, environmental degradation, and acute fiscal problems. At the same time, corporations attempting to develop the project may be hampered by lack of skilled workers, escalating construction costs because the necessary transportation and communications facilities are not in place, and by expensive lawsuits from environmental groups and local residents. Disruption and

Table 20

Components of the Boomtown Problem

Boomtowns represents different problems to different groups. There are positive aspects of energy development, but even some of those have negative side effects. Our case studies and the literature on boomtowns reveal eight components of the boomtown problem:

1. Social Disruption. Energy development causes sudden changes in the population mix and patterns of everyday life. These in turn cause social problems and social conflicts.[3] Rates of alcoholism, drug abuse, mental illness, divorce and juvenile deliquency increase. While many of these problems are experienced by newcomers unaccustomed to their living conditions, long time residents are the ones most affected by the disruption. For example, long time residents are more likely to become alcoholics or suffer from mental illness than newcomers.

2. Public Service Needs. Americans have come to expect certain basic public services such as roads, water, schools, police and fire protection, and social welfare assistance. During rapid growth these services are often overburdened, or unavailable to some groups. In addition, public services which a town did not provide before may be necessary to support energy development or to cope with its side effects (i.e., counseling may be needed for those suffering from community disruption). New residents sometimes expect more or different services than long time residents. Tax rates must often increase to cover the cost of providing new or expanded services. The lead time needed to design and build new facilities means that the costs are borne by those who live in the area before the boomtown population has actually arrived.

3. Shortage of Private Goods and Services. During a boom the private market rarely keeps pace with the demand for goods and services, especially housing. In some cases, housing shortfalls can restrict energy development: one hundred families recently found no housing when transferred to an oil boomtown and had to be transferred back to their previous positions.[4]

4. Inflation. Excess demand triggers inflation in prices, wages and rents. While price increases are welcomed by the storeowner whose costs usually do not rise as quickly as revenues, and increased housing prices are a blessing to the landlord, inflation is particularly harmful to the senior citizen and others on fixed incomes who cannot take advantage of rising wages. High construction wages, combined with a general labor shortage, cause other wages to rise. This can hurt an agricultural economy (though agricultural workers benefit from higher wages if their employers do not go out of business). Increased costs can also affect provision of public services. Two boomtowns had to increase salaries 40% in order to hold experienced employees. Increased costs for building materials raise municipal costs just when public facilities need to be expanded.[5]

5. Revenue Shortfalls. Even though growth expands sales and property tax bases, revenues increase more slowly than costs in the short run. Despite a 19% increase in sales tax revenue, one coal boomtown has already increased property tax *rates* several times; even with a 68% increase in its local sales tax revenue, an oil boomtown finds itself short of operating funds.[6] These revenue shortfalls are due to (i) delays between the time development begins and the time the locality realizes either property or sales tax revenue; (ii) delays in raising capital for constructing and improving public facilities; (iii) capital needs beyond local government's legal bonding capacity; (iv) location of high tax-yielding properties outside the communities hosting the newcomers and the resulting public costs.

6. Resources Lost to Other Uses.

Industry and its workers are notably consumptive of three resources needed by the agricultural economy; water, land and labor. As new industries use efficient collection techniques and cities exercise eminent domain over water rights, less is available for agriculture. In some states' energy development regions, groundwater use is unregulated by state permits. Increased consumption by energy development may mean water shortages for cities and agricultural producers drawing from the same aquifer.

Easily irrigated land near stream beds is particularly valuable to agriculture but it is also valuable to energy developers because, for example, coal is nearer the surface. When strip-mining removes land from agricultural production (for at least ten years in most places), local food processing industries fail. Even in oil boomtowns, where less land is disturbed, agricultural producers face a shortage of inexpensive labor, since high drilling salaries attract unskilled and semi-skilled farm workers.[7]

7. Aesthetic Deterioration.

Boomtown development sacrifices amenity to economy and ease of construction. Trailer courts are laid out without paving or landscaping; commercial establishments are built of sheet metal and often located in unsightly strips along major roads. Many people mention aesthetic deterioration as a problem, particularly if they considered the area attractive before the boom. The size of new developments causes part of the aesthetic problem. Many new neighborhoods, in which trees and shrubs have not had a chance to grow and which look barren, dwarf established parts of town.

8. Fundamental Change.

An important cost of boomtown development has nothing to do with conventional indicators of stress or inadequacy, since it results from change itself rather than from what the town changes to. The original residents of a boomtown chose their community—or chose to remain—because it was the best place for them (certainly the best they could afford). When development occurs, the appearance, social structure, friendship patterns, style of life, and nearly everything else about their community changes, and the community that supported them simply disappears. The injury such disappearance causes is only partly mitigated if the "new" town is clean and orderly.

Source: Susskind, Lawrence and Michael O'Hare, *Managing the Social and Economic Impacts of Energy Development,* Massachusetts Institute of Technology, 1977

---

delays occur not because residents and developers have divergent goals—indeed, they often share a long-run desire to encourage growth—but because there are few effective institutional mechanisms to resolve disputes and to determine how to finance and develop the necessary public infrastructure and services.

Boom town problems are the most obvious manifestations of problems that affect many jurisdictions—that is, private development projects, from shopping centers to factory branch plants, that are large, relative to the community in which they are located, and that create a permanent and widespread change in the local economic base and in the demand for public facilities and services. Although the discussion in this chapter focuses on energy-related boom towns, the types of policies discussed could easily be applied to communities dealing with growth induced by a private recreation development, a new airport, or a housing complex.

There are several costs that must be considered in developing a financing strategy to deal with large-scale developments.

☐ *Initial infrastructure costs.* Before a new project can start to function, new roads or other transportation systems will have to be developed, and the capacity of existing facilities will have to be expanded. Water supply and waste treatment systems will be needed. Utility hook-ups for the new populations must be provided. And the residential facilities—schools, libraries, and police and fire stations—must be built. These investments require front-end financing.

☐ *New Public Services.* After the initial building phase, the city or county must operate at a greatly expanded level—more police officers, teachers, and sanitation workers, and more money to be spent on infrastructure maintenance.

☐ *The "Bust Phase."* For most large-scale developments, the initial boom is followed by a decline in employment as construction labor leaves and as the project adjusts to its permanent operating level of employment. In some instances, the project may prove uneconomical and be closed completely. In other instances, the project may experience strong, cyclical fluctuations in activity as a result of changes in the world price of minerals or of recessions and expansions in the national economy. Because small communities do not have diversified economies, they are particularly vulnerable.

☐ *Compensating those harmed by development.* Some long-time residents will find their means of livelihood destroyed or their lifestyles so changed that they move away. Some will be compensated—at least in part—by increases in property values or by expansions of their businesses. A consistent compensation policy minimizes expensive lawsuits, protests, and other tactics employed by individuals and groups seeking relief.

State governments can provide a framework within which these costs can be allocated equitably and efficiently between public and private agencies and between the state and local governments. This chapter describes this framework. The first section discusses how to assess the social and economic impacts of a proposed project. The second section describes the overall management of state programs to deal with large-scale projects. In the third section, alternative revenue sources to finance necessary public capital investments are analyzed. Programs to provide state aid to impacted communities and individuals are outlined in the fourth section. The final section summarizes the lessons from these programs that are applicable to state public investment strategies. Much of the discussion is based upon an analysis of the experiences of western and mountain states with large-scale energy projects.[1] These lessons should prove invaluable to all states as they design complex but necessary programs to ensure that major developments are compatible with their long-run economic and social goals.

Project Impact Assessment

The purpose of project impact assessment is to develop the information necessary for the state and local governments to ensure that development and growth occur

209

in an orderly manner, that adverse effects are minimized, that those harmed are compensated, and that the costs of building public facilities and providing services can be covered through tax revenues and through cost sharing with the developer, where that is appropriate. The assessment must be able to predict economic, demographic, social, and environmental changes related to the project and relate these changes to resource needs and the requirements for public facilities and services.

The ability to predict the social, economic, and fiscal impacts of a large-scale development project is neither easy nor cheap, and is subject to considerable uncertainty. Between deciding in the spring of 1980 to undertake a massive oil shale project near Parachute, Colorado, and terminating the project in the spring of 1982, Exxon's estimates of its own costs had risen from between $2 and $3 billion to nearly $6 billion (*Fortune,* 5/13/82, p. 61).

Companies typically undertake detailed analyses of the socioeconomic impacts as well as engineering and marketing studies. However, it is difficult for state and local governments to rely upon the data supplied by the prospective developer, however, well-conducted. The research may be biased. Certainly, relying only on the developers' own estimates will arouse suspicion among those opposed to the development. In the case of Parachute, Exxon provided the state with the funds, with no strings, to develop its own impact-assessment study, a practice which has been followed by several companies in other states. A consulting contract of more than one quarter of a million dollars to assess the full impacts of a large project is not unusual. The development of a replicable "assessment model" that can be used on many different projects would reduce the costs of future impact assessments. Skimping on the development phase of the assessment model will lead to high costs later. Colorado, which has developed such a model under the auspices of a "Cumulative Impacts Task Force" (composed of representatives from state agencies, local governments, and industry), has found that the model tracks impacts accurately and can be an invaluable tool in negotiating fiscal mitigation strategies.

Effective impact assessment can meet two problems

that can undermine the process: (1) inadequate notice of the proposed project from the developer; and (2) inadequate access to data and information. Sufficient notice is no problem where the development will occur on federal or state lands. But where a private company already owns land and the necessary development rights, a massive project could occur with very little notice to local residents. One approach to ensure adequate notice is to require all major projects (defined by type of project, size of investment, or level of projected employment) to apply for a development permit from a state agency. Three states—North Dakota, Wyoming, and Montana—have developed effective mechanisms to ensure early notification and permitting processes that ensure that costs are negotiated with the private developer. Utah provides an example of a much less formal approach.

Impact assessment should not be confused with cost-benefit analysis although it should borrow many of the same analytic methods. The purpose is to lay out, as accurately as possible, the likely impacts of a project—both positive and negative—and how these costs and benefits will be shared among individuals, jurisdictions, and institutions. This information can then be used during the negotiation process that determines who pays for the additional costs and how the payments are made.

Obtaining project data is a problem that cannot easily be solved. Assessing a project's impacts requires highly technical data from the developer and also detailed financial data, both of which are usually confidential. Disclosure could lead to widespread financial harm to the corporation and its stockholders and could even jeopardize the viability of the project. In a project where passions run high, there is a very real danger that information could be leaked by parties anxious to block the project or impose their own conditions. A state that gains a reputation for indiscrete use of data will discourage private developers. At the same time, if excessive restrictions are placed upon what type of data can be released, then the results of the impact analysis cannot be verified by analysts employed by interested parties. If published findings are not believed, then interested parties may resort to costly and delaying legal battles.

211

North Dakota[2]

In North Dakota, a facility siting act was passed in 1975 which gives the Public Service Commission (PSC) authority to develop an inventory of potential sites for energy conversion plants and transmission lines (Lu, 1977). Utility companies—under the PSC's jurisdiction— are not restricted to these sites, but the PSC must evaluate any alternate locations chosen outside the existing inventory. Their evaluation is financed through an application fee of 0.05 percent of project cost—a user fee that ensures PSC of the resources necessary to conduct the study. The PSC has the power to override local regulations if a plan is approved. The process requires public hearings. The PSC has so far used its authority to either accept or reject utility siting proposals; it has not conditioned approval on the utility's commitment to provide infrastructure or other forms of impact assistance, such as front-end financing of public investments.

Project impact information is gathered and provided to communities by Interindustry Technical Assistance Teams (ITAT) made up of experts from the coal industry. ITAT uses computer models to provide employment projections through 1990, publishes biannual reports containing updates on development impacts, and works with state and local planners to suggest impact mitigation strategies.

Wyoming[3]

In Wyoming, the Industrial Development Information and Siting Act of 1975 created a council within the Governor's Office. All projects with a construction cost in excess of $50 million (as adjusted for inflation since 1975—the current level is $90 million) and all energy conversion projects in excess of a specific capacity must apply for a permit to the council (Foster, 1977).

The permit may impose conditions on developers, including requiring the provision of infrastructure. Information supplied to communities through the siting act is supplemented by technical assistance from thirteen advisory state agencies.

The siting act sets the stage for negotiations between

local communities and developers. Communities' zoning powers give them some bargaining power against developers and help them allocate their infrastructure resources efficiently. Moreover, local planning powers were reinforced by the Land Use Planning Act of 1975. This act mandated local planning of economic development and allocated up to $20,000 for this purpose to each county for a two-year period. The State also has extensive environmental protection legislation that requires detailed consideration of project impacts.

Montana[4]

Montana has the most complete system for assessing and controlling the impacts of coal (and, more recently, oil and gas) development projects. Most of the legislation, passed in the early 1970s and including the Major Facility Siting Act, was designed to deal with coal-related boom activities. Water pollution controls, air quality standards, and solid and hazardous waste management laws are directed to health and environmental concerns. In addition, special tax laws have been enacted. The Major Facility Siting Act requires anyone proposing energy generating and conversion plants and associated facilities above specified capacities to obtain a Certificate of Environmental Compatibility and Public Need before construction can proceed. The review and approval process is fully financed by a filing fee and sets time limits on the permitting process. The Department of Natural Resources has twenty-two months to study a proposal and to complete an Environmental Impact Statement. The Board of Natural Resources (citizens appointed by the governor) then has up to eleven months to conduct a hearing and issue a decision on the application. The board holds public hearings and, prior to issuing a certificate, must determine the basis of the need for the facility. The board also determines whether the facility represents the minimum adverse environmental impact allowed by available technology and looks into the nature of various alternatives.

When granting the certificate, the board has the right to impose conditions on the construction, operation, or maintenance of the facility. Since the enactment of the siting law in 1973, the board has exercised its power to impose conditions in every certification.[5] The act also requires developers to submit, annually, long-range plans for the construction and operation of covered facilities proposed to be constructed within the state in the ensuing ten years.

Utah[6]

Utah's only law relating to energy development has been on the books for about a year. The Natural Resources Development Act stresses cooperation and has no enforcement provisions. It requires only that a developer submit socioeconomic assessments and mitigation plans to local governments and the Community and Economic Development Department (CEDD), but approval is not required. Since an estimated 80 percent of development in Utah occurs on federal land, the most important weapon state and local officials can deploy is their ability to hold up water permits and building permits. In a few cases, communities have also been able to use conditional zoning to force developers to provide housing for project employees.

In summary, impact assessments can help a local community anticipate future problems, and, therefore, develop ways of resolving some of the problems identified in table 20, even if there are no state funds. But assessments coupled with resources and statutory powers to enforce negotiation between developer and community can be much more useful and equitable.

Managing Large-Scale Project Development

Local communities are rarely able to deal, unaided, with the consequence of large-scale development. First, the impacts of individual projects often cross jurisdictional boundaries. For example, coal development in Campbell County, Wyoming, has occurred outside the city of Gillette although the population expansion has occurred within the city. The county faces little difficulty in financing expanded public services through mineral tax revenues. The city, which does not control these revenues, has inadequate resources and faces a much more difficult task. The recent passage of the Wyoming Joint Powers Act attempts to reconcile these interjurisdictional problems by allowing combinations of local governments and districts to apply for loans to address growth problems.

Second, few small communities have the expertise and the resources to negotiate on equal terms with the developer. Many have only a few, low-paid public employees and may have only a part-time manager or mayor. They are unable to assess anticipated impacts and to prepare a detailed strategy for negotiating with the private developer.

Third, many large-scale resource development projects occur on federally or state-owned lands or on land in which some of the development rights (or rights-of-way) must be secured from a state or federal agency. Because it would deal with many different projects, a statewide agency could compile a wealth of experience in designing agreements that could not be duplicated at the local level.

Fourth, counties and municipalities are essentially creatures of the state and usually require state legislation in order to change the local tax base or to issue debt. Consequently, it is important that large-scale developments be coordinated statewide in order to ensure that projects are consistent with each other and do not incur unnecessary social or economic costs.

Development management should, therefore, be coordinated at the state level—even if the coordinating agency may decide, for any specific project, that no state actions are necessary and allow all negotiations to be conducted between local jurisdictions and the developer.

The Goals of a State Project Management Mechanism

The purpose of a state project management mechanism is to negotiate the allocation of costs among private and public agencies. It is *not* to bleed the project for the maximum tax revenues or to block projects that may be technically incompatible with environmental regulations. It certainly is *not* to add another layer of bureaucracy in what is already, all too often, a very tangled process. In fact, the mechanism, if it is correctly designed and if its procedures are adhered to, should streamline the permitting process for viable projects and allow the development to proceed with less fear of sudden changes in state and local taxes or regulations. The negotiation process should ensure that projects do not lead to sudden local fiscal crises requiring a state bail-out, that fluctuating employment does not require sudden changes in state taxes, and that harmful environmental impacts are reduced. It would enable local governments to anticipate with greater accuracy their capital construction and operating expenditures. Local residents will be more confident that their interests have been considered, that the best possible bargain with the private developer has been struck, and that those suffering most from the project have been compensated. Development interests have been served, while, at the same time, considerations of equity and environmental quality will have been included. Most important, the effort to balance interests is clearly visible and recognized by all concerned parties.

The state strategy should, therefore, include the following functions

1. Estimate the effects of development—social, economic, and fiscal—before final decisions are made by the developer and the community.
2. Coordinate the permitting process among the relevant public agencies.
3. Ensure the representation of all interested parties in discussing and negotiating the development.
4. Encourage the negotiation of an agreement between interested parties in a timely and equitable fashion.
5. Coordinate administrative and legislative changes necessary to carry out the project.
6. Monitor the development of the project to ensure compliance with the terms of the negotiation and to respond to any unforeseen problems and developments.

The Negotiating Process

For a negotiation to be successful, it is necessary to spell out several particulars in advance:

1. The topics to be negotiated;
2. Who can participate in the process;

3. An arbitration vs. mediation procedure that can be used if negotiations reach a deadlock;
4. A fixed time period within which the agreement must be reached.

Typically, the agreement will identify specific financial and administrative responsibilities and allocate them among the private developer and state and local governments. It may even carry conditional responsibilities that change the terms of the agreement if prescribed circumstances change during the course of the project. For example, the tax rate on mineral extraction may be reviewed if market prices of the mineral increase above, or fall below, predetermined benchmark levels.

Establishing a monetary value on all aspects of the negotiations may be neither possible nor efficient. For example, cnvironmcntalists may rcsist dircct paymcnt from a mining company in compensation for the spoiling of a natural area—questioning to whom the payment is made and what it is used for. They may prefer the company to purchase other, unspoiled, private land and turn it over to the state or county to be used as a wilderness area in perpetuity. The context of negotiations should be sufficiently broad to allow this type of exchange.

A negotiating process may seem alien to those firmly schooled in traditional cost-benefit project analysis. They might argue that if enough resources are devoted to developing economic, environmental, and other models, then the efficient and equitable allocation of costs can be determined. This is not the case. Such models and available data are notoriously unreliable. Many of the affected parties—both the local community and the developers—do not feel bound by outcomes computed by technicians, and thus challenge findings in courts or through the political process. The result may be a breakdown in the planning process and much greater uncertainty, which deters investment and multiplies distrust. Traditional cost-benefit analyses do not allow for the subtle trade-offs that must be made in a large-scale and complex development project.

Experience with negotiated investment strategies is limited. The complex negotiations that preceded the construction of the Alaska pipeline are probably an example

217

of what not to do. Agreements (between the federal government, the consortium of ARCO, Exxon, and Standard, and the state) were not based upon clearly established principles and were reopened several times. It is probably impossible to completely prevent renegotiation. Once a company has begun investing in a project, the negotiating power of the state or locality is strengthened. If the company strikes a bonanza, the state's position is further reinforced. More recent procedures established in Montana, Wyoming, and Colorado have been much more successful. They illustrate that major developers are aware of the benefits of a negotiated development and are prepared to act on this awareness. The process does not involve the surrender of any of the legal rights of those participating and, therefore, does not preclude any subsequent lawsuits, even though the fact of participation and public hearing in the negotiating process may deter later legal battles.

Determining who should participate in the negotiation is not easy. Which environmental group should negotiate on behalf of local citizens concerned about the possible environmental impacts? Will its negotiation strategy reflect the interests and preferences of the local community? How many state and national environmental concerns should be involved? How should delegates or representatives to the negotiation process be selected? What interest groups should be recognized? How should the results—preliminary and final—be communicated to the developers and to the local community?

There are no simple answers to these complex questions, although judicial solutions do provide examples. In the *United States v. Allegheny-Ludlum Industries* (5th Circuit, 1975), the trial judge created a panel of thirty-six people to represent six groups of plaintiffs. As experience with negotiations increases, we shall learn what approaches work most effectively. A brief description of a few examples of negotiated projects illustrates both the processes used and the outcomes that can be achieved.

North Dakota

Local governments use information from the Interindustry Technical Assistance Teams to manage local

218

growth patterns through zoning ordinances and through negotiations with utilities and mining companies. A good example is provided by the development of Coal Creek Station, North Dakota's largest mine mouth power plant. Total investment for the plant transmission lines and coal mine was about $1.2 billion. The construction work force at the plant in 1979 totaled 4,620 people while the permanent operating workforce during this period equaled 800. Coal Creek Station utilities contributed $40,000 for local public works, improved roads around their development site, organized a Citizen's Advisory Board to hear citizen concerns, and stimulated housing development before the start of the project by assembling a large tract of land and selling it to a residential developer.

The state also made contributions. Between 1975 and 1980, the Coal Impact Office made grants and loans to Washburn and Underwood, the two towns most directly impacted by Coal Creek, including, $747,000 in grants to the county for roads; $330,000 in grants to Washburn; $225,000 in grants to Underwood for expansion of water and sewer systems; $807,000 in grants to the county for additional police and fire protection services; and $570,000 in grants to Washburn and $520,000 in grants and $35,000 in loans to Underwood, all for schools.

State officials and industry representatives seemed satisfied with North Dakota's procedures for dealing with energy developments. Surveys of local residents during and after the Coal Creek construction revealed that, "almost all the persons interviewed indicated that the construction of the Coal Creek Station had a very positive effect on the community."[7]

Wyoming

The State's Industrial Siting Council successfully negotiated with the Missouri Basin Power Association to minimize the impact of the construction of the Laramie River power generating station in Wheatland. The Association agreed to provide up-front money for infrastructure development as well as planning assistance to the affected local governments.

Wyoming also provides examples where private developers have acted to coordinate their plans with local communities. In the development area known as the Overthrust Belt, which runs through Evanston, Kemmerer, and other small towns, the oil and gas developers formed the Overthrust Industrial Association (OIA). The OIA acted as local impact coordinator, providing interest-free loans to communities until a tax base was established, giving grants, constructing community improvements, providing impact projections, and helping with maintenance, such as snow plowing and road repair. In a more extreme example, ARCO, the developer of the Black Thunder Project, built the whole town of Wright. ARCO apparently had two reasons for this. Under the state's siting law, ARCO would have had to pay infrastructure costs in any case, and Gillette, the nearest town, was over forty miles away. A primary reason for ARCO's decision was that it was cheaper to build a town at the project site than to lose twenty work days each winter when snow storms close the roads. ARCO currently employs between 400 and 500 people at the development site.

Colorado[8]

Carbondale, once one of the towns most impacted by energy development projects, experienced most of the typical infrastructure problems associated with a development boom in the mid-1970s. Mid-Continent Coke and Coal Company responded to the town's request for assistance by providing a $10,000 planning grant, forming a housing corporation, and providing private buses to transport employees to and from the mines. On the whole, however, companies were reluctant to assume a substantial share of the front-end costs associated with capital intensive improvement projects. Localities had little bargaining power because they were worried that developers would go elsewhere and because they had little political leverage with the state legislature.

More recently, negotiations have proved much more successful both from the perspective of the local communities, which have benefited from private funding for public infrastructure, and for the developers, who have been able to proceed with the project in a more orderly fashion. Exxon provided nearly all the infrastructure needed for the Colony Oil Shale Project near Parachute, Colorado. When Exxon and Tosco started the project, the population of Parachute was about 400. When Exxon abruptly closed the project in the spring of 1982, it had to fire 2,100 employees working at the site. To support its workforce, Exxon started to build the town of Battlement Mesa, complete with stores, apartment complexes, a large recreational vehicle park, subdivisions (with $90,000 homes), and a partially completed recreation center costing more than $3 million. Exxon also loaned the local school district $12 million to finance front-end costs until a local tax base could be created.

Officials at the State Energy Impact Office attribute the greater cooperation between private developers and state and local officials in recent projects to several factors.

1. Possibly the most important reason is the formation in the state of an urban constituency interested in the social and environmental aspects of development projects. Major corporations cannot afford to antagonize large segments of the population.
2. Studies by these corporations have concluded that the increased productivity and lower project costs make it economical for the developer to support the provision of local public facilities and services.
3. State policies have encouraged cooperation. The state and local governments have shown in the past that they can stall projects by holding up building permits. The state has facilitated cooperation by conducting a voluntary permitting procedure, the Colorado Joint Review Process, that involves all interested parties at an early date. All parties are currently satisfied that cooperation is mutually beneficial.

Colorado uses several mechanisms to coordinate its energy policies. In 1975, Governor Lamm created the Energy Policy Council to develop state energy policy and to make recommendations on specific problems. Members of the council include the executive directors of the State Departments of Natural Resources, Local Affairs, Agriculture, and Health, as well as members of the governor's staff. The Western Slope Energy Impact Committee

(WSEIC), consisting of local citizens and staff from county planning agencies, was formed to provide the Energy Policy Council with local information. The Economic Impact Office works with developers to provide communities with periodic impact projections. Area-wide program coordination is carried out through thirteen councils of government. Each council is made up of the county commissioners of the area and municipal officials. The councils serve as the intermediaries between local government and the state and are the agencies through which reviews of many state and local funds pass.

The state and private developers have helped local governments with front-end financing and with community-specific impact projections. Communities have also used their own power to affect local development. Local governments, in addition to using their zoning powers, have switched to metered water to manage use and have tried to attract retail establishments into growing communities.

Revenues to Finance Public Infrastructure for Large-Scale Developments

Most large-scale resource projects have involved the extraction of minerals, principally gas, oil, coal, and oil shale. States have relied heavily on revenues generated by severance taxes to finance needed public facilities and services. Corporate income taxes, lease revenues, property taxes, sales taxes, and shared federal lease revenues have also been used. To secure up-front funds, some states and localities have required prepayment of taxes by the developers or have received low-interest-rate loans from the development corporations for public infrastructure construction. To ensure that revenues do not suddenly cease when the project is completed (or abandoned), some states pay a portion of their revenues into trust funds, funds whose principal or earnings can be used to diversify the local economic base during the bust phase. All states with trust funds protect the principal but allow the interest to be spent for more general purposes. During times of high inflation, spending all of the interest allows the principal to decline in value. Ideally, only the *real* interest would be spent, with the remaining interest returned directly to the fund to maintain its real value.

Before discussing specific state revenue-raising policies, some general remarks about the advantages and disadvantages of alternative taxes should be made.

☐ *Severance Taxes.* These are easy to collect and extremely popular among state governments. To the extent that project impacts are related to the volume of minerals extracted (for example, the volume of strip-mined coal is strongly related to the level of damages to the environment), a severance tax is an appropriate source of revenues. The principal impact of the tax is to reduce the value of mineral-bearing land and, therefore, the value of leases. A high severance tax (which is usually collected by the state) will reduce revenues from leases on state lands and from property taxes on private lands (which are locally collected). The tax is paid by a corporation regardless of its profitability (unlike the corporate income tax). This may deter the development of marginal mineral industries (such as coal in Alaska). It may also make local industries much more vulnerable to sudden declines in world mineral prices because they must continue to pay the tax even if the operation is no longer profitable. Severance taxes, because of their nature, are useful to finance infrastructure development costs and also, when deposited in trust funds, can finance the bust phase of the project and compensate those harmed.

☐ *Corporate Income Taxes.* Many states already have a corporate income tax which is paid by mineral extraction companies. The tax has the advantage of relating tax payments to the ability to pay. It will tend to spur a faster rate of mineral extraction. One disadvantage of the tax is that many mining companies are multinational, as well as multistate, and can allocate their income among different locations, placing it beyond the taxing-reach of individual states. It is also difficult to use the corporate income tax to recapture massive windfall benefits that may accrue from sudden increases in mineral prices. Revenues from this

223

tax are appropriate in funding ongoing state services to the project community.

☐ *Lease Revenues.* Many resource projects are located on state or federal land. Leases are usually sold determined in public auction. Revenues may provide the state with front-end revenues which may be shared with local communities. The federal government rebates to the state about 50 percent of the revenues from the sale of leases on federal land a share of which must be distributed to impacted counties according to a formula. These revenues can provide a useful source of front-end funds.

☐ *Property Taxes.* These are the primary source of revenues to finance local public services. Their principal disadvantage in rapidly growing communities is that revenues do not adjust as rapidly as public service demands. Also, much of the property on which the development occurs may lie outside the town or county that experiences most of the impacts.

☐ *Personal Income Taxes.* This tax can provide the state with revenues that track the boom-bust cycle, providing that temporary construction workers pay taxes within the state (company withholding can ensure that they do).

☐ *Other Taxes.* Sales taxes, especially if shared with localities, provide a revenue source that also tracks the boom-bust cycle. Both sales and property tax increments can be used to back local bond issues if permitted by the state.

An ideal revenue base to meet the needs of very rapid development would include all these tax elements. Excessive reliance on one tax source will not adequately meet the multitude of demands and the change in these demands over time. It may also distort the pattern of development.

The techniques used by mineral-rich states vary greatly. Montana has the most extensive financing system. Texas and Arizona have virtually no program to deal with fiscal mitigation and, therefore, no dedicated funds. The different approaches provide some insight into the alternative policies and their effectiveness.

Montana

Since 1975, Montana has imposed a coal severance tax set at 30 percent of the mine-mouth price, although the actual tax rate is about 22 percent due to numerous available deductions and credits for local property taxes paid by coal companies. In fiscal year 1981, total coal severance tax revenues were about $70.4 million. Coal tax revenues must by law go into separate funds or accounts. The division of coal tax revenues into these accounts is presented in table 21.

The permanent coal trust fund is designed to compensate future generations for the present exploitation of a nonrenewable resource. The interest earned on this fund is appropriated, but the principal can only be expended by a three-quarters vote of each house of the legislature. In 1981, all of the interest was appropriated for highway maintenance and construction. At the end of fiscal year 1981, the permanent fund totaled $75.2 million.

Wyoming

Wyoming's approach to development projects is similar to Montana's. Wyoming's coal severance tax is set at 10.5 percent, and has a net effective rate of about 9.5 percent after deductions and credits. The tax revenue goes into five funds, as shown in table 22.

The permanent fund, at the end of 1981, contained about $203 million. The principal of this fund is constitutionally protected; the interest goes into the state general fund. The Community Impact Fund and the Coal Impact Fund are both used for impact mitigation, with the latter fund reserved especially for communities impacted by coal mining and related activities. Both funds are administered by the Farm Loan Board (FLB). The Wyoming Community Development Authority (WCDA) has the power to float up to $100 million in tax-exempt bonds. The money the WCDA raises is loaned to local communities to finance public facilities and public housing. The grants given by the FLB are intended to be used as pledges to repay WCDA

225

Table 21

Distribution of Montana's Coal Tax Revenues

Fund or Account	% of Total Coal Tax Revenues
Permanent Coal Trust Fund	50%
State General Fund	19
Education Trust Fund	10
Local Impact Area Fund	8.75
Public School Equalization	5
Alternative Energy Research Fund	2.25
Park Acquisition & Cultural Trust Fund	2.5
Renewable Resource Development	0.625
Water Development	0.625
State Library Fund	0.5
Counties—Local Land Use Planning	0.5
Conservation Districts	0.25
TOTAL	100%

Table 22

Distribution of Wyoming's Coal Tax Revenues

Fund or Account	Tax Rate	% of Total Coal Tax Revenues
Wyoming Permanent Fund	2%	21%
Community Impact Fund	2	21
General Fund	2	21
Coal Impact Fund	1.5	16
Water Development Account	2	21
TOTAL	approx 9.5%	100%

loans. In the past, FLB grants have been restricted for use only on highways, road or street improvements, and water or sewer projects because these were the most pressing needs. Recent FLB grants have gone for other capital facility needs such as hospitals or mental health centers as well as for equipment such as fire engines.

In 1981, the state imposed a two percent oil and gas severance tax. Half of the proceeds will be distributed directly to cities, town and counties.

North Dakota

North Dakota has created an impact-assistance fund from the revenues generated by a coal severance tax. The current tax rate stands at $1.01 per short ton of coal; the rate is indexed to inflation, so that the tax rate increases $.01 for each four-point rise in the Wholesale Price Index. In 1981, the coal tax generated revenues of almost $17 million. The allocation of coal severance tax revenue is determined by statute and is shown in table 23.

The statute allocates coal tax revenues among different state funds and among different political subdivisions within the county where the coal was mined. If the tipple (loading facility) of a mine is within fifteen miles of a non-producing county, both counties receive a share of coal revenues according to a formula specified by statute.

A Coal Conversion Privilege Tax is applied to electrical generating plants and coal conversion (e.g., gasification) plants. This tax rate currently stands at $.25 per kilowatt-hour of power generation. In 1981, more than $3.4 million in conversion tax revenues were collected. These tax revenues are also allocated by statute as is shown in table 24.

Reflecting the growth in oil and gas developments in North Dakota, the state set up an Oil and Gas Impact Program in 1981. A direct appropriation of $10 million was made from the general fund to finance grants to local political subdivisions. The program parallels the Coal Impact Program. Local subdivisions submit applications for assistance for specific projects. The director meets with applicants and makes final funding decisions, based upon the degree of negative impacts resulting from oil and gas activity, the extent to which the proposed project will reduce those impacts, and the fiscal need of the applicant (which includes the local tax effort, the level of community cooperation, and the amount received by the applicant from the Oil and Gas Production Tax and other energy-related revenues).

Colorado

Colorado enacted legislation creating a coal severance tax, at a rate of $0.63 per ton (inflation adjusted) for surface coal and $0.31 per ton for underground coal, and setting up a Local Government Impact Assistance Fund in 1977. The state also has severance taxes on other minerals and oil and gas. In 1980, severance tax revenues totaled $31 million, $11 million from coal, $8 million from oil and gas, and the rest from other minerals. Since 1981, 50 percent of the severance tax revenues are distributed to the Local Government Severance Tax Fund, which funnels these revenues back to counties and municipalities affected by energy development loans. The other 50 percent is deposited in the Severance Tax Trust Fund to be utilized for the future consequences of the depletion of mineral resources and water project development. The interest from investments of the Severance Tax Fund is deposited in the general fund. As required by the federal government, Colorado distributes a share of federal mineral royalties to counties and school districts.

Utah

Since 1979, Utah has operated a Community Impact Account which has received 32.5 percent of the state's share of mineral lease revenues. It distributed over $20 million to energy-impacted communities. In 1982, the legislature, meeting in special session, created the Permanent Community Impact Fund and placed in it $35 million from oil shale bonus funds, 70 percent of all future bonus bid funds, and 32.5 percent of the state's share of mineral lease revenues. The fund will operate as a revolving loan fund to aid energy-impacted communities in making public capital investments.

Assistance to Localities

Since responsibilities for public services and public capital investments are shared between state and local governments, the funds to meet fiscal mitigation needs must also be shared. The type of aid provided, how it is allocated, and the conditions attached will significantly affect the ability of local jurisdictions to meet their needs. Again, examples from energy states provide useful lessons.

North Dakota

The county's share of the coal conversion tax revenues and the coal severance tax revenues are subdivided

Table 23
Distribution of North Dakota's Coal Tax Revenues

Fund or Account	Tax Rate in $		% of Total Tax Revenues	
State General Fund	$ .30		30%	
State Trust Fund	.15		15	
Coal Impact Fund	.35		35	
County Where Coal Mined	.20		20	
— County General Fund		$.08		8
— Incorporated Municipalities (based on relative population)		.06		6
— School Districts (based on number of pupils)		.06		6
TOTAL	$1.00	$ .20	100%	20%

Table 24
Distribution of North Dakota's Conversion Privilege Tax

Fund or Account	Tax Rate ($s/kw-hr)		% of Total Tax Revenues	
State General Fund	.1625		65%	
County Where Facility Located	.0875		35	
— County General Fund		.035		14
— Incorporated Municipalities		.0263		10
— School Districts		.0263		10
TOTAL	.25/ kw-hr	.0875/ kw-hr	100%	35

according to the statutory formula shown in tables 23 and 24: 40 percent of the county's share goes into the county general fund, 30 percent goes to incorporated municipalities within the county, and 30 percent goes to school districts within the county.

The funds created to receive coal severance and conversion tax revenues are very similar to those created by Montana and Wyoming. The coal impact fund is administered by the Energy Development Impact Office (EDIO), which makes funds available ($6.5 million in 1981) to local political subdivisions to help them to pay for public services and facilities. The EDIO evaluates each request for impact assistance according to the specific needs of the locality.[9]

Aside from Coal Trust Fund loans and grants from the EDIO, communities can also draw upon the coal tax revenues that are returned directly to them. There are no restrictions as to how counties, municipalities, and school districts may make use of this money. Communities receive additional state aid through general revenue sharing; North Dakota, however, does not have a coal or mineral property tax that communities can draw on. Federal mineral leasing royalty payments go only into a school trust fund.

Wyoming

In addition to loans from the Wyoming Community Development Authority, impacted communities also receive state aid from two other sets of funds and accounts. Wyoming, with nearly 50 percent of its land under federal ownership, receives substantial federal mineral leasing royalties (over $100 million in 1981). While many states just add these royalty payments to the general funds, Wyoming puts 50 percent of the royalty *bonus* payments into the Government Royalty Impact Assistance (GRIA) account administered by the Farm Loan Board (FLB). The state share of the royalty payments themselves are placed into nine different funds. About 14 percent of the returned royalties are given directly to local political subdivisions for local expenditures including roads and schools. A further 16 percent of the state's royalty funds are earmarked for additional special impact assistance.

These two programs provide considerable assistance to communities. In fiscal year 1980, $60 million in coal tax revenues were collected and something less than $100 million in federal royalty payments were received, while about $28 million in impact assistance was given out. Almost all of this money is administered by the FLB. Most communities are eligible only for loans and conditional grants because they will eventually be able to pay back current deficits with future increases in tax revenues. FLB loans and conditional grants are forgiven if the anticipated economic development and tax revenues do not occur. Communities receive additional funds from the state through intra-state revenue sharing programs, and, since

1973, counties can—by referendum—impose an optional 1 percent sales tax. Seven counties, including those containing Gillette and Rock Springs, had enacted the optional tax by the beginning of 1977.

In 1981, the state created a program that allocates funds from the state's share of the increase in sales and use taxes collected in counties where a facility is under construction with a permit issued from the siting council. Only those counties levying the 1 percent local option are eligible to receive the funds from the state. The funds are distributed within the impact counties to the jurisdictions according to each's share of the sale tax distribution. The siting council may determine that an adjoining county is impacted and provide for a ratio-of-impact formula to be used to distribute the funds between the counties. The revenues from the oil and gas severance tax, enacted in 1981, will provide an estimated $250–$300 million in aid to localities by fiscal year 1986. Finally, Wyoming addresses the problem of interjurisdictional cooperation within the state by allowing local governments to form Joint Powers Boards, which act strictly as administrative agencies, consolidating the borrowing and lending authorities of local governments.

Montana

The local impact fund in Montana is administered by the State Coal Board and is used for local impact assistance. After passing through an application process, loans and grants are given to local governments for governmental services and facilities needed as a direct consequence of coal development. Since its inception, the State Coal Board has awarded 122 local impact assistance grants, totaling $40.2 million (twenty-three to the Colstrip area). Most of the funds were used for public facilities and capital equipment.

Unlike most states, Montana does not have a revenue sharing plan with local governments, but portions of specific taxes or fees are distributed to local governments on a formula basis and often for specific uses. For instance, Montana returns to all counties a portion of state liquor revenues. The School Foundation program helps to fund maintenance and operating costs but not capital expenditures in local school districts. Counties collect a gross proceeds tax on the production of coal within their boundaries. Montana has not yet resolved the issue of interjurisdictional cooperation when the benefits of development are enjoyed in one jursidiction but most of the costs are incurred in another.

Colorado

Of the monies placed in Colorado's Local Government Fund (50 percent of severance tax revenues), 15 percent are automatically distributed to impacted jurisdictions in proportion to the number of employees of each mine who reside in each county's unincorporated area or in each municipality. The remaining 85 percent is distributed at the discretion of the executive director of the Department of Local Affairs (DLA) to impacted communities for planning, construction, and maintenance of public facilities and for the provision of public services. The tax resources and tax effort of the communities are considered in awarding the grants.

The Local Government Severance Tax Fund and the Local Government Mineral Impact Fund (which receives federal leasing royalties) are coordinated by the Division of Commerce and Development (C and D) in the DLA. C and D has encouraged the formation of local impact assistance teams, composed of local and county officials, industry representatives, and the general public, to assign priorities for local funding requests.

The Oil Share Trust Fund, established in 1974, receives funds from federal oil shale leases. The entire proceeds are spent in the four impacted counties for public facilities and services—appropriated by the state legislature. Overall, the extent of assistance that can be provided by the state is limited because of the state's constitutional prohibition against indebtedness.

Texas[10]

Texas provides an example of development with little assistance to local governments. Typical boom town problems exist in southwest Texas due to oil and lignite development, and in East Texas as a result of lignite mining and the construction of coal-fired power plants.

> While previous oil and natural gas development has taught Texans to protect the physical environment, they have drawn a different conclusion about the social environment: cities with serious rapid growth problems during the oil boom days have survived (Stinson, 1977, p. I-5).

Perhaps as a result, Texas has no state financial impact assistance program, very little monitoring or predicting of community-specific impacts, and also very little local government power to zone or otherwise negotiate with developers. Public and private utilities were recently denied the power of eminent domain for mineral development. Counties in Texas do not have the power to pass ordinances or zone, and most towns have very limited powers to annex or pass ordinances. As a result, developers have given communities little help in providing infrastructure.

Although many communities have suffered, some have come up with innovative means of controlling economic development even without state assistance. For example, the town of Pearsall charges utility rates that are 50 percent higher outside the city than inside. The town of Dilley gives no guarantees that utility connections will ever be provided outside the city limits. However, owners of land outside the city limits who petition for annexation often receive priority treatment. The town of Mt. Pleasant took the unusual step of seeking cooperation with the county and school district so that they could share infrastructure (e.g., paving equipment, buildings, fire protection).

Conclusions and Recommendations

Our limited experience with large-scale project development suggests several lessons for all states and localities that can be applied to developing an equitable and efficient process for allocating the costs of public facilities and services and for ensuring orderly development.

233

Intergovernmental Responsibilities

The capacity to finance the public facilities and services necessary for large-scale projects involves federal, state, and local governments as well as the private developers. Indeed, many of the project sites span federal, state, and private lands. New initiatives will be necessary at all three levels of government if a fully successful strategy is to be constructed.

Federal Government. The federal government has so far seemed unwilling to get involved in discussions about infrastructure responsibilities. It has not provided significant amounts of impact mitigation assistance (all state officials interviewed agreed that the amount of federal aid was so small as to have no effect on socioeconomic impacts) nor has it explicitly considered impact mitigation planning in its decision on whether to lease particular portions of federal land. In addition, the federal government may constrain state policy choices for future negotiations between state and local governments and developers by unilaterally making the decision to lease a particular portion of federal land.

At present, the federal government does reimburse a part of the lease revenues to the originating state, which proved important to Colorado in its negotiations with Exxon for financing the Colony development. But the federal lease payments are often lower than the price paid on comparable private land, and the amount returned to the states is not large—usually much less than is returned from state-owned land. The development of a coherent state investment strategy could be strengthened by a more consistent leasing approach and more active communications between state and federal officials.

State Responsibility. The state government has three levels of responsibility. First, it must promulgate a consistent overall policy toward large-scale resource development projects. This policy must involve a clearly delineated siting policy, a consistent environmental framework, the fiscal framework for financing these projects, and the clear delineation of the role of the state relative to local governments. Second, it must provide a framework within which local governments can negotiate with private developers, the subjects that are negotiable, and the broad procedures that must be followed during a negotiation process. Third, it must provide real resources—both technical and fiscal—to local government units that provide them with the tools and power to negotiate effectively. These must include a detailed estimate of possible impacts and the power to improve the necessary tax or to issue the necessary debt to pay for the "public" side of the negotiated strategy.

In order for a state to negotiate or to legislate an effective capital investment infrastructure strategy, it must first be clear about its own values and about its goals. These values do differ among states. Residents of Montana are worried about the environmental and social damage resulting from development projects. Montana thus retains tight control of the development process and charges a high severance tax. Utah and Texas apparently want more energy development and so put very few restrictions on the development process. Each state must examine its collective values in order to make an intelligent cost-benefit analysis of what it stands to gain by pursuing economic development in general or the continuation of a specific project in particular. Some of the important factors to be considered by the state include the costs and the benefits that have been discussed in this chapter.

The state should also evaluate specific possible outcomes. It should consider, for example, how much it values the revenues or economic activity induced by the project. It must judge the value of the private developer's commitment to contribute further to the state's economic development in the future. For example, a commitment by the developer to build processing, refining, or manufacturing facilities in the state would be very valuable. And the state must assess the value of the developer's provision of infrastructure.

The goals of the state should include, at a minimum, that it not suffer a net loss by adopting a particular development policy. If costs and benefits are defined broadly enough, and weighed by the state's own collective values, this goal could be interpreted as choosing the development policy that would maximize the net benefits to the state.

Local Governments. The responsibility for negotiating the development of a large-scale project will rest, ultimately, with the local government units—townships or counties—that house most of those directly affected by the project. However, the responsibility for setting the overall framework within which these negotiations are conducted, for conducting evaluations and analyses of options, and for providing fiscal resources, must rest with the states. In states where local capacity is clearly not sufficient to undertake sophisticated negotiations, the state must be prepared to take primary responsibility in conjunction with representatives from the impacted communities.

Having recognized that a favorable settlement on infrastructure responsibilities must be weighed against other possible bargain outcomes, it next becomes necessary to consider the fiscal tools that the state and its communities can bring to the negotiating table.

Financing Tools

States and localities can use a variety of fiscal and regulatory tools to finance project evaluation, public services, and infrastructure necessary for large-scale project development.

Impact Assessment and Evaluation. A state office to undertake impact assessment and to coordinate the negotiation process is an essential component of an effective strategy. This could be located within the governor's office or within a line agency with jurisdiction over resource development. This operation can be successfully financed by a "project application fee" as in North Dakota and Montana. It could also be financed through the prepayment of a portion of taxes from the project.

Infrastructure Development. Where most of the development of a new town can be attributed to a single project, a large part of the costs can be imposed directly upon the developer. Other mechanisms that do not involve the issue of public debt include: (1) the prepayment of taxes; (2) proceeds from lease sales on state land;[11] (3) federal "revenue sharing" from the proceeds of lease sales on federal land; or (4) a development fee that reflects the cost of extending roads and sewer and water services to the project. If public debt is used, then limited obligation bonds can be issued backed by: (1) the increment in sales tax or property tax revenues; (2) the revenues from a severance tax or corporate profits tax imposed on the development companies; (3) the revenues from special district taxes—a multi-county area affected by the development could be granted special district status and allowed to impose a supplementary sales or property tax.

Public Services and Mitigation Payments. These should be financed by the additional tax revenues that are generated by the project, including all additional revenues from the development companies, local businesses, and residents. If their costs are not covered then the project is being implicitly subsidized by other taxpayers in the state, which may lead to reduced development elsewhere. It will be important to monitor public sector revenues and costs attributable to the project to minimize such subsidies. Some states—notably Alaska, Texas, and Louisiana—have chosen to use revenues from oil and gas production to subsidize all other sectors of economic activity. These subsidies cannot be sustained in the long-run which may lead to traumatic adjustment problems when oil and gas tax revenues decline. There is little evidence to suggest that subsidies are necessary to "prime" development, and therefore, wherever possible, the development of new industries or regions should proceed on a pay-as-you-go basis.

The Bust Phase. Most mineral-rich states have recognized that booms cannot continue indefinitely. Resource prices fluctuate widely over time, and easily recoverable resources are eventually depleted. Most states set aside some of their annual revenues in trust funds that have three major purposes: (1) to invest in new industry that will diversify the local economy; (2) to provide state and local revenues that will continue as severance taxes and other resource-related revenues decline; and (3) to repair the environmental damages incurred as a result of resource development. Although this is a prudent course, the typical level of investment in trust funds—with the exception of Montana and Wyoming—is insufficient to provide very much cushion. In most states, revenues are used

237

overwhelmingly to fund state operations—a procedure that promises severe fiscal pain in the future.

Large-scale development is not necessarily harmful nor is it necessarily an unmixed blessing. A carefully designed procedure to negotiate an equitable and efficient allocation of the costs among state and local governments and private developers and the appropriate deployment of fiscal policies can lead to a harmonious and mutually beneficial development that will build and sustain healthy local economies. This would involve a much greater state commitment to impact assessment and negotiated development then has yet been made in most states.

CHAPTER VI NOTES

1. The information presented in this chapter relies heavily on the excellent study conducted by the Laboratory of Architecture and Planning, Massachusetts Institute of Technology, which examined policies and practices of fiscal mitigation in mountain states. This study is summarized in Susskind and O'Hare (1977), but see also Foster (1977) and Gilmore and Duff (1975) for a discussion of Wyoming; Sanderson (1977), Texas; Monaco (1977), Colorado; Lu (1977), North Dakota. Overviews of policy issues are contained in Freudenberg (1976); Sanderson and O'Hare (1977); O'Hare (1977); Brody (1977). The discussion of specific state programs is based upon a paper prepared by Klaus Kolb of the Kennedy School of Government, under the supervision of Professor Herman Leonard.

2. Information for North Dakota is summarized from Lu (1977); from correspondence from James Luptak, Deputy Director, Energy Development Impact Office, State of North Dakota, and Darrell Ohlhauser, Acting Federal Aid Coordinator, State of North Dakota; and from a telephone interview with August Keller, Director, Energy Development Impact Office, State of North Dakota.

3. Information for Wyoming is summarized from Foster (1977); from a telephone interview with Warren White, Director, State Planning Coordinator's Office, State of Wyoming; and from correspondence from W. Don Nelson, Governor's Office, State of Wyoming.

4. Information for Montana is summarized from a telephone interview and correspondence with Lee Berry, Director, Department of Natural Resources; Nancy Owen, Don MacIntyre, Frank Culver, Carol Massman, and Paul Cartwright, Department of Natural Resources,

State of Montana; Mike Shields, Lieutenant Governor's Office; Terry Cohea, Governor's Office; and Carol Ferguson, Department of Commerce.

5. For example, the certificate for the power plants known as Colstrip 3 and 4 contains twenty-six conditions, including:
   1. keeping a 50-day water supply,
   2. building sealed sludge ponds,
   3. placing air quality monitoring equipment on the nearby Northern Cheyenne Indian Reservation, and
   4. providing for the training and employment of members of the Northern Cheyenne Tribe.

6. Information for Utah summarized from telephone interviews and correspondence with Kent Briggs, Executive Assistant, Office of the Governor, State of Utah, and Gary Tomsic, Deputy Director, Department of Community and Economic Development, State of Utah.

7. Gilmore et al., Case Study #1: (1977) Coal Creek Station, McLean County, North Dakota, in Leistritz and Maki, (1977, pp. 70–71).

8. Information for Colorado summarized from Monaco (1977) and telephone interviews and correspondence with Lee White, Director, Office of State Planning and Budgeting, State of Colorado, and Randy Russell, State Energy Impact Office, Department of Local Affairs, State of Colorado. Articles on the closing at the Colony Shale Oil Project in *The New York Times Magazine*, May 3–17, 1982.

9. For example, in the case of a temporary population surge, the EDIO may agree to reimburse 100 percent of the cost of portable classrooms. If the community wants to invest in permanent school additions, the EDIO will pay only a portion of the total expenses. However, the community would also be eligible for loans from the Coal Trust Fund. These loans, administered by the State Land Board, are made at 6 percent interest with ten-to-twenty-year payback periods. The state deducts loan payments from a county's share of coal tax revenues. If a coal mining project ceases, the loan is forgiven.

10. Information for Texas is summarized from Stinson (1977) and from a telephone interview with Mr. Mike Martin, Staff member, Senate Committee on Natural Resources, State of Texas.

11. The use of proceeds from lease sales on state lands is restricted in Wyoming. State lands were granted to the State by the federal government under this Act of Admission. Under the terms of the trust created by this Act, income from these lands can only be used for the betterment of Wyoming's public schools and other public institutions.

CHAPTER VII

Using Tax Incentives
to Finance
Public Investment[1]

A MORE DRAMATIC ALTERNATIVE for financing public infrastructure than those discussed in preceding chapters is to involve directly the private sector by transferring ownership of a public facility to a private firm in order to take advantages of the tax incentives offered to private investment. Harnessing tax incentives for public purposes is hardly new. To finance low-income housing and industrial development, the public sector has devised programs explicitly using tax shelters available to private investors. Over the past two decades, special provisions have been added to the Federal Tax Code to encourage private investment or expenditure that meets policy goals. These provisions do not reduce the cost to government of achieving its objectives but shift the cost from direct on-budget expenditures to less-direct tax expenditures. This chapter analyzes how state and local governments can take advantage of federal business tax incentives as a means of cutting the cost of infrastructure finance. It describes the limits to private participation and examines the circumstances under which private funds might be used to finance public facilities[2] that have traditionally been conceived of as purely public in nature.

The mechanisms described in this chapter—lease financing, service contracts, and outright sale—are, essentially, fiscal gimmicks. They do not reduce the actual cost of making the investments. They do not improve the efficiency of public investments through improved planning and management. They simply export a part of the cost of a local project to federal taxpayers. As such, they are fiscally equivalent to a federal categorical grant program that may fund between 10 and 15 percent of a project's cost.

Unfortunately these mechanisms operate less efficiently than federal categorical grants. Part of the federal tax expenditures—the federal corporate income tax revenues foregone—flow not to the municipality but to the private corporation entering into the financial agreement and to the financial institution negotiating the deal. Indeed, not all the tax burden is necessarily shifted across jurisdictional boundaries. For example, a large share of the cash payment by Metromedia to the New York Metropolitan Transit Authority for the purchase of buses reflected not saved federal taxes but reduced state and city corporate income taxes.

However, what may be a relatively inefficient national policy may be attractive to individual states and cities. After all, even if a categorical program provides grants to localities worth less than the cost of raising the necessary federal revenues, localities that do not apply gain nothing. With federal direct grants sharply curtailed and tax-exempt interest rates remaining stubbornly high, tax-incentive financing is worth considering. The appeal of this approach to state and local government is similar to the appeal of Industrial Revenue Bonds (IRBs) since, in both cases, federal tax expenditures fund part of the costs. There is a certain amount of irony here. Through IRB financings, state and local governments assist private, taxable businesses by creating the convenient fiction that tax-exempt IRBs have a fully public character. The same governments, through lease finance arrangements, seek federal tax subsidies for a purely public project by depicting the project as a private, taxpaying entity.

Transferring ownership of a public facility to a private corporation—even if only for tax purposes—raises the issue of why the facility was public to begin with. The belief in the appropriateness of public ownership extends beyond mere cost considerations and cannot be simply answered. In determining whether tax-incentive financing can be applied to a given facility, the following general questions must be answered:

1. If a facility cannot or, it is determined, should not cover its costs (because it is in part a public good or merit good), is it possible to channel public funds to a private facility operator to capture the tax advantages of private ownership? Theoretically, the cost to the public sector of operating the facility might be reduced by the value of tax breaks for private investors.

2. Where the facility possesses the characteristics of a social good, can conversion to private ownership—with appropriate regulations—allow cost savings and, at the same time, meet public use requirements?

3. Where the facility has all the characteristics of a private facility, including the ability to generate surplus revenue, can the outright sale to a private company generate increased revenues to the public sector?

The first section, below, reviews the tax advantages of private ownership in terms of the investment tax credit and accelerated cost recovery and analyzes the legal impediments to the public sector capture of these benefits. The subsequent three sections describe, respectively, how leasing, service contracts, and sale arrangements can be used to reduce the costs of public facility financing. The final section summarizes the main conclusions and outlines the policy concerns that such arrangements may create for state and local governments. The discussions in the three major sections are highly technical. The reader interested in reviewing the policy issues may wish to turn directly to the final section.

The Tax Advantages of Private Ownership

Government use of various business tax subsidies[3] for public purposes faces certain legal restraints. This section briefly describes the structure of federal tax incentives for business investment, outlines the legal impediments to their capture by state and local government, and defines the types of arrangements that can be made between public and private investors.

242

Federal Tax Incentives
for Business Investment

Under present federal tax law, business investment in plant and equipment is subsidized in two ways. The most straightforward is through an investment tax credit, which is a relatively clear and discrete subsidy. A taxpayer making a qualifying capital investment may deduct a percentage of the cost of the investment directly from the taxes due to the federal government under the corporate (or personal) income tax. The Economic Recovery Tax Act of 1981 (ERTA) established the following percentages:

3-year class life equipment	6%
5-year and 15-year class life equipment	10%
Rehabilitation of structures 30 to 39 years old	15%
Rehabilitation of structures at least 40 years old	20%
Rehabilitation of certified historic structures	25%
Investment in research and development in excess of the level of investment in 1980	20%

In addition, ERTA significantly revised the method by which businesses depreciate capital assets by adding an implicit subsidy to what had been ostensibly a system for merely recovering capital costs. Prior to ERTA, businesses were allowed to depreciate an asset by deducting from income a percentage of an asset's capital cost over the asset's presumed economic life, creating, for tax purposes, a series of expenses that conformed with a hypothetical rate at which the asset was used up. Of course, any such series of expenses can only be approximations in practice. The system that preceded ERTA was extremely complex—classifying eligible plant and equipment under 130 categories that could be depreciated over periods between eighteen months and forty years, and, for most assets, allowing a choice of three ways in which depreciation provisions could be apportioned over the life of the asset. However, no allowance was made for varying rates of inflation, since depreciation was against the purchase price of the asset. Therefore, the effective corporate tax rate on capital rose and fell with the inflation rate. This makes it extremely difficult to devise a depreciation schedule that is equitable for all types of assets and for all rates of inflation.[4]

243

Despite such practical and theoretical difficulties, it is clear that, beyond a certain reasonable range approximating the true or economic depreciation rate, a radical shortening of asset life for tax purposes and allowance for a more rapid write-off in early years, which ERTA has done through the Accelerated Cost Recovery System (ACRS), is an implicit subsidy for capital investment. ACRS groups all assets into one of only four categories that can be depreciated over fifteen years (structures), ten years (investments by public utilities), five years (most equipment) and three years (transportation equipment and machinery previously depreciated over four years or less).

The changes in the rate at which assets can be depreciated for tax purposes are:

Type of Asset	Pre-ERTA Asset Depreciation Range System (ADR)	Post-ERTA Accelerated Cost Recovery System (ACRS)
Short fixed equipment (weighted average)	5 years	3 years
Other equipment (weighted average)	8 years	5 years
Structures	40 years	15 years

ACRS subsidies are harder to quantify than ITC subsidies. The amount of the subsidy is the increased tax forgiveness over that which would be available if only economic depreciation were allowed. Consider a machine costing $1,000 that wears out evenly over ten years. The real value of depreciation is $100 a year for ten years. Under ACRS the equipment will be depreciated over five years at $200 each year. The total value of the depreciation allowances is the same—$1,000. But with ACRS, the benefits are enjoyed sooner and are therefore more valuable. If we discount future depreciation benefits to compute the *present value* of depreciation under the two systems, the implicit subsidy under ACRS becomes apparent. Assuming a 10 percent discount rate and a 46 percent marginal tax bracket, the present value of depreciating over ten years is $283, and the present value of depreciation over five years is $349. Thus, a business that is confident that it can earn at least 10 percent interest on cash in hand would be prepared to pay at least $66 ($349 minus $283) for the ability to use ACRS rather than the true depreciation rate.

Since there is no rigorous way of calculating the true depreciation rate, we can only approximate the extent of the subsidy. The combined effect of both ACRS and ITC allows for negative tax rates under certain conditions. Alan Auerbach (1982), in a recent examination of ACRS, found the following effective tax rates for assets purchased during 1981–94 with inflation at 12 percent:

Life of Asset	Effective Tax Rate
3 years	– 0.85
5 years	– 0.74
15 years	+ 0.15

A negative tax rate is a difficult concept to understand. Essentially it means that the present value of the tax credit and depreciation subsidies is considerably greater than the present value of the expected earnings from the equipment and therefore will create an internal "tax loss" that the corporation can write-off against its earnings on existing capital. Of course, these estimates are based on hypothetical assumptions about the rate of inflation and the earnings from the investment. But these data illustrate an important conclusion: Because of these changes in the tax law, the after-tax cost of capital investments by private corporations—particularly in relatively short-lived equipment—has been substantially reduced. Therefore the potential benefits of private investment relative to public investment have been dramatically increased.

Legal Impediments to Tax Benefit Transfers

In order to capture private sector tax benefits, agreements between state and local governments and private firms must comply with federal tax laws and regulations. There are many legal impediments that must be overcome. The clearest prohibitions in federal law affecting the ability of government to utilize tax benefits arise with respect to so-called "Section 38 property"—which is defined as property eligible for the federal investment tax credit. Since the ITC was clearly and explicitly designed to be an investment stimulus to private business, Section 38 of the tax code excludes from ITC eligibility property used by government. ERTA qualified this general prohibition by excepting expenditures for the rehabilitation of public structures. Property owned by government but used by the private sector may qualify for the ITC under certain conditions.

Since depreciation is (at least in principle) merely a method of recovering capital costs, there has been no attempt to apply Section 38-type restrictions to depreciation claimed under ACRS. Generally, ACRS may be taken by any taxpayer with respect to property held for production of income or in a business or trade. Thus, while government property *per se* is not depreciable since it is typically tax-exempt by definition, property owned by the private sector and leased for profit to a state or local (or even the federal) government may be depreciable. Similarly, property owned by the government and leased to the private sector for business purposes, such as publicy owned industrial space, may be depreciable under certain circumstances.

If tax subsidies more than offset the traditional advantages of tax-exempt financing available to the public sector, government can save money by leasing facilities and equipment that have been built and are owned by the private sector instead of purchasing them. The lease payments by a government to the private owner for an office building, for example, could be less than the public debt service payments that would be necessary had the government itself financed the building through issuing bonds. However, the IRS limits the type of transactions that can be characterized as a lease.

1. The lessor must have a positive cash flow and profit from the lease independent of the tax benefits.

246

2. The lessee must not have an investment in the lease and must not lend any of the purchase costs to the owner.
3. The lessee must not have the right to purchase the property at less than fair market value.
4. The use of the property at the end of the lease term by a person other than the lessee must be commercially viable.
5. The lessor must have a minimum investment at risk of 20 percent throughout the lease term.

These standards, which apply with most force to equipment,[5] are meant to ensure that a transaction is truly a lease—that is, the private company owns and maintains the property for profit. They were not originally developed to deny government the ability to capture tax subsidies. They were created to inhibit the unlimited transferability of tax shelter benefits between private firms. In the absence of any such standards defining what constitutes a lease, a firm with no taxable income would never acquire a capital asset. Instead it would lease the asset from a firm with a positive taxable income. The lease payments to the high bracket lessor might create a negative, or breakeven, before-tax cash flow, but a positive after-tax cash flow; the lessee could purchase the asset for a nominal sum at the close of the lease.

These so-called true lease requirements reduce the potential benefits that a state or local government can enjoy. However, they can be circumvented under certain conditions.

1. ERTA specifically allowed for certain transactions to be characterized as leases, regardless of the IRS standards discussed above. Such leases, known as "safe-harbor" leases, allow for the unfettered flow of tax benefits between firms with different brackets, the same flow that earlier IRS rulings had attempted to limit. But safe-harbor leasing activity is limited by ERTA to Section 38 property, which excludes property used by government. (ERTA even excluded from safe-harbor provisions Section 38-eligible rehabilitation expenditures leased to government.) The two ex-

ceptions made by ERTA were mass transit rolling stock and equipment used by volunteer fire departments. New York's Metropolitan Transit Authority realized savings of 22 percent on subway cars and 13 percent on buses by entering into a safe-harbor arrangement; similar savings could be expected in non-transit areas, depending on the tax benefits associated with each type of property. Massive federal deficits, however, led to the immediate curtailment and eventual phase-out of safe-harbor benefits under the 1982 Tax Act. For as long as the provisions do remain in effect, small- to medium-sized public transit operators should explore the benefits of safe-harbor leases, particularly, if purchases by a number of operators can be made jointly, providing for economies of scale in the sale of tax benefits to outside investors.

2. Real property is not fully subject to the IRS guidelines. In particular, the lessee may participate in the financing, and the 20 percent minimum interest rule does not apply. This liberalization, combined with ERTA provisions allowing the ITC to be claimed in connection with real property leased to government, allows for quite deep federal tax subsidies with respect to certain government real property.

3. Arrangements may be structured between governments and private corporations that are explicitly not leases, thereby avoiding IRS lease restrictions. One such mechanism is the service contract, discussed later.

4. In the case of a revenue-producing facility, outright sale to the private sector may be the most advantageous policy for the state or local government.

Even if these three loopholes cannot be used for a particular project, a true lease may still be a cost-effective financing option. True lease requirements do not prohibit a private firm from enjoying certain tax benefits from property leased to government. Since ERTA allows the ITC to be taken along with ACRS with respect to rehabilitation expenses associated with property leased to government, it is possible that capital costs incurred by the public sector under a true lease arrangement may be lower than

248

through alternative financing mechanisms, especially for projects involving rehabilitation of existing structures. The local government will have to provide for a positive before-tax cash flow to the investor and for sufficient funds to purchase the asset at a more than nominal price at the close of the lease, unlike a safe-harbor lease. Yet the tax benefits may still be deep enough to offset these additional public sector costs.

Leasing

This section describes how a true lease agreement between a local government and a for-profit corporation can be used to finance a project, and shows the cost savings that are possible. To show more concretely how leasing restrictions may affect the flow of tax benefits, let us examine a simple case of a safe-harbor arrangement. The main effect of the safe-harbor provisions is to replace existing IRS restrictions with far looser guidelines for defining a lease. Most importantly, they eliminate the requirements that the lessor have a positive cash flow during the lease term and that any repurchase be at fair market value. Although the Tax Equity and Financial Responsibility Act of 1982 limits safe-harbor activities, it is worthwhile examining a safe-harbor transaction, because it shows the workings of tax-incentive financing in its simplest form.

Table 25 presents the data from such a hypothetical transaction. In this example, five-year ACRS property owned by a government, which is eligible for the ITC, is sold to a corporation paying a marginal corporate tax rate of 46 percent and then leased back to the government. The transaction involves a down payment plus a note from the lessee (the government) to the lessor (the private owner). The annual lease payment from the lessee to the lessor is exactly equal to the amount due on the note; the two cash payments cancel each other out (columns 6 and 9). The lessor, however, depreciates the property on an accelerated basis over five years and takes a credit in the initial year of 10 percent of cost. These two factors combine to create significant paper losses in the first five years, allowing the lessor to shield other income from taxation at the

249

Table 25

Sale/Leaseback Example

($ in millions)

| Year | ITC | Depreciation Deductions | | Tax Savings | | Total debt Service |
		Actual	Dis-counted	Actual	Dis-counted	
0	10	15.0	15.0	6.9	6.9	—
1		22.0	19.1	10.1	8.8	15.4
2		21.0	15.9	9.7	7.3	15.4
3		21.0	13.8	9.7	6.4	15.4
4		21.0	12.0	9.7	5.5	15.4
5		—	—			15.4
6		—	—			15.4
7		—	—			15.4
8		—	—			15.4
9		—	—			15.4
10		—	—			15.4
11		—	—			15.4
12		—	—			15.4
13		—	—			15.4
14		—	—			15.4
15		—	—			15.4
TOTAL +	10	100.0	75.8	46.1	34.9	230.9

Notes: * Assumptions: Property worth $100 million and eligible for 5-year ACRS treatment is sold by the lessee. The buyer/lessor puts $10 million down and pays the remaining $90 million, plus interest at 15 percent, in 15 equal annual installments. (The lease also runs for 15 years.) Future amounts are discounted at a 15 percent annual rate to yield present values as of year zero. 10% ITC, 46% tax rate.

Columns may not add up to totals due to rounding.

Debt service		Rental Payments	Rent Minus Interest Costs (taxable income)		Tax payable	
Interest	Principal		Actual	Dis-counted	Actual	Dis-counted
—	—	—	—	—	—	—
13.5	1.9	15.4	1.9	1.6	.9	.7
13.2	2.2	15.4	2.2	1.6	1.0	.7
12.9	2.5	15.4	2.5	1.6	1.2	.7
12.5	2.9	15.4	2.9	1.6	1.3	.7
12.1	3.3	15.4	3.3	1.6	1.5	.7
11.6	3.8	15.4	3.8	1.6	1.8	.7
11.0	4.4	15.4	4.4	1.6	2.0	.7
10.4	5.0	15.4	5.0	1.6	2.3	.7
9.6	5.8	15.4	5.8	1.6	2.7	.7
8.7	6.7	15.4	6.7	1.6	3.1	.7
7.7	7.7	15.4	7.7	1.6	3.5	.7
6.6	8.8	15.4	8.8	1.6	4.1	.7
5.3	10.1	15.4	10.1	1.6	4.7	.7
3.8	11.6	15.4	11.6	1.6	5.3	.7
2.0	13.4	15.4	13.4	1.6	6.1	.7
140.9	90.0	230.9	90.0	24.7	41.5	11.8

Net tax benefits are equivalent to column 1 (PV of ITC) plus column 5 (PV of depreciation benefits) minus column 13 (PV of tax). Deep tax subsidies in early years more than offset tax due.

Maximum price = 10 + 34.9 − 11.8 = 33.1

Source: Adapted from Mark Willis, "Leasing—A Financial Option for States and Localities," *Federal Reserve Bank of New York Quarterly Review,* March 1982.

46 percent marginal bracket (columns 1–5). However, holding aside the lessor's depreciation deductions, the taxpayer's taxable income grows each year, since his cash rental income is subject over time to smaller interest deductions, which results in net taxable income after the sixth year (columns 10–13). However, these taxes are significantly less in present value terms than the tax savings during the first five years. In fact, the positive difference between the tax savings and tax liability in present value terms defines the amount of equity the investor will be willing to advance. In short, the present value of the ITC plus the present value of tax savings from depreciation minus the present value tax liability from rent income net of interest deductions is the value of the transaction to the private investor and will be the maximum amount that the investor will be willing to pay the government for the right to own the facility for tax purposes.

In this case, the investor should be willing to increase his equity position above $10 million. With each increment in equity, the rate of return drops because of the higher equity contribution and the reduced interest deductions. The investor will continue to add to his equity—in this case up to about $25 million, assuming a typical rate of return—with the offsetting public sector lease costs declining with each increment. The tax benefits provide the private sector lessor the required return to equity to make the transaction possible and profitable.

This transaction shows how IRS restrictions may depress the value of the transaction. In this example, the lessee's net benefit would be about $25 million, since no real economic transactions take place after the initial cash payment. However, if the lessor is required to show a before-tax profit, the lessee's (the government's) $25 million windfall will be reduced because the lessee will have to pay higher lease payments to ensure the lessor's profit. Similarly, the lessee's gain will be reduced by the present value of the repurchase cost in excess of the nominal sum allowed under safe-harbor rules. The IRS guidelines reduce—but may not eliminate—the potential dividend to the local government. But once it is realized that a dividend is legally possible, any number of structures are possible.

☐ *An existing assest may be refinanced.* Certain public facilities may be sold to the private sector and leased back. The financing might be obtained privately or, in some instances, through the issuance of industrial development bonds. In the safe-harbor analysis presented, the maximum amount of the private sector contribution in order to secure tax benefits on $100 million of equipment was judged to be approximately $25 million. In an equivalent non-safe-harbor arrangement, the $25 million in potential tax benefits would not accrue in its entirety as a dividend to government. It will be split three ways: Some must fund IRS profitability tests; a portion must be used to establish a separate "sinking fund" used to repurchase the asset; the balance represents the net fiscal dividend. How much of the maximum $25 million must be used to fund federal compliance depends on a number of factors, including the jurisdiction's estimate of residual value. However, since government retains some ability to depress residual value (through separate ground leases or renewal options at reasonable rates), a substantial portion of free cash is left.

☐ *Sale/Leaseback for renovation.* In the case of a public facility in need of rehabilitation, a sale/leaseback arrangement may provide all or part of the funds that would otherwise be raised publicly. In this case, private monies can fund profitability tests and repurchase, but the balance would be applied toward the rehabilitation of the facility. Since the ITC on real property rehabilitation may be as high as 20 or 25 percent as compared with 10 percent in the equipment safe-harbor analysis, the benefits might be substantial.

☐ *Sale/Leaseback for new construction or acquisition.* Both real property and equipment would qualify for sale leaseback for these purposes.

Service Contracts

A second method by which tax benefits may be put to public use involves service contracts. A service contract is the use by a private vendor of its own equipment to provide a service to a client for a fee. It can be distinguished from a traditional lease (in which the client purchases the right to use an asset for a specified period) and from a lease-purchase arrangement (by which the client acquires the asset over time). But distinguishing a service contract from a lease, while apparently simply a matter of draftmanship, is conceptually difficult and legally hazardous. Perhaps the best way to approach the issue is by examining a relatively clear case of what a service contract is and discussing, later, the limits of the concept.

Copying machines are a fixture in most government offices. "Property used by government" is not Section 38 property, and, therefore, expenditures by the company supplying the government with the copying machines would appear to be ineligible for the federal ITC. However, the Xerox Corporation maintained a service contract agreement with the federal government, through which the federal government purchased copying services for a fee. Xerox claimed the ITC for the cost of the machines positioned in federal offices and defended the action by maintaining that the copying machines in question were not used by government, but rather by the Xerox Corporation, which used them to provide a service to government. The federal government's payments therefore represented a fee for copying services rather than a lease payment on a machine. IRS disagreed. The Court of Claims, in *Xerox Corp. v. the United States*, (I.R.S. Court of Claims, Washington, D.C., 1978) sided with Xerox and the opinion provides some guidelines in terms of what constitutes a legal service contract.

In general, the court agreed that it is not sufficient merely to characterize an agreement as "not a lease" to avoid the "use by government" prohibition. Rather, the actual nature of the owner's possessory interest requires examination on a case-by-case basis. Xerox was able to show, among other things, that it still had responsibility to maintain the equipment and that, since the machines were readily substitutable in the event of mechanical problems, government was not intending to rent a particular machine but rather the benefits associated with any such machine.

In addition, the court put forward, as a second test, the notion that the equipment, to be eligible, should be part of a larger network in which the taxpayer has additional responsibilities. Again, Xerox was able to qualify.

However, two problems arise in attempting to broaden this line of reasoning to make it suitable for wide application. First, the Court of Claims decision, while attempting to set firm standards, inevitably created some ambiguity. Automobiles and trucks, for instance, were specifically mentioned in the decision as equipment not eligible for service contract treatment. Yet an automobile driven by a government employee is not unlike a Xerox machine. Both machine and auto provide a service; both are substitutable; both may be maintained by a vendor; and both may be part of a larger network.

Legal ambiguity does not, of course, necessarily result in prohibition. Depending on the risks the parties are willing to run and the extent to which the equipment user is willing to provide indemnification to the investor, service contracts may be possible for infrastructure or related equipment. In particular, as the notion of infrastructure grows broader through technological change to include sophisticated telecommunications systems and data processing equipment, service contracts on such equipment may be defended more easily than, say, a truck fleet to maintain county roads, if only because analogies to copying machines may be clearer and more direct. However, truck fleets and other traditional infrastructure-related uses ought not to be overlooked by enterprising governments; the fact that the courts have been able to distinguish a particular automobile lease from a particular copying machine service contract does not imply that all arrangements involving automobiles are necessarily leases. Structuring a service contract for vehicles may well involve altered management and control responsibilities, and it will certainly involve adroit legal draftmanship, but such agreements seem theoretically possible.[6]

Not all service contract arrangements, however, are likely to run into severe legal challenges, particularly if the actual use of the equipment in question is arguably private in nature. Resource recovery facilities, for example, may be operated privately or publicly, depending on

255

governmental preferences, market conditions, and other factors. A government may choose to construct and operate such a facility directly, or it may choose to allow for private operation, with a portion of the revenues to the operator to be pledged by government in the form of guaranteed minimum tipping fees. A group of Massachusetts localities have, in fact, recently adopted this approach. It is unlikely that the private owners will be denied the relevant investment and energy credits since they clearly maintain a possessory interest in the facility. From the public's point of view, such privatization is minimized as a political issue if the facility is new, if public sector jobs are therefore not at stake, and if the jurisdiction is relatively indifferent to the issue of public or private control.

In order to determine how cost savings are effected by means of a service contract, we will contrast a service contract with the most likely alternative method of property acquisition—a lease-purchase arrangement.

How a Lease-Purchase Works

A government wishing to acquire a capital asset, but unwilling to incur debt to do so, may enter into an agreement with a private entity, such as a bank, which provides credits for the purchase and then leases the asset with all responsibilities of ownership to the government. Provided the agreement is properly structured, the lease payment by government to the private sector may be treated for tax purposes as though it were a debt service payment, with separate principal and interest components. The tax benefit that accrues to the private lessor (the bank) is the ability to deduct the implied interest portion of government's lease payments from income. In this sense, cost savings to government are effected in the same manner as are all facilities or equipment financed with tax-exempt debt. Lease-purchase agreements typically differ from government debt-financed transactions in terms of security— usually because repayment is conditioned upon annual appropriations rather than through bond convenants— but it is fair for our purposes to conceive of lease-purchase and tax-exempt debt as roughly equivalent in terms of cost, rate, interest, and use of the asset.

How a Service Contract Works

In a service contract arrangement, the private sector provides the financing for the asset, as is the case under a lease-purchase. However, the private firm does not then lease the asset to government. Rather, it maintains ownership and enters into a contract with government to provide a service with the asset in return for a fee. Since government is neither acquiring, paying for, or even legally using the asset, the fee has no principal and interest components. And since the private firm receives no interest, it is afforded no interest deduction and consequently pays tax on the entire fee as ordinary income.

In the absence of depreciation deductions or tax credits, the inability to deduct interest income would drive up the after-tax cost of capital relative to lease-purchase, and the higher cost would be passed along to government in the form of higher fees. However, the private firm will be willing to lower its service contract fees below lease payments if the tax subsidies associated with ownership exceed the tax subsidies stemming from the ability to deduct interest, all else being equal.

Whether the tax breaks associated with private ownership are greater than the interest income deduction on what amounts to public debt depends on: (1) the life of the asset, (2) the type of depreciation and/or credit for which it is eligible, (3) the ability of the private firm to leverage debt for acquisition, (4) the residual value of the asset at the end of the lease, and (5) the investor's tax bracket. We can determine the relative importance of these variables by examining a hypothetical lease-purchase transaction as a base line for comparison. Let us assume the private firm invests $10 million to acquire a piece of equipment that government wishes to use, and that the firm will effectively invest $10 million in cash since IRS regulations prohibit double-dipping—that is, the firm may not incur debt, investing such borrowed funds in tax-exempt securities, in order that it may simultaneously deduct the interest payments on the debt incurred and enjoy tax-exempt interest income.

The equipment is leased to a jurisdiction with provision for purchase for a nominal sum at the close of the lease term. Although the lack of a bond covenant for security may raise the implicit interest rate above that associated with a traditional government debt instrument, let us assume that the timing and amount of lease payments generates a yield equal to a tax-exempt issue—in this case, say, 12 percent.

The data relevant to investor are shown in table 26. Since interest income is deducted, and no tax is paid on

---

Table 26

Hypothetical Lease Purchase Agreement (Cash flow, tax consequences and return on investment (ROI) $10 million lease-purchase 12% implicit interest rate, five years)

($ in thousands)

Initial investment: $10 million

Year	Lease Payment	Interest	Principal	Tax	After-Tax Cash
1	2,774	1,200	1,574	0	2,774
2	2,774	1,011	1,763	0	2,774
3	2,774	800	1,975	0	2,774
4	2,774	563	2,211	0	2,774
5	2,774	297	2,477	0	2,774

After-tax ROI = 12%

Table 27

Hypothetical Service Contract (Cash flow, tax consequences and return on investment (ROI) $10 million service contract 175% d-b; 10% ITC; no residual value; 50% bracket)

($ in thousands)

Initial investment: $10,000

Year	Before Tax Fee Income	Depreciation	Taxable Income	Tax Benefit	ITC	After-Tax Cash
1	2,774	3,500	(726)	334	$1,000	4,108
2	2,774	2,275	499	(230)		2,545
3	2,774	1,479	1,295	(596)		2,178
4	2,774	1,373	1,401	(644)		2,130
5	2,774	1,373	1,401	(644)		2,120

ROI = 11.1%

principal repayments, the firm's after-tax cash flow and before-tax cash flow are equivalent, and provide the firm, therefore, with a 12 percent after-tax return on investment (ROI).

One way of comparing a service contract with a lease-purchase is to ask if the same payment by government as a contract fee, will allow for an equivalent or greater internal rate of return to the firm. Table 27 shows that, under a service contract, the firm's ROI drops to 9.5 percent, assuming a $10 million cash investment, 150 percent declining balance depreciation over five years, a 10 percent investment tax credit, and no residual value. Choice of a less-rapid method of cost recovery will depress the return further; a positive residual value will increase the return. Compared with the relatively straight-forward return discernable under a lease-purchase, the firm's after-tax cash flow under a service contract agreement is subject to a variety of influences.

In this case, the fee payment that the public sector would have to generate to provide a 12 percent return on investment would be slightly higher than $2.774 million per year. But what would be the effect of changing certain of our assumptions? Table 28 shows how variations in assumptions alter the private sector ROI, using a lease-purchase agreement yielding 12 percent as a base line in each instance.

The data presented in this table demonstrate that two variables will be decisive in determining whether, and to what extent, financial savings can be expected under a service contract arrangement. First, for short-lived assets, the jurisdiction's estimate of the residual value of the equipment at the end of the service contract is crucial. Under a lease-purchase, government has acquired the asset over the period of the agreement; under a service contract the vendor will typically control the asset at the close of the contract. Private ownership will not be a problem if the asset is obsolete at this point, but ACRS asset-lives are often shorter than assets' useful lives.

A more important consideration, however, is the ability of the private firm to leverage debt—that is, its ability to purchase the asset with the minimum commitment of its own cash. Since interest payments on borrowed funds may not be deducted from income if such funds are used to purchase tax-exempt securities, the firm's investment in a lease-purchase may not be leveraged as in a typical purchase. The ability to deduct interest expenses distorts investment preference in favor of debt over equity, all else being equal; the double-dipping prohibition effectively neutralizes this distortion and converts the lease-purchase investment in equipment or structures into a tax-exempt security. However, no such prohibition exists with respect to a service contract.

Therefore, even if the two tax-benefit scenarios (interest income deductions versus business tax write-offs) have equivalent effects on a given transaction, the ability of the firm to incur debt as a means of reducing equity while also deducting debt service interest payments may create a preference for service contracts. Put another way, the preferential tax treatment of service contracts would allow for a fee payment lower than the corresponding lease-purchase payment, still generating a rate of return satisfactory to private investors. For example, table 28 shows that the private sector ROI increases to 65.2 percent given the following conditions: (1) 90 percent debt financing, (2) private debt financing interest rates 2 percent above the public tax-exempt rate, (3) zero residual value, (4) a three-year asset, and (5) 150 percent declining balance depreciation. This would allow for a significantly lower fee payment by government in place of the lease purchase payment in order to equalize the private sector rate of return at 12 percent.

Outright sale by Government to Private Companies

State and local governments own and operate a variety of facilities that generate revenues in excess of costs—toll bridges, waste disposal facilities, recreation areas, ports, water supply systems, electric and gas utilities, and even transit lines. Sale of these facilities can provide the jurisdiction with substantial revenues. However, private ownership and unregulated pricing may not lead to effi-

Table 28

Return on Investment Under Alternative Service Contract Assumptions
Comparison in Each Case: Lease-Purchase at 12% and 14% ROI

Type of Asset		3-Year Asset				5-Year Asset				1-Year Asset			
Depreciation Method		Straight Line		150%		Straight Line		150%		Straight Line		150%	
Cost of Capital[1]		12	14	12	14	12	14	12	14	12	14	12	14
Debt/Equity Ratio	Residual Value (% of cost)												
0/100[2]	0	8.5	8.5	9.0	9.0	9.0	9.0	9.5	9.5	7.9	7.9	8.1	8.1
	50	23.6	23.6	24.6	18.0	18.0	18.0	18.7	18.7	10.0	10.0	10.3	10.3
50/50	0	11.2	10.1	12.6	11.5	12.6	11.5	13.9	12.7	10.3	9.1	11.1	9.8
	50	35.9	35.9	38.5	37.8	27.0	26.3	28.7	28.0	13.6	12.8	14.4	13.5
90/10	0	40.4	29.5	77.9	65.2	65.0	54.9	101.0	92.3	62.6	52.2	101.0	70.6
	50	96.2	91.7	125.4	119.8	84.5	79.1	112.1	105.8	63.8	52.8	80.0	70.7

Notes: Costs discounted at the public sector financing rate.

6% ITC assumed on 3-year assets
10% ITC assumed on 5-year assets
No ITC assumed on 15-year assets

1. 12% assumes financing costs equivalent to lease-purchase; i.e., tax-exempt IDB financing available.
14% assumes private financing available at 2% above lease-purchase rate.

2. Cost of capital not relevant since 100% equity is assumed.

Source: Based on calculations by Jeffrey Apfel, Office of Development Planning, New York State.

261

cient or equitable outcomes. In some cases—a toll bridge, for example—unregulated private ownership would lead to monopoly pricing which would lead to an inefficiently low level of use, as well as considerable public opposition. In other cases—state-owned office buildings, for example— the problem of monopoly pricing is much less since the facility would have to compete with surrounding privately owned buildings. This section describes the potential financial benefits to be gained by selling a public facility. But the issue of which facilities ought to be sold must be left for each jurisdiction to decide on a case-by-case basis. Clearly, an important element in this decision is the size of the potential revenue enhancement.

The relevant question is, Can the imposition of a tax on a given net revenue stream actually enhance the present value of that revenue stream? An example will help answer the question.

Let us assume the public sector owns a facility that costs $1 million per year to operate but generates annual gross revenues of $2.5 million. The financial value of the asset to the public sector is therefore $1.5 million per year—the amount of the net revenue stream. Let us further assume that the private sector agrees to buy the facility, paying a certain amount in cash up-front and incurring debt for the balance of the purchase price; the public sector borrowing rate is 12 percent; the private sector borrowing rate is 14 percent; and a purchase-money mortgage of $10 million is extended by the public sector at 14 percent over 20 years. The annual debt service to the public sector is $1.5 million—the same amount it would have received had it retained title. But in addition, the public sector will receive an up-front cash payment, the amount of which will be determined by the investor's required rate of return. Assuming the investor pays $2 million in cash on closing, his fifteen-year financial outlook is depicted in table 29. A $2 million cash investment up-front would yield the tax benefits depicted in the last column, resulting in a 12.1 percent rate of return.

The present value of government's net revenues, assuming continued public ownership, (discounted at the 12 percent public sector rate) is approximately $10 million. A year-one cash infusion of $2 million can therefore

Table 29

Cash and Tax Consequences of Sale
46% marginal bracket

(in millions)

	Investment	Income	Expenses	Current Debt-Service Payment	Current Interest	Depreciation	Taxable Income	Tax Benefit	Cash	After-Tax Income
0	-2000								-2000	-2000
1		2500	1000	1500	1400	1200	-1100	506	0	506
2		2500	1000	1500	1386	1080	-966	444	0	444
3		2500	1000	1500	1370	972	-842	387	0	387
4		2500	1000	1500	1351	874	-726	334	0	334
5		2500	1000	1500	1331	787	-618	284	0	284
6		2500	1000	1500	1307	708	-516	237	0	237
7		2500	1000	1500	1230	708	-489	225	0	225
8		2500	1000	1500	1249	708	-458	210	0	211
9		2500	1000	1500	1214	708	-423	194	0	195
10		2500	1000	1500	1174	708	-383	176	0	176
11		2500	1000	1500	1129	708	-337	155	0	155
12		2500	1000	1500	1077	708	-286	131	0	131
13		2500	1000	1500	1018	708	-226	104	0	104
14		2500	1000	1500	950	708	-159	73	0	73
15		2500	1000	1500	873	708	-82	37	0	38

ROI = 12.2%

be considered a 20 percent increase in facility revenues over the fifteen-year period.

This simplified analysis does not, of course, treat several significant issues, including public sector revenues beyond the recovery life, legal mechanisms for sale, and state legal and constitutional issues. But the figures do highlight the potential revenue increment.

State and Local Policy Concerns

In the future, state and local decision makers will be confronted with proposed tax-subsidy finance arrangements. While business tax incentives remain in the federal tax code, and while state and local governments face fiscal problems, these arrangements will remain attractive. This section raises policy concerns that should be considered when evaluating these opportunities. Underlying all the concerns is the assumption that cost is only one factor among many in the public investment decision process.

1. *The importance of public sector control.* Clearly, facilities differ with respect to the need for public control. The public sector may wish to own a facility in order to preserve accountability in management, to protect public employment, or to preserve the external benefits provided by the facility. Some of these concerns can be addressed without maintaining public ownership. For example, the public employment effects of privatization might be lessened if the financing is for a new facility and new employment. Or a private manager might be compelled to provide external benefits through regulation of price or service. It may be helpful to conceive of the instruments discussed in this chapter as lying along a continuum of public control.

Public Control and Financing Instruments

Low need for public control		High need for public control
sale service contract	lease	safe-harbor lease

264

At the end of the continuum—low need for public control—is outright sale. While title can be passed to the private sector with strings attached, outright sale normally implies an abdication of basic management responsibilities. Thus, sale can be seen as particularly appropriate where government has assumed quasi-private functions in such areas as real estate and industrial development.

Service contracts, similarly, might be most appropriate only when the public sector is comfortable with the notion of abdicating a relatively high level of management control, since IRS will allow the ITC only when the private sector can document possession and use.

Leases provide a wider degree of public sector control, depending on the terms of the lease. However, current federal restrictions on what constitutes a lease mandate at least some control by the private sector.

Only with the extreme case of safe-harbor leases is private influence negligible, since private ownership is for tax purposes only.

2. *The level of public sector risk.* The public sector may be called upon to assume certain risks in the transactions that must be balanced against the cash generated. One risk is the ability to repurchase. Because non-safe-harbor leases may not contain provisions for nominal public sector repurchase, government must hope that it will have sufficient funds to repurchase a leased facility in the future at the price requested by the lessor. For example, the Suffolk County Sewer District Sale/Leaseback calls for repurchase of the sewer system at market value with reinvested residual bond proceeds. But if today's judgments as to the level of funds required are not accurate, repurchase may be made more expensive or difficult.

Another type of risk the public sector may encounter is indemnification risk. Typically, tax subsidy finance transactions contain provisions to indemnify the investors in the event of legal changes or adverse IRS actions. Such provisions create the possibility that government may be required to compensate the in-

265

vestors in the amount of their lost tax advantages. Because many of the transactions are complex and certain areas of the tax law are untested, this risk may be large.

3. *The effect of the financing on the existing structure of state and local finance.* Leases and service contracts convert what might otherwise be a public operation into a private operation, at least for tax purposes. Thus, the restrictions that many states have on public debt may not apply if the transaction is characterized as private. For example, New York State requires that the principal component of any local debt service payment not exceed by more than 50 percent the principal component of any other debt service payment from the same obligation. This restriction prohibits level-debt service schedules and forces an early amortization of debt. Refinancing a sewer through an IDA, however, allows for level-debt service on the new debt, violating the intent of state law. Additionally, private financing may, like lease purchasing, provide for a way to circumvent constitutional limitations on debt issuance.

4. *The effect on the tax-exempt market.* Changes in institutional behavior, increases in IDB financing, and other factors have already raised tax-exempt rates relative to taxable rates. It is probable that new tax-exempt instruments will exacerbate the problem. In the Suffolk County Sewer District refinancing, $370 million in debt will be retired and $625 million will be issued, all with no new construction to show for it, only a reduction and stabilization of sewer charges at the local level.

5. *Fiscal prudence.* The flexibility afforded by some transactions may allow for a lack of prudence by government or by private firms. Traditional government finance markets impose standards, in part, to assure the long-term soundness of financial systems. Innovation generally brings flexibility, but flexibility can create potential hazards. For example, a municipality, in establishing a fund to reduce local assessments, might be tempted to draw on the fund to subsidize

266

rates more heavily during the early years of the lease term, leaving much less money to offset assessments in the future. No standards or laws exist to limit this type of borrowing against the future.

6.   *In-state financial incidence.* Not all the tax expenditures at work are borne by out-of-state taxpayers. Depending on the relationship of state and local tax systems to the federal tax system, some portion of the cost may be shifted back to in-state taxpayers.

Conclusion

At a time of increasing needs and decreasing resources, state and local governments should explore the possibilities of tax-subsidy finance. Jurisdictions should carefully examine transactions on a case-by-case basis and, additionally, attempt to set general standards in line with the considerations outlined above. Governments should also recognize that tax-subsidy finance will not be a magic cure for infrastructure problems. It may, however, prove a valuable method, in the short run, for reducing costs.

CHAPTER VII NOTES

1.   This chapter was prepared by Jeffry Apfel, Assistant Director of the Governor's Office of Development Planning, New York State.

2.   The term "facility" in this chapter is used broadly to include not only public structures but other capital items such as transportation equipment, medical equipment and computers.

3.   While "business tax subsidies" will be referred to in this chapter, it should be pointed out that such subsidies may also be available to individuals. Partnerships composed of individuals, for instance, are often the recipients of investment subsidies in the real estate area. Generally, the term "business tax subsidies" will refer, then, to both businesses and individuals.

4.   The system that meets an economist's definition of equity and efficiency is known as the first-year cost recovery system.

5.   A current view is that judicial confusion and disagreement have to

a large extent rendered these standards obsolete, even with respect to equipment. See Freida Wallison, "Benefits of ERTA Available to State and Local Governments," *New York Law Journal,* Vol. 63, No. 1, March 25, 1982.

6. A case for just such an arrangement has been made by Robert Lamb, "The Service Contract vs. The Lease," New York State Department of Transportation, 1982, unpublished.

CHAPTER VIII

Summary
and
Recommendations

THE NATION IS FACING a crisis precipitated by insufficient and inefficient investment in the development and maintenance of public infrastructure. The crisis can only be averted by radical changes in planning, managing, and financing public capital investments. State and local governments are trapped between the need to arrest the rate of deterioration and to provide for new development and the shrinking resources available to pay for public infrastructure. Failure to increase public investments will jeopardize local and national economic recovery, will weaken governments' ability to deliver public services, and will threaten public safety and health. Yet, the ability of states and localities to raise the necessary revenues is constrained by local revenue and debt limitations, by sharp cuts in federal aid, and by high interest rates.

None of these factors is likely to change significantly in the near future. Budget cutting, small tax increases, and creative financing will not yield the resources to bridge the yawning gap between present levels of investment and what is needed to sustain economic growth through the 1980s.

A comprehensive public capital investment strategy is needed for all levels of government. States can build their strategies around eight elements:

1. Developing cost-effective maintenance, replacement, and design standards for public works projects. The

present engineering standards lead to inflated estimates of needs and are insufficient as guides for assigning investment priorities.

2. Reducing public subsidies for private sector investments and the termination of public sector programs and facilities that could be provided by private firms. Scarce public funds must be used to maintain and develop only those projects necessary to fulfill public obligations.

3. Improving planning, budgeting, and management procedures for capital investment. Costly delays, inefficient priorities, and poor management of public facilities inflate costs and accelerate deterioration.

4. Imposing user fees—charges and dedicated tax revenues—to pay for both the construction and operating costs of public facilities. User fees are *not* simply an additional source of revenues and a way to circumvent tax limitations. Efficiently designed user fees are public prices for public goods and services. They will encourage more efficient use of facilities—which will reduce investment needs—and more efficient public investment decisions.

5. Improving bond-financing mechanisms to avoid the proliferation of small issues that increase financing costs. Bond banks, state loans to localities, and state guarantee programs are initiatives that can yield substantial savings.

6. Shifting a larger share of the costs of public facilities associated with large-scale projects onto private developers. For major private projects, state and local governments will have to negotiate the allocation of infrastructure costs with the developers. Also, lease financing and service contracts offer indirect ways of leveraging private sector tax incentives to reduce public sector costs.

7. Negotiating the allocation of capital financing responsibilities among federal, state, and local governments to avoid needless duplication and to ensure that all jurisdictions have adequate resources to make needed investments.

8. Increasing state and local taxes to support increased spending on public works.

None of these steps is easy—either to design or to carry out. Data on the condition of the public capital stock, the cost of repair or replacement, and local priorities are not readily available. There have been few attempts to assess how the changing structure of local economies and rapidly evolving technologies will shape the future demand for public facilities. Yet political leaders can educate the public in the need for new policies only if they can present a coherent and comprehensive public investment strategy.

A durable and effective solution to our deteriorating infrastructure will require initiatives by all levels of government—initiatives undertaken with mutual agreement on the fundamental principles of infrastructure financing. There are four principles that can guide the design of an evolving partnership between federal, state, and local governments.

1. Wherever possible, those who benefit from a particular facility or the services it provides should pay for it. Road users should pay for roads; water users should pay for water; and visitors to a park should pay for the privilege.
2. The capital costs of a facility should be amortized over the expected life of that facility and maintenance costs should not be deferred. This avoids intergenerational transfer of costs.
3. The costs of a facility or program should be paid by the jurisdiction in which the benefits are provided. This reduces the tendency to fund pork-barrel projects. However, some allowance should be made for differences in the fiscal capacities among localities.
4. Where user fees may deny access to a facility or service to the poor, special provisions should be made for low-income households.

These general principles should guide public capital investment policies for all levels of government. In the following sections, the major policy options for state and local

271

governments are briefly discussed. But state and local policies must be developed within the context of federal actions. Many of the factors that have made public infrastructure such an important issue have their roots in federal policies—the poor design of federal grants programs, changes in the tax structure, and mismanagement of the national economy. In the next few years, increased fiscal and economic responsibility for capital investments will devolve onto state governments. This shift is compatible with many of the recommendations discussed in this book. States and localities have the greater potential for obtaining more sound information than federal agencies on what type of capital investments are needed and a much stronger incentive to ensure that investments are wisely made and well managed. But that decentralization must be accompanied by the delegation of necessary powers and the commensurate fiscal resources. For example, the federal government may delegate to states increased responsibility for major transportation programs. But that transfer may be accompanied by other policies to reduce the cost of bond financing and with the delegation of much broader powers to state governments—to impose tolls on sections of the interstate highway or to modify current engineering standards, for example. The National Governors' Association has argued that increased state and local responsibility for "bricks and mortar" programs—projects with relatively local impact—should be balanced by increased federal responsibility for income maintenance and human resource investments, programs that are aimed at national objectives. The final structure of President Reagan's New Federalism initiative is still being negotiated, and the process may take several years to complete. The following section discusses some of the possible changes in federal policies toward infrastructure investment that will shape the way state and local governments develop their own capital investment strategies.

The Federal Context

There are dozens of bills circulating in Congress that would affect the infrastructure issue and the ability of states to finance and manage their public investments.

272

These initiatives can be divided into four types of federal action.

☐ *Subsidies for state and local capital borrowing.* These have been proposed through two mechanisms: (1) low-cost loans from a federal development bank or Reconstruction Finance Corporation or (2) direct interest subsidies of the interest costs of taxable bonds issued by states and localities for public infrastructure projects.

☐ *Decentralization of infrastructure financing and administration.* Proposals include greater reliance on block grants, user fees for inland water transportation, and increased revenues into the Interstate Highway Trust Fund, perhaps accompanied by a flexible arrangement with state governments for administration and financing of the system.

☐ *A countercyclical public works jobs program.* This could either repeat the Local Public Works Program enacted in 1976 that provided 100 percent federal funding to state and local projects or use a direct federal expenditure program based on depression-era models.

☐ *Increased federal planning and managing of public works investments.* Proposals range from a federal capital budget to a reauthorized and expanded Economic Development Administration that would finance state and local planning activities.

Borrowing Subsidies

The purpose of these initiatives is to address the weakening of the tax-exempt bond market, which resulted from tax reforms and changing behavior by institutional investors, and the deteriorating fiscal positions of state and local governments. The two types of recommendations are (1) to provide low-interest-rate loans to state and local governments for major capital investment projects and (2) to subsidize directly the interest costs on taxable infrastructure bonds issued by state and local governments.

Federal Loans. A reauthorized EDA or a Reconstruc-

273

tion Finance Corporation have been proposed to make low-interest-rate loans and/or capital grants to municipalities and states for major capital projects. Under most proposals, the subsidies would be at the discretion of the administering agency and would be negotiated. The federal loans would be financed through the issue of federal debt (which may exacerbate the competition with municipal borrowing in the capital market) and by direct appropriations to provide grants and interest write-downs. It would be, in essence, a very-large-scale Urban Development Action Grant program.

The proposal would allow federal agencies to ensure that local capital spending was targeted at areas of national need and would extend the fiscal capacity of local jurisidictions. But the initiative may be subject to the same problems that have surrounded many similar, if smaller, federal programs in the past. First, it may encourage states and localities to develop projects that would receive federal aid rather than projects that are needed and to "over-design" the projects in order to prove that they could not be paid for out of state and local resources. Second, year-to-year funding would create considerable uncertainty. Third, ensuring a regional allocation of funding would lead to different needs criteria in different areas. Fourth, some projects may be funded for political rather than economic reasons. Finally, the program would be very expensive.

Taxable Bond Option. During the last decade, there were several proposals, both by Congressional committees and by analysts of the municipal bond market, to provide state and local governments with the option of issuing taxable bonds, for which they would receive a direct subsidy equal to 30 or 35 percent of the interest costs from the U.S. Treasury. The proposal was argued for three reasons.

☐ First, there is growing belief that exemption of interest from personal income taxes was unnecessarily expensive. Some research indicates that as much as one-third of the revenues not collected by the U.S. Treasury are essentially subsidies to high-income individuals (Vaughan, 1980). A direct subsidy from the U.S. Treasury could be designed that would be cheaper in terms of revenues lost and would provide a greater borrowing subsidy to state and municipal governments.

☐ Second, a taxable bond would compete in a much broader capital market than a tax-exempt bond and would, therefore, make it easier to market public debt.

☐ Third, the taxable bond market is more stable than the tax-exempt market; therefore, a public taxable bond would offer the public sector the opportunity for more stable long-term financing.

However, several studies have called into question these arguments. Mussa and Kormendi (1979) argue that those that have asserted that the exemption benefits very-high-income households at the expense of low-income households are wrong because at least two-thirds of all tax-exempt bonds are held by institutional investors (pension funds, trust funds, insurance companies, and so forth) whose investments benefit a very broad class of income groups. Mussa and Kormendi also question the efficiency of providing a deeper subsidy for state and municipal borrowing. However, their arguments were made before the Economic Recovery Tax Act of 1981, before the withdrawal of institutional investors from the tax-exempt market, and before the sharp reductions in federal grants for public infrastructure. For these reasons, the proposal is being reconsidered.

The proposal is fairly simple and inexpensive. States and localities would be empowered to issue taxable bonds and would receive an annual cash payment of between 25 and 35 percent of the interest cost from the U.S. Treasury. Since the marginal tax rate of bond purchasers is at least 35 percent, the tax revenues collected by IRS would be about equal to the cost of the subsidy (Koepke and Kimball, 1979). If the long-term taxable bond rate were 13 percent, the post-subsidy cost to a locality would be 8.45 percent, nearly 200 basis points below the 10.4 percent on tax-exempt bonds that has prevailed during the last quarter of 1982.

Three features could distinguish most planned versions of this from past proposals. First, the taxable bond

275

would be an option for state and local governments. It would not replace tax-exempt bonds. Second, the taxable bond option would be made available for only certain types of public investments—including public education and health facilities, roads, water treatment facilities, and ports and terminals. It could explicitly exclude public bonds whose revenues were used to finance private facilities, or facilities with private tenants—including not-for-profit health care institutions, industrial facilities, and pollution control projects for private firms.

Third, the interest subsidies would be an entitlement and not be subject to annual budget appropriations. Placing the subsidy as a line budget item would make it vulnerable to the vagaries of the annual appropriations process, which will create sufficient uncertainty to deter rational long-term planning by state and local governments. The taxable bond option may be offered as an entitlement to states and localities in exchange for increased state assumption of financing responsibilities.

The cost of the program would be borne by high-income households whose 50 percent marginal tax rates make municipal bonds at 10 percent the equivalent of a taxable bond earning 20 percent. The program is less cumbersome than categorical grant programs or a direct federal loan initiative because it would entail no expensive allocation procedure or costly mandates and regulations.

Dencentralization of Infrastructure Responsibilities

Decentralization of both fiscal and administrative responsibilities for infrastructure construction and maintenance seems inevitable. State governments will have to pay a larger share of the costs and undertake more of the planning, management, and administration of the facilities and systems. From the state perspective the important issues are (1) what fiscal responsibilities are assumed by the federal government, (2) what programs are decentralized, and (3) what funding sources accompany the decentralized programs.

The first issue is too broad to be discussed here. The second question is also highly complex because more than

400 federal categorical programs remain on the books, many of which have a capital facilities component. Two of the most important broad federal programs with the greatest impact on infrastructure are water projects and the interstate highway system (including the repair of bridges).

Water projects. Most major water projects concerned with inland freight transportation are 100 percent financed and managed by the Army Corps of Engineers. Many water projects concerned with electricity generation, irrigation, and municipal water supply are undertaken by the Bureau of Reclamation. Studies by the U.S. General Accounting Office have found that some of these projects are not cost-effective. Because no state or local funds are involved, localities have no incentive to identify and undertake only those projects that are economically viable. Senators Moynihan and Domenici have proposed to convert water project funding into a block grant program, which would require a state match for each project funded. This proposal is consistent with the administration's New Federalism and, since it could yield substantial savings to the federal government, may receive more attention in the future. State administration of these funds could be effectively undertaken through a statewide water authority that would issue bonds, backed by user fees, to undertake major projects and to lend money to localities. New York State has already completed feasibility studies and proposed enabling legislation for such an authority. The experience of irrigation districts in many western states also provides useful models.

Decentralization of the Interstate Highway Program. The deteriorating condition of the interstate highway system will be one of the most expensive infrastructure programs during the next decade. The four cents per gallon gasoline tax, unchanged in two decades, is no longer adequate. Inflation in construction costs and the switch to smaller cars has eroded revenues drastically. Replacement, reconstruction, and rehabilitation costs are escalating rapidly. The increase in the tax, enacted in December 1982, was a necessary element in developing an effective solution (CBO, 1982). A long-term solution

277

might also include a decentralization of management and administration of the system that would allow states to set up their own trust funds that would receive federal monies but would be augmented by revenues from state gas taxes, tolls (if the present requirement that tolls be phased out is relaxed), and other dedicated fees and taxes.

Allocations to the state trust funds could be made in a manner similar to the present allocations, with a state match required (which could include toll revenues), but the states would have much greater flexibility over choosing which, among presently eligible projects, to undertake. States that elected this option could choose which incomplete sections to complete, which bridges to repair, and which sections to upgrade, ending the time-consuming and highly political negotiations that currently attend these decisions. All states would be required to set up trust funds by some prescribed date, and all federal highway expenditures would be channeled through these funds. The trust fund structure would allow long-term comprehensive planning at the state level. Washington could define minimum standards to ensure the maintenance of a uniform system. The combination of increased gasoline tax revenues, tolls, and enforced local setting of project priorities could provide for a long-term solution to crumbling roads.

Countercyclical Public Works

The high rate of unemployment—it approached one quarter of all employees in the construction industry in September 1982—has led to a proliferation of legislative proposals to provide federal funds for public works projects. Such a program might be modeled on the Local Public Works Program (LPWP), initiated in 1976, which provided 100 percent federal financing through grants to state and local governments, or modeled on President Roosevelt's Works Progress Administration (WPA), under which the federal government directly hired workers for federally financed projects.

Past experience suggest that neither approach would provide a long-term solution to the infrastructure problem, although they may provide some fiscal relief to state and local government (see Vernez and Vaughan, 1978). The LPWP was beset with many problems (summarized in Vaughan, 1980). Most of the funds were not spent until four years after the 1975 recession, and the average job created lasted only a month. There was little increase in state and local capital spending, since federal funds simply supplanted local spending. In fact, there was a sharp decline in state and local spending, while these governments waited to see which of their project applications would be federally financed. And many of the projects undertaken were paid for because they could be started quickly, not because they were a high local priority. The WPA model may be very difficult to undertake today because public construction requires a labor force versed in skills that few of the unemployed have acquired.

Increased Federal Planning and Management

The mounting concern over the deterioration of public works and the lack of data from which to assess the extent of the problem and to evaluate alternative solutions has led to several proposals to increase the public capital planning and managing activities of the federal government. These include the development of a national capital budget that would divide federal expenditures between operating and capital and would calculate the rate of depreciation of existing capital facilities, federal planning grants to states and localities, and investment strategies negotiated between federal agencies and state and local governments.

The federal government may help develop new techniques for setting user fees and improve other analytic techniques discussed in academic journals but not applied to state and local decision making. The privatization of some public activities will only be possible after some complex research, reform of regulatory procedures, and the establishment of markets for public goods and services where none currently exist. This, too, could be aided by a federal commitment to funding research and demonstration projects.

The dissemination of information may be a function

279

best performed by a federal agency. State and local governments should be able to draw upon data on technological innovations in construction and maintenance practices, on needs assessment techniques, and on evaluations of policy and program innovations carried out by other states and areas.

The State Role

The greatest increase in fiscal and administrative responsibility for public capital investments will fall upon state governments. Not only will states have to change their own practices and levels of effort, but they will have to provide increased assistance—fiscal, technical, regulatory, and administrative—to local units of government. Many of the state functions will be unfamiliar—regulating private water suppliers, entering into leasing arrangements with private firms, or managing hazardous waste disposal sites, for example. All actions will require public education and leadership to secure the passage of enabling legislation or budgetary obligations against the efforts of individual interest groups who have benefited from implicit and explicit subsidies in the past and who will face higher taxes or user fees in the future. It will be necessary to present a comprehensive strategy in which the general principles and all the elements of them are outlined.

Setting the State House In Order

The first step in developing an effective state capital investment strategy is to develop state capital budgets. Increased spending must be based upon much more careful analysis of needs and costs of alternative actions. Capital budgets should include more than a wish list of future projects. They must include a discussion of the underlying values and principles that guide the strategy, an analysis of public and private sector responsibilities, a discussion of the mechanisms that will be used to finance both construction and operating costs, and a careful analysis of the impacts of capital projects on future operating expenditures. Without this long-term framework (discussed in detail in volume 1 of this series, *Planning and Managing*),

Table 30

User Fees for State Infrastructure Programs

Type of Infrastructure	Possible User Fees
Road Systems	— Ad valorem vehicle registration fee — Gasoline taxes — Other transportation-related sales taxes — Bridge and highway tolls (peak load pricing)
Research and Higher Education	— Tuition assistance with "royalty payback" — State match to private R&D grants — Patent policy reform — Tax incentives for corporate donations — Technology user fees
Transit	— Increased fares (especially during peak hours) — Subsidy from gasoline tax — Special district assessments — Para-transit licensing
Water Supply	— Metered water use — Full cost pricing for utility hook-ups — Peak-load pricing
Waste Water Treatment	— Industrial and commercial effluent charges
Waste Disposal	— Full-cost coverage from disposal fees
Ports and Terminals	— Full-cost coverage from fees and charges to users
Recreation	— Peak-load pricing of seasonal facilities — Special assessment district revenues — Tax increment financing

a sound strategy will not be designed nor will consistent principles be followed.

The state must undertake a long-term review of the way it manages its public facilities, including assessing whether the institutional framework (state agency, public authority, special district, and so forth) leads to efficient cost control, what type of analytic techniques are used to establish investment needs, and what revenue sources are

281

available. Public referendums will be required for some actions (tax increases, tax dedication, bonding power for public authorities, and so forth), a process that takes several years.

States can undertake specific policies to address infrastructure needs. These actions will include:

☐ Privatization of existing public facilities and services (accompanied by appropriate changes in regulatory policy).

☐ Reduced use of public bond issue revenues to subsidize private projects.

☐ Closing discretionary tax abatement and exemption programs and using the increased revenues to finance infrastructure programs.

☐ Imposition of user fees for a broad array of state capital investment programs (see table 30).

☐ Increased use of private tax incentives to finance public infrastructure.

☐ Negotiated investment strategies with developers of large-scale projects, especially in small communities.

These changes may involve the loss of discretionary power over the annual budget process and will challenge the states to develop mechanisms to make public authorities and the increasing numbers of private suppliers of facilities and services fully accountable to state agencies. But without these changes, decisions with long-term implications will continue to be made with short-term procedures. And capital projects will be undertaken for reasons of political expediency rather than as sound economic investments.

State Assistance to Localities

In addition to reforming their own planning, budgeting, and financing techniques, state governments will have to work much more closely with localities to develop a coordinated investment strategy. The state can ensure that local financing and management policies do not lead to interjurisdictional pricing competition and that local investment practices are consistent with broad state objectives. The state must increase its expenditures on research and evaluation of public capital investment needs and of alternative financing mechanisms, and share the results with localities. Many of the issues that surround the design of an effective user fee system, the transfer of responsibility to the private sector, or the negotiation of cost-allocation with private developers are complex and are beyond the capacity of local government units.

Some states will also have to amend the taxing powers of local governments to allow appropriate user fee systems and create more flexible local administrative mechanisms to make public investments. But this delegation of responsibility must be accompanied by increased state oversight of local government policies and practices. Procedures must be developed to allow more flexible negotiations between state and local governments to establish investment priorities.

The sharp reduction in federal aid will create special problems for jurisdictions with high concentrations of low-income households and with distressed local economies. States must review their intra-state revenue-sharing programs and sharpen the targeting where possible. Categorical aid programs could also be refocused, with the state share to nondistressed communities cut back and aid to needy areas increased.

State regulatory policy should also be carefully reviewed for its effects on the costs of local public works investments. State labor law, contract-letting procedures, tax policies, permitting procedures, and construction codes can all contribute to inflated costs and unnecessary delays (NCSL, 1982).

Table 31 lists the major initiatives that states can undertake to assist localities in reducing infrastructure financing costs. While these measures will not dramatically reduce debt issuing and servicing costs, programs such as bond banks and low-interest-rate loans can prove very valuable to distressed communities. They can also help create an atmosphere of cooperation between states and their component jurisdictions that will allow for more radical, and sometimes painful, steps to be taken.

Table 31

Possible Actions for State Governments*

Action	Suitable States
Improve technical assistance programs.	All
Create a loan program for water & sewer construction.	All
Create a municipal bond bank.	Rural states with many small issuers
Earmark state aid for debt service.	States with fiscally distressed communities
Assist local governments with creative financing (through technical assistance Programs and enabling legislation).	All
Create loan programs for energy impact assistance.	Energy-rich states
Increase state supervision of local debt management.	States with cities having poor credit ratings or histories of poor financial management.
Guarantee local debt.	Most states

Note: *The most effective measures are listed first.

Source: National Conference of State Legislatures, Watson, 1982.

Benefits	Drawbacks
Facilitate bond issuance and encourage responsible debt management.	Local governments may fear state intrusion.
Stimulate investment in water and sewer facilities, and supplement federal wastewater program. Provide loans at favorable rates, particularly for distressed communities and small or infrequent Issuers.	Increase state general obligation debt and thereby lower state credit rating.
Reduce borrowing costs for small or infrequent Issuers.	Local banks, bond counselors, and underwriters may suffer a loss in business.
Improve rating of bond issues (reduce interest rate) for large, fiscally distressed communities.	Requires a large, permanent state aid program and some state supervision.
Increase local flexibility. Facilitate use of beneficial techniques, and discourage improper use.	Many techniques are untested. May result in excessive short-term debt, or high interest rates in future.
Finances rapid capital construction in energy boom towns. Supplement to grant programs.	Local governments prefer grants or sharing of severance revenues.
Encourage responsible debt management, and Improve credit ratings.	Increased administrative costs for local governments, possible restriction on local actions.
Improve rating on local bonds.	May seriously weaken state credit rating.

285

Conclusion

There is no simple and cheap way to pay for public works. There is no easy way to cut back on existing services and programs, to charge user fees, or to raise taxes. Yet failure to devise a rational and effective way of investing in public works will surely prevent any significant improvement in the national and state economies. We must use this crisis as an opportunity to redefine public investment priorities. A sound fiscal strategy and a clear allocation of responsibility between the public and private sectors are much more powerful development incentives than speculative projects, tax subsidies, and uncertainty over the condition of vital public works. Sustained economic growth will require increases in taxes to pay for the maintenance and development of roads, bridges, ports, water supply and treatment systems, and facilities for the disposal of hazardous waste. States can no longer afford to delay designing a complete capital investment strategy.

Annotated Bibliography

The following annotated bibliography is intended as a brief guide to the overall bibliography. It classifies references under the major topics covered in this book.

For overall statistical data on public investments the most useful sources are the *Survey of Government Finances*, annually; various articles in the *Survey of Current Business* (monthly, published by the Bureau of Economic Analysis); the Office of Management and Budget; and various reports by the Bureau of Economic Analysis. There are also reports published by various interest groups including the American Public Works Association, Federal Highway Users Association, American Public Transit Association, and Association of Metropolitan Sewage Agencies.

The best single source on public capital finance issues is the Municipal Finance Officers' Association, which has an extensive set of publications. The National Conference of State Legislatures, the Council of State Planning Agencies, and the Urban Institute also have extensive sets of publications and reports.

Bond Banks:
Forbes and Renshaw, 1972; Jarrett and Hicks, 1977; Katzman, June 1980 and March 1980; Solano and Hoffman, 1982.

Bonds: *(see also Bond Banks, Credit Ratings, Debt, Housing Bonds, Industrial Development Bonds, Taxable Bonds)*
For an overview of municipal bonds and definitions and descriptions of the bond market see ACIR, 1976; Amdursky, 1981; Lamb and Rappaport, 1980; Peterson, J., 1976; Public Securities Association, 1981. See also Durst, 1981; Fischer et al., 1980; Klapper, 1980; Robinson, 1981; and White, 1979. Basic data on bonds and bond markets is reported in the *Daily Bond Buyer* and in *Moody's Bond Survey* (weekly) and is summarized in the annual reports of the Public Securities Association.

For an analysis of the behavior of the bond market, including the effects of federal tax changes, see Browne and Syron, 1979; Forbes and Peterson, 1975; Hendershott and Koch, 1977; Her-

287

ships and Karvelis, 1981; Kaufman, 1981; Kimball, 1977a; Kopcke and Kimball, 1979; Mumy, 1978; Peterson, J., 1982; Twentieth Century Fund, 1976; Viscount, 1982; and U.S. Congress, Joint Economic Committee, 1981.

Insurance: Miralia, 1980.

Marketing: MFOA, 1976.

New Jersey Qualified Bond Program: Jones, 1978; Peterson and Miller, 1981.

Small Denominations: Lehan, 1980.

Underwriting: Cagan, 1978; Silber, 1980.

Boom Towns: *(see also Energy Development)*
Brookshire and D'Arge, 1980; Gilmore and Duff, 1975; O'Hare, 1977; O'Hare and Sanderson, 1978; U.S. Department of Defense, Office of Economic Adjustment, 1981a and 1981b.

Capital Budgeting: *(see also Debt, Management and Planning)*
For a discussion of the process and benefits of capital budgeting, see Choate and Walter, 1981; Devoy and Wise, 1979; Douglas, 1977; Fujardo, 1976; Howard, 1973; Matson, 1976; U.S. GAO, 1982, 1981, and 1980; Wacht, 1980; and White, 1978. For examples of state initiatives, see Alexander, 1980; American Public Works Association, 1979; Maryland, 1980; and Rumowicz, 1980.

Condition of Public Works: *(see also Financing Public Investment)*
For a brief account of the problem, see Choate and Walter, 1981, and *Newsweek* 8/2/82. For more detailed discussions of the extent of the problem, see Abt Associates, 1980; CONSAD, 1980; Dossani and Steger, 1980; U.S. Department of Commerce, 1980. The study of the capital stock in 12 cities conducted by the Urban Institute is exhaustive: see Grossman, 1979; Humphrey and Wilson, 1980; Humphrey et al., 1979; Peterson and Miller, 1981; Wilson, 1980. See also American Public Works Association, 1981 and 1976; Beals, 1981; Buckley, 1982; Choate, 1982; Finck and Pike, 1981; Hatry, 1980; Lindsay, 1979; and MacDonald, ed., 1982.

Countercyclical Public Works:
See CBO, 1978; Kaus, 1982; Vaughan, 1980a, 1980b, and 1976; and Vernez and Vaughan, 1978.

Credit Rating: *(see also Bonds, Debt, Fiscal Capacity)*
The most comprehensive guides are Ingram and Copeland, 1982; Peterson, J., 1974; Smith, 1979. See also American

Bankers Association, 1968; Aronson and Marsden, 1980; Boyett and Giroux, 1978; Osteryoung, 1978; Reilly, 1967.

Debt: *(see also Bonds, Credit Ratings, Fiscal Capacity)*
ACIR, 1976; Gold, 1981; Irwin, 1979.
Danger Signals: Aronson, 1976.
Limitations: ACIR, 1980; Baer, 1981.
Management: Brown et al., 1978; Moak, 1970; Peterson, J., 1979a, 1978; Small Cities Financial Management Project, 1978; Steiss, 1975. State Assistance to Localities: Alaska Legislative Affairs Agency, 1967; Forbes and Peterson, 1978; Glaser, 1978; Peterson, 1977 (see also Bond Banks).

Energy Development: *(see also Boom Towns)*
Foster, 1977; Kolb, 1982; Leistritz and Murdock, 1981; Lu, 1977; Monaco, 1977; Rocha, 1982; Sanderson, 1977; Schnell and Krannich, 1977; Susskind and O'Hare, 1977; and West, 1977.

Federal Government: *(see also Bonds, Intergovernmental Relations)*
Grants: Executive Office of the President, 1980 and 1978; National Governors' Association, 1977 (see also Intergovernmental Relations).
And Local Fiscal Conditions: Herships and Karvelis, 1981 (see also Fiscal Capacity).
Impact on Infrastructure: Gramlich and Galper, 1973; Hatry, 1980.

Financing Public Investment: *(see also Capital Budgeting, Condition of Public Works, Lease Financing, User Fees)*
For summaries of policy alternatives, see Pagano and Moore, 1980; Peterson, n.d.; Peterson and Miller, 1981; Stanfield, 1980; Watson, 1982. For bibliography, see Buss, 1981. See also Buckley, 1982; Getzels and Thurow, 1980; McWatters, 1979; Saffran, 1979; Shaul, 1981; Wolman and Reigeluth, 1980.

Fiscal Capacity: *(see also Bonds, Debt, Intergovernmental Relations)*
ACIR, 1971; Crinder, 1978; Herships and Karvelis, 1981; Howell and Stamm, 1979; Hubbell, 1979; Matz, 1980; Rothschild, Unterberg, Towbin, 1982; U.S. Joint Economic Committee, 1981; and Wolman and Davis, 1981.

Highways: *(see also User Fees)*
For a discussion of financing, see Congressional Budget Office, 1982; Langton, 1981; "Forty States Eye Motor Fuel Tax Boost," 1981.

Housing Bonds: *(see also Bonds)*
Bates and Wolfson, 1981; Harrington, 1979; Levatino-Donoghue, 1979; National Conference of State Legislatures, 1980; Peterson, G., 1979; Worsham, 1980.

Industrial Development Bonds:
Edmonds and Hoyd, 1981.

Intergovernmental Relations:
For an overview, see ACIR, 1980, 1979, and 1978. See also CBO, 1978, and Zimmerman, 1976.

Lease Financing: *(see also Financing Public Investment)*
Barnes, 1981; Dyl and Joehnk, 1978; Lubick and Galper, 1982; Mentz et al., 1980; Schellenbach and Weber, 1978; Shubnell and Cobb, 1982.

Management and Planning: *(see also Capital Budgeting)*
Amara, 1979; American Society of Planning Officials, 1977; Bologna, 1980; Corr, 1980; Donnelly, 1980; Hall, 1979; Hatry, 1980; Higgins, 1978; Holloway and King, 1977; International City Managers Association, 1981; Korbitz, 1976; Kunde and Berry, 1982; Naylor, 1979; Naylor and Neva, 1980 and 1979; Schmidt, 1979; Schneider and Swinton, 1979; Sheeran, 1976; Shepard and Goddard, n.d.; and Steiss, 1975.

Public Authorities:
Beyer, 1972; Edelman, 1976; Holland, 1972; and, for the most detailed analysis, Walsh, 1976.

Special Assessment:
Shoup, 1980.

Taxable Bond Option:
Kimball, 1978; Kopcke and Kimball, 1979; Mussa and Kormendi, 1979.

Taxes:
And Economic Development: Kieschnick, 1981, and Vaughan, 1979.
Of Mineral Resources: Zeller, 1982.
Limitations on Revenues: Bacon, 1981; Baer, 1981; Benson, 1980; McWatters, 1979; Pascal, 1980; Saffran, 1979.

User Fees:
The best overview of the principles and applications of user fees is in Mushkin, 1972. See also ACIR, 1974; Buss, 1981; Downing, 1980; Feldstein, 1972; Galambos and Schreiber, 1978; Gold, 1979; Mick, 1981; Mushkin, 1979 and 1977; Mushkin and Vehorn, 1977; Stanfield, 1980.

Airports: Feldman, 1967, Littlefield and Thompsen, 1977.
Health: Badgley and Smith, 1979, Berki in Mushkin, ed., 1977.
Highways: Abouchar, 1974; Feuer, 1978; Henion and Ford, 1981; Higgins, 1979; Langton, 1981; Smith, 1980.
Recreation: Artz and Bermond, 1970; Economics Research Associates, 1979.
Residential Infrastructure: Bacon, 1981.
Transit: Institute for Public Administration, 1980.
Waste Disposal: Albert, Hansen, and Wilkinson, 1972; Dales, 1970; DeLucia, 1974; Hanke and Wentworth, 1981.
Water: Angelides and Bardach, 1978; Barry, 1976; Carey, 1976; Grover, 1980; Hanke, 1981 and 1976; Hoggan, 1977; Keller, 1977.

Water: *(see User Fees)*
Grossman, 1979b; Keller, 1977; Kish, 1980; Lake, 1979.

Bibliography

Abt Associates, Inc., *National Rural Community Facilities Assessment Study*, Boston, MA, 1980.

Abouchar, Alan, "A New Approach to the Evaluation and Construction of Highway User Charges," *Eastern Economic Journal*, 1974, pp. 34–38.

Adams, Charles F., Jr., and Dan L. Crippen, "The Fiscal Impact of General Revenue Sharing on Local Governments," unpublished report prepared for the Office of Revenue Sharing, U.S. Department of the Treasury, November, 1978.

Advisory Commission on Intergovernmental Relations, *Significant Features of Fiscal Federalism, 1979–80 Edition*, Washington, DC: GPO, 1980.

_____, *Restructuring Federal Assistance: The Consolidation Approach*, Bulletin No. 79–6, October, 1979.

_____, *The Intergovernmental Grant System: An Assessment and Proposed Policies*, (B-1), September, 1978.

_____, *State Mandating of Local Expenditures*, (A-67), July, 1978.

_____, *A Catalog of Federal Grant-in-Aid Programs to State and Local Governments: Grants Funded FY 1975*, (A-52a), October, 1977.

_____, *Categorical Grants: Their Role and Design*, (A-52), May, 1977.

_____, *Improving Federal Grants Management*, (A-53), February, 1977.

_____, *The Intergovernmental Grant System as Seen by Local, State and Federal Officials*, (A-54), March, 1977.

_____, *Community Development: The Workings of a Federal-Local Block Grant*, (A-57), March, 1977.

_____, *The States and Intergovernmental Aids*, (A-59), February, 1977.

293

————, *Federal Grants: Their Effects on State-Local Expenditures, Employment Levels, and Wage Rates*, (A-61), February, 1977.

————, *Pragmatic Federalism: The Reassignment of Functional Responsibility*, (A-49), July, 1976.

————, *Local Revenue Diversification: Income Sales Taxes and User Charges*, (A-47), June, 1974.

————, *Multistate Regionalism*, (A-39), April, 1972.

————, *Measuring the Fiscal Capacity and Effort of State and Local Areas*, (M-58), March, 1971.

Alaska, Legislative Affairs Agency, *State Assistance to Local Governments on Bonding Problems*, Juneau, AL: Legislative Council, Legislative Affairs Agency, January, 1967.

————, Legislative Budget and Audit Committee, *Alaska's Public Corporations: A Framework for Assessment*, prepared by the Institute for Public Administration, New York, January, 1982.

Aldrich, Mark, *A History of Public Works in the United States, 1790–1970*, Washington, DC: U.S. Department of Commerce, 1979.

Alexander, Governor Lamar, *The Five Year Capital Budget for the State of Tennessee. 1980–81, 1984–85*, Nashville: The Government of the State of Tennessee, January, 1980.

Amara, Ray, "Strategic Planning in a Changing Corporate Environment," *Long-Range Planning*, Vol. 12, February, 1979, pp. 2–16.

Amdursky, Robert S., *Municipal Bond Law: Basics and Recent Developments: A Course Handbook*, New York: New York Practicing Law Institute, 1981.

American Bankers Association, Bank Management Committee, *A Guide for Developing Municipal Bond Credit Files*, New York, 1968.

American Enterprise Institute, *Waterway User Charges*, Washington, DC, 1977.

American Public Works Association, *Revenue Shortfall: The Public Works Challenge of the 1980s*, Chicago, 1981.

————, *Administration of State Capital Improvement Programs: Nine Selected Profiles*, Chicago, 1979.

————, *A History of Public Works in the United States*, Chicago, 1976.

American Society of Planning Officials, *Local Capital Improvements and Development Management: Literature Synthesis*, Washington, DC: GPO, July, 1977, prepared for the U.S. Department of Housing and Urban Development and the National Science Foundation.

Angelides, Sotirios, and Eugene Bardach, *Water Banking: How to Stop Wasting Agricultural Water*, San Francisco: Institute for Contemporary Studies, 1978.

Aronson, J. Richard, *Determining Debt's Danger Signals*, International City Management Association, Management Information Service, Vol. 8, no. 2, December, 1976.

Aronson, J. Richard, and James R. Marsden, "Duplicating Moody's Municipal Credit Rating," *Public Finance Quarterly*, Vol. 8, no. 1, January, 1980, pp. 97–106.

Aronson, J. Richard, and Eli Schwartz, *Management Policies in Local Government Finance*, Washington, DC: International City Managers Association, 1975.

Artz, Robert M., and Hubert Bermond, "The Fee" in *Guide to New Approaches to Financing Parks and Recreation*, New York: Acropolis, 1970.

Association of the Bar of the City of New York, Committee on Municipal Affairs, *Local Finance Project: Proposals to Strengthen Local Finance Law in New York State*, New York, November, 1978.

Bacon, Kevin, "Paying for Public Facilities after Proposition Thirteen," *Western City*, August, 1981, pp. 8–11.

Badgley, Robin F., and R. David Smith, *User Charges for Health Services*, Toronto: Ontario Council of Health, 1979.

Baer, Jon A., "Municipal Debt and Tax Limits: Constraint on Home Rule," *National Civic Review*, Vol. 70, no. 4, April, 1980, pp. 204–10.

Barnes, Garry, "Going Into Lease Financing," *The Bankers Magazine*, Vol. 164, no. 4, July/August, 1981, pp. 9–14.

Barr, James L., "Rational Water Pricing in the Tucson Basin," *Arizona Review*, Vol. 25, October, 1976.

Bates, John C., and Barry M. Wolfson, "New Mortgage Bond Arbitrage Restrictions: The Problems and Potential Solutions," *Weekly Bond Buyer*, September, 1981, pp. 5, 45.

Beals, Alan, *Cities: Infrastructure Problems and Needs*, Washington, DC: National League of Cities, September 10, 1981.

Benson, Earl D., "Municipal Bond Interest Cost, Issue, Purpose and Proposition 13," *Governmental Finance*, September, 1980, pp. 15–19.

Beyer, Stuart, *Statewide Public Authorities in New York: The Question of Control*, Ph.D. Thesis, State University of New York at Albany, University Microfilms, NY, 1972. (Ann Arbor, MI).

Bologna, Jack, "Why Managers Resist Planning," *Managerial Planning*, January/February 1980, pp. 51–56.

Boyett, Arthur S., and Gary A. Giroux, "The Relevance of Municipal Financial Reporting to Municipal Security Decisions," *Governmental Finance*, May, 1978, pp. 29–34.

Braun, J. Peter, et al., "Dollars for Debt: A Case for Planned Debt Management," *New Jersey Municipalities*, November, 1978, pp. 1–7.

Brody, Susan E., *Federal Aid to Energy Impacted Communities: A Review of Related Programs and Legislative Proposals*, Cambridge, MA: Lab of Architecture and Planning, MIT, 1977.

Brookshire, David S., and Ralph C. D'Arge, "Adjustment Issues of Impacted Communities or, Are Boomtowns Bad?" *Natural Resources Journal*, Vol. 20, July, 1980.

Browne, Lynn E., and Richard F. Syron, "The Municipal Market Since the New York City Crisis," *New England Economic Review*, July, 1979, pp. 11–26.

Buckley, Michael Patrick, "Assessing the Issues and Trends in Public Utilities Financing: Planning and Policy Considerations for State and Local Governments in Oregon," master's thesis, University of Oregon, Salem, 1982.

Burchell, Robert W., and David Listokin, *Cities Under Stress*, New Brunswick, NJ: Rutgers University, Center for Policy Research, 1981.

Burr, Eugene, *Preparation of a Capital Improvement Program*, MTAS Technical Report, Knoxville: Municipal Technical Advisory Service, Institute for Public Service, University of Tennessee Municipal League, November, 1975.

Buss, Terry F., *Innovative Financial Mechanisms for Urban Economic Development: A Bibliography*, Public Administration Series, Monticello, IL: Vance Bibliographies, May, 1981. Bibliography P-732, p. 14.

_____, *Public/Private Partnerships for Urban Economic Development: A Bibliography*, Public Administration Series, Monticello, IL: Vance Bibliographies, May, 1981. Bibliography P-731.

Cagan, Phillip, "The Interest Savings to States and Municipalities from Bank Eligibility to Underwrite All Nonindustrial Municipal Bonds," *Government Finance*, May, 1978, pp. 40–48.

Carey, D.I., "Conservation Water Pricing for Increased Water Supply Benefits," *Water Resources Bulletin*, Vol. 12, December, 1976, pp. 111–123.

Centaur Associates, Inc., *Economic Development Administration Title 1 Public Works Programs Evaluation*, Washington, DC, May, 1979.

Choate, Pat, "Special Report on U.S. Economic Infrastructure," unpublished paper, The House Wednesday Group, May 18, 1982.

_____, *As Time Goes By: The Costs and Consequences of Delay*, Columbus, OH: The Academy of Contemporary Problems, 1980.

_____, "Urban Revitalization and Industrial Policy: The Next Steps," testimony before the Subcommittee on the City, Committee on Banking, Finance, and Urban Affairs, U.S. House of Representatives, hearings on Urban Revitalization and Industrial Policy, Washington, DC, September 7, 1980.

Choate, Pat, and Susan Walter, *America in Ruins: Beyond the Public Works Pork Barrel*, Washington, DC: Council of State Planning Agencies, 1981.

Citizen's Budget Commission, Inc., *A Plan to Expedite the Rebuilding of New York City's Infrastructure*, New York, 1979.

Clyde, Larry F., "Statement before the Senate Committee on Finance," U.S. Senate, Washington, DC, 1982.

Coltman, Edward, and Shelley Metzenbaum, *Investing in Ourselves: Strategies for Massachusetts: A Report to the Task Force on Public Pension Investments of the Massachusetts Social and Economic Opportunity Council*, Conference on Alternative State and Local Policies, Washington, DC, 1979.

297

Congressional Budget Office, *The Interstate Highway System: Issues and Options*, Washington, DC: GPO, June, 1982.

_____, *Countercyclical Uses of Federal Grant Programs*, Washington, DC: GPO, November, 1978.

Congressional Research Service of the Library of Congress, *Review of Title V Commission Plans*, Washington, DC: GPO, 1977.

CONSAD Research Corporation, *A Study of Public Works Investment in the United States*, Washington, DC: GPO, 1980. In volumes.
Vol. 1 *Historical Analysis of PWI Trends and Financing Mechanisms.*
Vol. 2 *Analysis of Maintenance, Condition and Financing of Urban Capital Stock.*
Vol. 3 *Effects of Federal Capital Grants on the State-Local Functions: Water Systems, Sewer Systems, Streets and Highways, Bridges and Mass Transit.*

Corr, Arthur, "Capital Investment Planning," *Financial Planning*, August, 1980, pp. 12–15.

Council for Urban Development, *Coordinated Urban Economic Development*, Washington, DC, 1978.

Council of State Community Affairs Agencies, *State Financial Management Resource Guide*, Washington, DC, 1980.

Crinder, Robert A., *The Impact of Inflation on State and Local Government*, Urban and Regional Development Series, no. 5, Columbus, OH: Academy for Contemporary Problems, 1978.

Daily Bond Buyer, New York: Daily Bond Buyer, issued weekdays.

Dales, J.H., *Pollution, Property and Prices*, Toronto: University of Toronto Press, 1970.

Daniels, Belden, and Nancy Barbe, *New England Innovation: Paradigm for Reindustrialization*, Cambridge, MA: Counsel for Community Development, Inc., February 9, 1981.

Darst, David M., *The Handbook of the Bond and Money Markets*, 2d edition, New York: McGraw-Hill, 1981.

DeLucia, R.J., *An Evaluation of Marketable Effluent Permit Systems: Final Report*, Washington, DC: U.S. Environmental Protection Agency, GPO, 1974.

Denver Regional Council of Governments, *Capital Improve-*

ments Programming for Local Governments, Denver, 1975.

Devoy, Robert, and Harold Wise, *The Capital Budget*, Washington, DC: Council of State Planning Agencies, 1979.

Donnelly, Robert M., "Strategic Planning For Better Management," *Managerial Planning*, November/December, 1980, pp. 3–6, 41.

Dossani, Nazir, and Wilbur Steger, "Trends in U.S. Public Works Investment: Report on a New Study," *National Tax Journal*, Vol. 33, no. 2, June, 1980, pp. 97–110.

Douglas, Scott, "Determinants of Capital Budgets," paper presented at the 1977 national meeting of the American Society for Public Administration, Atlanta.

Downing, Paul B., *User Charges and Service Fees*, Tallahassee: Florida State University Press, 1980.

Dyl, Edward A., and Michael D. Joehnk, "Leasing As a Municipal Finance Alternative," *Public Administration Review*, November/December, 1978, pp. 557–62.

Economic Development Administration of the U.S. Department of Commerce, *An Updated Evaluation of the EDA-Funded Industrial Parks—1968–74*, Washington, DC: GPO, 1974.

Economics Research Associates, *Impacts of Fees and Changes on Urban Recreation and Cultural Opportunities*, San Francisco, 1979.

Edelman, Seth, *The Career of the New York State Public Authority*, Albany, NY: State University of New York at Albany, 1976.

Edmonds, Charles P., and William P. Hoyd, "Industrial Development Bond Financing," *Financial Executive*, April, 1981.

Executive Office of the President, *Small Community and Rural Development Policy*, Washington, DC: GPO, December 20, 1979.

_____, Office of Management and Budget, *Managing Federal Assistance in the 1980s*, Washington, DC: GPO, March, 1980.

_____, Office of Management and Budget, *Special Analyses, Budget of the United States Government—Fiscal Year 1980*, Washington, DC: GPO.

_____, Office of Management and Budget, *Public Works as Countercyclical Assistance*, Washington, DC: GPO, November, 1979.

299

————, Office of Management and Budget, *Reorganization Study of Local Development Assistance Programs*, Washington, DC: GPO, December, 1978.

Feldman, Paul, "On the Optimal Use of Airports in Washington, D.C." *Socio-Economic Planning Science*, Vol. 1, 1967, pp. 21–39.

Feldstein, Martin, "Distributional Equity and the Optional Structure of Public Prices," *American Economic Review*, March, 1972, pp. 231–247.

Feuer, Albert, "Motor Fuel Tax Alternatives," *State Government*, 1978, pp. 11–17.

Finck, John A., and Howard Pike, *Infrastructure Rehabilitation: Where Do We Go from Here?* Albany, NY: New York State Department of Environmental Conservation, October 28, 1981.

Fischer, Philip J., et al., "Risk and Return in the Choice of Revenue Bond Financing," *Governmental Finance*, September, 1980, pp. 9–13.

Forbes, Ronald W., and John E. Peterson, *State Credit Assistance to Local Governments*, Boston: First Boston Corporation, 1978.

————, *Cost of Credit Erosion in the Municipal Bond Market*, Chicago: Municipal Finance Officers Association, December, 1975.

Forbes, Ronald W., and Edward F. Renshaw, *State Bond Banks: Review of Present Developments and Needs for Bond Banks*, Chicago: Municipal Finance Officers Association, 1972.

Forty States Eye Motor Fuel Tax Boost, Washington, DC: Highway Users Federation, January, 1981.

Foster, Robert, *State Responses to the Adverse Impacts of Energy Development in Wyoming*, Report published by Laboratory of Architecture and Planning, MIT, Cambridge, MA, 1977.

Fujardo, Richard P., *Capital Budgeting: Guidelines and Procedures*, Research Reports in Public Policy, no. 9, Santa Barbara: Urban Economics Program, University of California at Santa Barbara, July, 1976.

Galambos, Eva, and Arthur Schreiber, "Pricing for Local Government: User Charges in Place of Taxes" in *Making Sense*

Out of Dallas, Washington, DC: National League of Cities, 1978.

Getzels, Judith, and Charles Thurow, *Local Capital Improvements and Development Management: Analyses and Case Studies,* Chicago: American Planning Association, June, 1980.

Gilmore, John S., and Mary K. Duff, *Boom Town Growth Management: A Case Study of Rock Springs–Green River, Wyoming,* Boulder: Westview Press, 1975.

Glaser, Sidney, "New Jersey's Limits on State and Local Spending: A Model for the Nation," *New Jersey Municipalities,* November, 1978.

Gold, Steven D., *How Restrictive Have Limitations on State Taxing and Spending Been?* Legislative Finance Paper no. 13, Denver: National Conference of State Legislatures, January, 1982.

_____, *Trends in the Magnitude and Character of State Debt,* Denver: National Conference of State Legislatures, 1981.

_____, *Property Tax Relief,* Lexington, MA: Lexington Books, D.C. Heath, 1979.

Gramlich, Edward M., and Harvey Galper, "State and Local Fiscal Behavior and Federal Grant Policy" in *Brookings Paper on Economic Activity, no. 1,* 1973.

Grossman, David A., *The Future of New York City's Capital Plan,* Washington, DC: The Urban Institute, 1979a.

_____, *Water Resources Priorities for the Northeast,* Washington, DC: The Consortium of Northeast Organizations, September, 1979b.

Grover, Kathryn, "Wholesale Water Pricing: A Cost-to-Serve Plan That Works," *American City and County,* Washington, D.C., November, 1980.

Hall, William K., "Changing Perspectives on the Capital Investment Process," *Long-Range Planning,* Vol. 12, February, 1979, pp. 37–40.

Hanke, S.H., "On the Current Crisis in Urban Water Supply," unpublished paper, Washington, DC: President's Council of Economic Advisors, 1981.

_____, *Options for Financing Water Development Projects,* Baltimore: Johns Hopkins University Press, 1976.

301

Hanke, S.H., and R.W. Wentworth, "On the Marginal Cost of Wastewater Services," *Land Economics,* November, 1981, pp. 196–210.

Harrington, John, *Packaging Housing Mortgage Loans: Strategies for California,* Washington, DC: Conference on Alternative State and Local Policies, 1979.

Hatry, Harry P., *Local Government Capital Infrastructure Planning: Current State-of-the-Art and State-of-Practice,* Washington, DC: The Urban Institute, 1980.

_____, *Maintaining the Existing Infrastructure,* Washington, DC: The Urban Institute, August 28, 1980.

Hendershott, Patric H., and Timothy W. Koch, *An Empirical Analysis of the Market for Tax-Exempt Securities,* New York: New York University, Graduate School of Business Administration, Center for the Study of Financial Institutions, 1977.

Henion, Lloyd, and Mark Ford, "Financing Highway Maintenance," *Journal of Contemporary Studies,* Vol. 4, no. 2, Spring, 1981, pp. 38–47.

Herships, David, and Leon Karvelis, *Effects of the Reagan Administration's Economic Recovery Plan on the Credit Standing of State and Local Governments,* New York: Merrill Lynch, Pierce, Fenner and Smith, Inc., December, 1981.

Higgins, James M., "Strategic Decision Making: An Organizational Behavioral Perspective," *Managerial Planning,* March/April, 1978, pp. 9–13.

Higgins, Tom, "Road Pricing: Should and Might It Happen?" *Transportation,* Vol. 8, June, 1979, pp. 1–17

Hoggan, D.H., *A Study of Feasibility of State Water Use Fees for Financing Water Development,* Logan, UT: College of Engineering, Utah State University, 1977.

Holland, Stuart, *The State as Entrepreneur,* London: Weidenfeld and Nicholson, 1972.

Holloway, Clark, and William King, "Evaluating Alternative Approaches to Strategic Planning," *Long-Range Planning,* Vol. 12, August, 1977, pp. 74–78.

Howard, Kenneth S., *Changing State Budgeting,* Lexington, KY: Council of State Governments, 1973.

Howell, James M., and Charles F. Stamm, *Urban Fiscal Stress:*

A Comparative Analysis of 66 U.S. Cities, Lexington, MA: Lexington Books, D.C. Heath, 1979.

Hoyle, Robert S., "Capital Budgeting Models and Planning: An Evolutionary Process," *Managerial Planning,* November/December, 1978, pp. 78–89.

Hubbell, Kenneth L., editor, *Fiscal Crisis in American Cities: The Federal Response,* Cambridge, MA: Ballinger Publishing Company, 1979.

Humphrey, Nancy, George E. Peterson and Peter Wilson, *The Future of Cincinnati Capital Plant, America's Urban Capital Stock Series, vol. 3,* Washington, DC: The Urban Institute, 1979.

Humphrey, Nancy, and Peter Wilson, "Capital Stock Condition in Twenty-Eight Cities," Washington, DC: The Urban Institute, unpublished, February, 1980.

Illinois Bond Watcher, Springfield, IL: Illinois Economic and Fiscal Commission, July, 1981.

Illinois General Assembly, Joint Committee on Long-Term Debt, *Report,* Springfield, IL, January 10, 1079.

Ingram, Robert, and Ron Copeland, "State Mandated Accounting, Auditing and Finance Practices and Municipal Bond Ratings," *Public Budgeting and Finance,* Spring, 1982, pp. 21–33.

Institute of Public Administration, *Financing Transit: Alternatives for Local Government: Executive Summary,* Washington, DC: GPO, 1980.

Irwin, David T., "Debt Management for State Government," *State Government,* 1979, pp. 9–17.

Jarrett, James E., and Jimmy E. Hicks, *The Bond Bank Innovation: Maine's Experience,* Lexington, KY: Council of State Governments, February, 1977.

Jones, Benjamin, *Restoring Municipal Credit: The New Jersey Qualified Loan Bond Program,* Lexington, KY: Council of State Governments, June, 1978.

Katzman, Martin T., "Measuring the Savings From Municipal Bond Banking," *Governmental Finance,* March, 1980, pp. 19–25.

———, "Municipal Bond Banking: The Diffusion of a Public Finance Innovation," *National Tax Journal,* Vol. 33, no. 2, June, 1980, pp. 149–60.

303

Kaufman, Henry, *The Crowding of the Municipal Bond Market,* Salomon Brothers, New York City, August, 1981.

Kaus, Robert, "Jobs for Everyone," *Harpers,* October, 1982, pp. 11–17.

Kaynor, Edward R., "Uncertainty in Water Resources Planning in the Connecticut River Basin," *Journal of the American Water Resources Association,* December, 1978.

Keller, Charles W., "Pricing of Water," *Journal of the American Water Works Association,* Vol. 69, January, 1977, pp. 92–103.

Kidwell, David S., and Patric H. Hendershott, "The Impact of Advanced Refunding Bond Issues on State and Local Borrowing Costs," *National Tax Journal,* Vol. 3, no. 1, March 1978, pp. 93–100.

Kieschnick, Michael, *Taxes and Growth,* Washington, DC: Council of State Planning Agencies, 1981.

Kimball, Ralph C., "The Effect of a Taxable Bond Option on Borrowing Costs of State and Local Governments in the Northeast," *New England Economic Review,* March, 1978, pp. 21–31.

————, "Commercial Banks, Tax Avoidance, and the Market for State and Local Debt Since 1970," *New England Economic Review,* January/February, 1977a, pp. 21–32.

————, *Commercial Bank Demand and Municipal Bond Yields,* Boston: Federal Reserve Bank of Boston, 1977b.

Kish, T., "A Look at Self-Supporting Utilities," *Water Pollution Control Federation Journal,* Vol. 52, no. 11, November, 1980.

Klapper, Byron, "Municipal Commercial Paper," *Government Finance,* September, 1980, pp. 10–15.

Kolb, Klaus J., "Economic Development in Alaska: Responsibilities for Providing Infrastructure," unpublished paper, Kennedy School of Government, Harvard University, May, 1982.

Kopcke, Richard, and Ralph C. Kimball, "Investment Incentives for State and Local Governments," *New England Economic Review,* January/February, 1979, pp. 20–40.

Korbitz, William E., editor, *Urban Public Works Administration,* Washington, DC: International City Management Association, 1976.

Kunde, James E., and Daniel E. Berry, "Restructuring Local Economies through Negotiated Investment Strategies," forthcoming *Policy Studies Journal* symposium on "Public Policy for Communities in Economic Crisis."

Lake, Elizabeth R., et al., *Who Pays for Clean Water?: The Distribution of Water Pollution Control Costs,* Boulder: Westview Press, 1979.

Lamb, Robert B., and Stephen P. Rappaport, *Municipal Bonds: A Comprehensive Review of Tax-Exempt Securities and Public Finance,* New York: McGraw-Hill, 1980.

Langton, John, *Toll Road Financing: Description and Policy Implications,* Washington, DC: Association of American Railroads, 1981.

Lehan, Edward Anthony, "The Cast for Directly Marketed Small Denomination Bonds," *Governmental Finance,* Vol. 5, no. 9, September, 1980, pp. 3–7.

Leistritz, Larry F., and Steven H. Murdock, *The Socioeconomic Impact of Resource Development: Methods for Assessment,* Boulder: Westview Press, 1981.

Levatino-Donoghue, Adrienne, "Local Bonds for Housing," *Journal of Housing,* Vol. 36, no. 6, June, 1979, pp. 306–9.

Levine, Charles H., and Ira Rubin, editors, *Fiscal Stress and Public Policy,* Sage Publications, Beverly Hills: 1980.

Lindsay, Robert, editor, *The Nation's Capital Needs: Three Studies,* New York: New York Committee on Economic Development, 1979.

Littlefield, S.C., and G.F. Thomsen, "Aircraft Landing Fees: A Game Theory Approach," *The Bell Journal of Economics,* Vol. 8, 1977, pp. 201–232.

Litvak, Lawrence, and Belden Daniels, *Innovations in Development Finance,* Washington, DC: Council of State Planning Agencies, 1979.

Lu, Catherine, *State Responses to the Adverse Impacts of Energy Development in North Dakota,* Cambridge, MA: Laboratory of Architecture and Planning, MIT, 1977.

Lubick, Donald C., and Harvey Galper, "The Defects of Safe Harbor Leasing and What to do about Them," *Tax Notes,* March 15, 1982.

MacDonald, Keith, editor, *Northeast Urban Infrastructures: A*

305

Reader, Boston: Coalition of Northeast Municipalities, 1982.

McWatters, Ann Robertson, *Financing Capital Formation for Local Governments*, Research Report, 79-3. Berkeley: University of California, March, 1979, Institute of Governmental Studies.

Management Policies in Local Government Finance, Washington, DC: International City Management Association, 1981.

Maryland, Capital Debt Affordability Committee, *Report on Recommended Debt Authorization for Fiscal Year 1983, Submitted to the Governor and the General Assembly of Maryland*, Annapolis, August 1, 1981.

Matson, Morris C., "Capital Budgeting: Fiscal and Physical Planning," *Governmental Finance*, August, 1976, pp. 42–50, 58.

Matz, Deborah, *Trends in the Fiscal Condition of Cities: 1978–80*, Washington, DC: GPO, 1980.

Mentz, J. Robert, et al., "Leveraged Leasing and Tax-Exempt Financing of Major U.S. Projects," *Taxes*, August, 1980. pp. 553–60.

Mick, Susan R., *User Charges and Fees*, Washington, DC: The Urban Institute, 1981.

Miralia, Lauren M., "Municipal Bond Insurance Gaining in Acceptance," *ABA Banking Journal*, February, 1980, pp. 63, 65, 66.

Mitchell, William E., "Debt Refunding: The State and Local Government Sector," *Public Finance Quarterly*, Vol. 7, no. 3, July, 1979, pp. 323–37.

Moak, Lennox L., *Administration of Local Government Debt*, Chicago: Municipal Finance Officers Association of the United States and Canada, 1970.

Moak, Lennox L., and Kathryn W. Killian, *A Manual of Suggested Practice for the Preparation and Adoption of Capital Budgets by Local Governments*, Chicago: Municipal Finance Officers Association of the United States and Canada, 1964.

Monaco, Lynne, *State Responses to the Adverse Impacts of Energy Development in Colorado*, Cambridge, MA: Laboratory of Architecture and Planning, MIT, 1977.

Moody's Bond Survey, New York: Moody's Investors Service, Inc. weekly. *Moody's Municipal and Government Bonds: News*

Report, New York: Moody's Investors Service, Inc. Issued every Tuesday and Friday.

Moody's Municipal and Government Manual—American and Foreign, New York: Moody's Investors Service, Inc. Since 1955, annually.

Morgan Guaranty Survey, *Fiscal Stress for States and Localities,* New York: Morgan Guaranty Trust Co., November, 1981.

Mumy, Gene E., "Issue: Costs and Competition in the Tax-Exempt Bond Market," *National Tax Journal,* Vol. 3, no. 1, March, 1978, pp. 81–91.

Municipal Finance Officers Association of the United States and Canada, *A Guidebook to Improved Financial Management in Smaller Municipalities,* Chicago, August, 1978.

_____, *Costs Involved in Marketing State/Local Bonds,* Chicago, 1976.

Mushkin, Selma J., "The Case for User Fees," *Taxes and Spending,* April, 1979, pp. 49–82.

_____, editor, *Public Prices for Public Products,* Washington, DC: The Urban Institute, 1972.

_____, "Prices as an Alternative to Reorganization," paper presented at Conference on Government Reorganization, Woodrow Wilson School, September, 1977.

Mushkin, Selma J., and Charles L. Vehorn, "User Fees and Charges," *Governmental Finance,* Vol. 6, November, 1977, pp. 61–75.

Mussa, Michael L., and Roger C. Kormendi, *The Taxation of Municipal Bonds: An Economic Appraisal,* Washington, DC: American Enterprise Institute for Public Policy Research, 1979.

National Association of Counties, *Bridging the Revenue Gap,* Washington, DC, 1980.

National Conference of State Legislatures, *Guidelines for Single-Family Tax-Exempt Mortgage Revenue Bonds,* Denver, 1980, p. 30.

National Governors' Association, *Federal Roadblocks to Efficient State Government,* Washington, DC, 1977.

National Governors' Association for Policy Research, *Bypassing the States: Wrong Turn on Urban Aid,* Washington, DC, November, 1979.

Naylor, Thomas H., "Organizing for Strategic Planning," *Managerial Planning,* July/August, 1979, pp. 3–9, 17.

Naylor, Thomas H. and Kristin Neva, "The Design of a Strategic Planning Process," *Managerial Planning,* January/February, 1980, pp. 3–7.

———, "The Planning Audit," *Managerial Planning,* September/October, 1979, pp. 31–37.

Neuner, Edward, Dean Dopp, and Fred Sebold, "User Charges versus Taxation as a Means of Funding a Water Supply System," *Journal of the American Water Works Association,* Vol. 69, 1977, pp. 256–281.

Newsweek, "The Decaying of America," August 2, 1982, p. 25.

Northeast-Midwest Institute, *Urban Water Supply and Sewer Needs in the Midwest,* Washington, DC, December, 1980.

Oates, Wallace E., "The Use of Local Zoning Ordinances to Regulate Population Flows and the Quality of Local Services" in *Essays in Labor Market Analysis,* edited by Orly Ashenfelter and Wallace E. Oates, New York: John Wiley and Sons, 1977.

O'Hare, Michael, "Not on My Block You Don't—Facility Siting and the Strategic Importance of Compensation," *Public Policy,* Vol. 25, no. 4, 1977, pp. 78–93.

O'Hare, Michael, and Debra Sanderson, "Fair Compensation and the Boomtown Problem," *Urban Law Annual,* Vol. 14, 1978, pp. 29–37.

Osteryoung, Jerome S., "State General Obligation Bond Credit Ratings," *Growth and Change,* Vol. 9, no. 3, July, 1978, pp. 95–103.

Pagano, Michael, and Richard J. Moore, "Emerging Issues in Financing Basic Infrastructure," unpublished paper, September, 1981.

Pascal, Anthony, *User Charges, Contracting Out, and Privitization in an Era of Fiscal Retrenchment,* P-6471, Santa Monica, CA: The Rand Corporation, April, 1980.

Peterson, George E., *An Examination of State and Local Governments' Capital Demand, Alternative Means of Financing 'Public' Capital Outlays and the Impact on Tax-Exempt*

Credit Markets, Washington, DC: The Urban Institute, n.d., pp. 65–69.

_____, *Tax-Exempt Financing of Housing Investment,* Washington, DC: The Urban Institute, 1979.

Peterson, George E., and Mary John Miller, *Financing Infrastructure Renewal: Policy Options,* Washington, D.C., Urban Consortium, December, 1981.

Peterson, John E., "Has the Municipal Bond Market Undergone Fundamental Change?" unpublished paper, May, 1982.

_____, "Current Research in State and Local Government Debt Policy and Management, parts 1, 2, *Government Finance,* March/June, 1979a, pp. 45–48: November, 1978, pp. 33–35.

_____, *State Roles in Local Government Financial Management: A Comparative Analysis,* Washington, DC: Government Finance Research Center, 1979b.

_____, *State and Local Government Finance and Financial Management: Compendium of Current Research,* Chicago: Municipal Finance Officers Association of the United States and Canada, 1978, p. 27.

_____, *Watching and Counting: A Survey of State Assistance to and Supervision of Local Debt and Financial Administration,* Denver, National Conference of State Legislatures and the Municipal Finance Officers Association, 1977.

_____, *Changing Conditions in the Market for State and Local Government Debt,* Washington, DC: GPO, 1976.

_____, *The Rating Game,* New York City, Twentieth Century Fund, 1974.

"Preserving U.S. Roads: A Rough Time Ahead," *Journal of American Insurance,* Winter, 1977–78, pp. 16–20.

Public Securities Association, *Fundamentals of Municipal Bonds,* New York, 1981.

"Reform of the Municipal Bond Market: Alternatives to Tax-Exempt Financing," *Columbia Journal of Law and Social Problems,* Vol. 15, no. 3, Fall, 1979, pp. 233–75.

Reilly, James F., *Municipal Credit Evaluation and Bond Ratings Diagnosis, Prognosis and Prescription for Change,* Berkeley, CA: Institute for Local Government, 1967.

Robinson, Donald J., et al., *Municipal Bonds 1981—A Course Handbook,* New York: Practicing Law Institute, 1981.

Rocha, Luis M., "Post-Development Costs in Rural Communities in Alaska," unpublished paper, Kennedy School of Government, Harvard University, May, 1982.

Rothschild, L.F., Unterberg, Towbin, Municipal Research Department, *The Fifty States: Will Budget Problems Continue?* New York, January 11, 1982.

Rumowicz, Madelyn, "In New Jersey: Capital Budgeting and Planning Process," *State Government,* Spring, 1980, pp. 99–102.

Saffran, James S., "Proposition 13: Effect Upon the Bond Market," *Western City,* February, 1979.

Sanderson, Debra, *State Responses to the Adverse Impacts of Energy Development in Texas,* Cambridge, MA: Laboratory of Architecture and Planning, MIT, 1977.

Schellenbach, Peter W., and James S. Weber, "Leasing: An Alternative Approach to Providing Governmental Services and Facilities," *Government Finance,* November, 1978, pp. 23–27.

Schilling, Paul R., "Wisconsin Municipal Debt Finance: An Outlook for the Eighties," *Marquette Law Review,* Vol. 63, no. 4, Summer, 1980, p. 539–92.

Schmidt, Richard, "Strategic Planning: Off-Limits for Financial Managers?" *Management Review,* June, 1979, pp. 71–77.

Schneider, Mark, and David Swinton, "Policy Analysis in State and Local Government," *Public Administration Review,* January/February, 1979, pp. 12–17.

Schnell, John F., and Richard S. Krannich, *Social and Economic Impacts of Energy Development Projects: A Working Bibliography,* Monticello, IL: Council of Planning Librarians, 1977.

Schramm, Gunter, *The Value of Time in Environmental Decision Processes,* Ann Arbor, MI: The University of Michigan, November, 1979.

Schwartz, Gail Garfield, and Pat Choate, *Being Number One: Rebuilding the U.S. Economy,* Lexington, MA: Lexington Books, D.C. Heath, 1980.

Schwertz, Eddie L., Jr., *The Local Growth Management Guidebook,* Washington, DC: The Southern Growth Policies Board, 1979.

Shaul, Marnie S., "The Determinants of City Borrowing," Ph.D. dissertation, Ohio State University, 1980, pp. 135–37.

_____, "Capital Financing Options for Local Government," unpublished paper, National Urban Policy Roundtable, 1980.

Sheeran, Burke F., *Management Essentials for Public Works Administrators*, Chicago: American Public Works Association, 1976.

Shepard, Kevin, and Haynes C. Goddard, "New Approaches to Capital Planning and Financing," National Urban Policy Roundtable discussion paper, n.d.

Shoup, Donald C., "Financing Public Investment by Deferred Special Assessment," *National Tax Journal*, Vol. 33, no. 4, December, 1980, pp. 413–29.

Shubnell, Larry, and Bill Cobb, "Creative Capital Financing: A Primer for State and Local Governments," *Resources in Review*, May, 1982, pp. 7–11.

Silber, William L., *Municipal Revenue Bond Costs and Bank Underwriting: A Survey of the Evidence*, New York: New York University, Graduate School of Business Administration, Salomon Brothers Center for the Study of Financial Institutions, 1980.

Small Cities Financial Management Project, *A Debt Management Handbook for Small Cities and Other Governmental Units*, Chicago: Municipal Finance Officers Association of the United States and Canada, 1978.

Smith, Fred L., *Alternatives to Motor Fuel Taxation—Weight-Mileage Taxes*, Washington, DC: Association of American Railroads, 1980.

Smith, Wade S., *The Appraisal of Municipal Credit Risk*, New York: Moody's Investor Service, Inc., 1979.

Solano, Paul, and Steven Hoffman, "Municipal Bond Banking: A Comment," *National Tax Journal*, March, 1982, pp. 64–79.

Stamm, Charles F., and James M. Howell, "Urban Fiscal Problems: A Comparative Analysis of 66 U.S. Cities," *Taxing and Spending*, Fall, 1980, pp. 41–58.

Stanfield, Rochelle, "Building Streets and Sewers Is Easy—It's Keeping Them Up That's the Trick," *National Journal*, May 24, 1980, pp. 1141–1145.

Stanley, David T., *Cities in Trouble*, Columbus, OH, Academy for Contemporary Problems, 1976.

Steiss, Walter Alan, *Local Government Finance: Capital Facilities Planning and Debt Administration*, Lexington, MA: D.C. Heath, 1975.

Sternlieb, George, *Housing Development and Municipal Costs*, New Brunswick, NJ: The Rutgers Center for Urban Policy Research, 1974.

Susskind, Lawrence, and Michael O'Hare, *Managing the Social and Economic Impacts of Energy Development*, Cambridge, MA: Laboratory of Architecture and Planning, MIT, 1977.

_____, Task Force on Municipal Bond Credit Rating, *The Rating Game*, New York: Twentieth Century Fund, 1974.

U.S. Bureau of the Census, *1977 Census of Governments*, Washington, DC: GPO, 1980. In 7 volumes.

_____, *Statistical Abstract of the United States: 1980*, Washington, DC: GPO, 1979.

_____, *State Government Finances*, Washington, DC: GPO, 1964.

_____, *Local Government Finances in Selected Metropolitan Areas and Large Counties*, Washington, DC: GPO, 1964.

U.S. Conference of Mayors, *Transit Financing: An Overview of the National Transit Financing Picture in Terms of Federal and State Funding Levels, Fare Structures and Local Revenue Sources*, Washington, DC: GPO, October, 1980 (DOT-P-30-80-34).

U.S. Congress, House Subcommittee on the City of the Committee on Banking, Finance, and Urban Affairs, *City Need and the Responsiveness of Federal Grant Programs*, Peggy L. Cuciti Subcommittee Print, Washington, DC: GPO, 1978.

_____, Committee on Public Works, *A National Public Works Investment Policy*, Washington, DC: GPO, December, 1974.

_____, Joint Economic Committee, *Chaos in the Municipal Bond Market*, Washington, DC: GPO, September 28, 1981.

_____, Joint Economic Committee, *Trends in the Fiscal Conditions of Cities, 1979–1981*, Washington, DC: GPO, May, 1981.

_____, Joint Economic Committee, *Public Works as a Counter-cyclical Tool*, Washington, DC: GPO, 1980.

312

_____, Joint Economic Committee, Subcommittee on Economic Growth and Stabilization, *Deteriorating Infrastructure in Urban and Rural Areas: Hearing, August 30, 1979*, Washington, DC: GPO, 1979.

_____, Senate Committee on Public Works, United States Senate, 93rd Congress, 2d session, *Construction Delays and Unemployment*, Washington, DC: GPO, 1974.

_____, *Senate Committee on Environment and Public Works, Hearings on the Inland Energy Development Impact Assistance Act of 1977 (S 1493)*, Washington, DC: GPO, 2 parts, August 2, 27, 1977, and May 10, June 19, 1978.

_____, Senate Committee on Governmental Affairs, Subcommittee on Intergovernmental Relations, *Intergovernmental Fiscal Impact of Mortgage Revenue Bonds: Hearing, July 18, 1978*, Washington, DC: GPO, 1979.

U.S. Department of Agriculture, *Rural Development Progress, January 1977–June 1979*, Washington, DC: GPO, 1979.

_____, *Social and Economic Trends in Rural America*, Washington, DC: GPO, October, 1979.

U.S. Department of Commerce, *Establishment of a National Development Bank*, unpublished paper, National Public Advisory Committee on Regional Economic Development, Washington, DC: GPO.

_____, *Governmental Finances in 1979–80*, Washington, DC: GPO, 1981.

_____, *A Study of Public Works Investment in the United States*, Washington, DC: GPO, 1980.

U.S. Department of Defense, *Boom Town Annotated Bibliography*, Washington, DC: The Pentagon, 1981a.

_____, *Boom Town Business Opportunities and Management Development*, Washington, DC: The Pentagon, 1981b.

_____, Office of Economic Adjustment, *Base Closures: Are the Economic Impact Predictions Realistic? An Analysis of the Post-Closure Economic Impact of Military Installations on Local Communities*, Washington, DC: The Pentagon, 1979.

_____, *Communities in Transition, Community Response to Reduced Defense Activity*, Washington, DC: The Pentagon, 1978.

U.S. Department of Housing and Urban Development, *Stream-

313

lining Land Use Regulation: What Local Public Officials Should Know, Washington, DC: GPO, 1980.

———, *The President's National Urban Policy Report,* Washington, DC: GPO, 1980.

———, *Causes and Consequences of Delay in Implementing the Community Development Block Grant Program,* Washington, DC: GPO, June, 1980.

———, *Advance Project Planning for Public Works: A Systematic Approach,* Washington, DC: GPO, 1979.

U.S. Department of Transportation, *The Status of the Nation's Highways: Condition and Performance,* Washington, DC: GPO, January, 1981.

———, Federal Highway Administration, *1981 Federal Highway Legislation: Program and Revenue Options,* Washington, DC: GPO, June, 1980.

———, *Draft Transportation Agenda for the 1980s: The Issues,* Washington, DC: GPO, March, 1980.

———, *Financing Transit: Alternatives for Local Government,* Washington, DC: GPO, July, 1979.

U.S. Environmental Protection Agency, *1990: Preliminary Draft Strategy for Municipal Waste Water Treatment,* Washington, DC: GPO, 1981.

———, *Clean Water: Fact Sheet,* Washington, DC: GPO, April, 1980.

———, *The Cost of Clean Air and Water: A Report to the Congress,* Washington, DC: GPO, August, 1979.

U.S. General Accounting Office, *Effective State and Local Capital Budgeting Practices Can Help Arrest the Nation's Deteriorating Infrastructure,* Washington, DC: GPO, June, 1982.

———, *Better Targeting of Federal Funds Needed to Eliminate Unsafe Bridges,* Washington, DC: GPO, August, 1981.

———, *More Can Be Done to Insure that Industrial Parks Create New Jobs,* Washington, DC: GPO, December 2, 1980.

———, *Foresighted Planning and Budgeting Needed for Public Buildings Program,* Washington, DC: GPO, September 9, 1980.

———, *Perspectives on Intergovernmental Policy and Fiscal Relations,* Washington, DC: GPO, June 28, 1978.

314

_____, *Federally Assisted Areawide Planning: Need to Simplify Policies and Practices*, Washington, DC: GPO, March, 1977.

_____, *Long-Range Analysis Activities in Seven Federal Agencies*, Washington, DC: GPO, December, 1976.

Vance, Mary A., *Municipal Bonds: A Bibliography*, Monticello, IL: Vance Bibliographies, August, 1981.

Vaughan, Roger J., "Federal Tax Policy and State and Local Fiscal Conditions" in *The Urban Impacts of Federal Policies*, Norman Glickman, ed., Baltimore: Johns Hopkins University Press, 1980.

_____, *Inflation and Unemployment: Surviving the 1980s*, Washington, DC: Council of State Planning Agencies, 1980a.

_____, "Countercyclical Public Works: A Rational Alternative," testimony given before the Joint Economic Committee of the United States Congress, June 17, 1980b, Washington, DC.

_____, *State Taxation and Economic Development*, Washington, DC: Council of State Planning Agencies, 1979.

_____, *Public Works as a Countercyclical Device: A Review of the Issues*, Santa Monica, CA: The Rand Corporation, July, 1976.

Vernez, Georges, and Roger J. Vaughan, *Assessment of Countercyclical Public Works and Public Service Employment Programs*, Santa Monica, CA: The Rand Corporation, 1978.

_____, and Robert K. Yin, *Federal Activities in Urban Economic Development*, Santa Monica, CA: The Rand Corporation, April, 1979.

_____, and Burke Burright, and Sinclair Coleman, *Regional Cycles and Employment Effects of Public Works Investments*, Santa Monica, CA: The Rand Corporation, 1977.

Viscount, Francis, *Municipal Bonds: The Need to Regulate*, Washington, DC: National League of Cities, May, 1982.

Vogt, John A., *Capital Improvements Programming: A Handbook for Local Officials*, Chapel Hill: Institute of Government, University of North Carolina, 1977.

Wacht, Richard F., *A New Approach to Capital Budgeting for City and County Governments*, Research Monograph no. 87, Atlanta: College of Business Administration, Georgia State University, 1980.

315

Wallace, Holly, "Infrastructured: Maintain It Now or Pay the Price Tomorrow" in *City Economic Development*, Washington, DC: National League of Cities, May 12, 1980.

Walsh, Ann Marie Hauck, *The Public's Business: The Policies and Practices of Government Corporations*, Cambridge, MA: MIT Press, 1978.

West, Stanley, *Opportunities for Company-Community Cooperation in Mitigating Energy Facility Impacts*, Cambridge, MA: Laboratory of Architecture and Planning, MIT, 1977.

White, Anthony G., *Municipal Bonding and Taxation*, New York: Garland, 1979.

White House Conference on Balanced National Growth, proceedings, Washington, DC: GPO, 1978.

White, Michael J., "Capital Budgeting," in *State and Local Government Finance and Financial Management*, ed. John E. Petersen et al., Chicago: Municipal Finance Officers Association, 1978.

White, Michael J., and Scott Douglas, "An Interpretation of Capital Programming as a Political Process in No-Growth Municipalities," paper presented at the 1975 annual meeting of the American Political Science Association, San Francisco.

White, Sharon S., *Municipal Bond Financing of Solar Energy Facilities*, Washington, DC: GPO, 1980.

Wildavsky, Aaron, *Budgeting: A Comparative Theory of Budgetary Processes*, Boston: Little, Brown and Company, 1975.

Wilson, Peter, *The Future of Dallas' Capital Plant*, Washington, DC: The Urban Institute, 1980.

Wolman, Harold, and Barbara Davis, *Local Government Strategies to Cope with Fiscal Pressure*, Washington, DC: The Urban Institute, 1980.

Wolman, Harold, and George Reigeluth, *Financial Urban Public Transportation: The U.S. and Europe*, New Brunswick, NJ: Transaction Books, 1980.

Worsham, John P., Jr., *Tax-Exempt Mortgage Bonds: Revenue Aids to Homeownership*, Monticello, IL: Vance Bibliographies, November, 1980.

Zeller, Martin, *The Management of Mineral Revenues in the Western Energy-Producing States*, unpublished paper prepared for the Council of State Planning Agencies, Washington, DC, 1982.

Zimmerman, Joseph, *Reassignment of Functional Responsibility*, U.S. Advisory Commission on Intergovernmental Relations, Washington, DC: GPO, July, 1976.

INDEX

320

Motor vehicle inspection, 161; registration fees, 170
Municipal bonds, 194
Municipal debt, rated, 195; reduced demand for, 192–94
Municipal securities, disclosure requirements lax, 195; no organized exchanges, 195
Municipal spending, limited, 128
Museums, lease-back, 102; and low-income households, 154; two-tier pricing for, 149

National capital budget, 279. See U.S. capital budget
National Development Bank, 34–35
National Economic Recovery Tax Act, 104
National Governor's Association, balance between federal and state, 272
National objectives, role of levels of government, 116–17, 120
National Public Works Investment Strategy, 69
Natural resources, definition of, 117; management of, 111
Needs assessment, lack of, 104. See also Impact assessment
Negative tax rate, definition of, 245
Negotiated development, state commitment to, 238
Negotiating process, versus cost-benefit project analysis, 217–18
New Federalism, block grant for water, 277; effect of, 120–21, 137; negotiations on, 272
New Hampshire, bond banks in, 199–200; state guarantee of local debt, 202
New Jersey, state grants for debt service, 201; state supervision in local bond issues, 198
New Orleans, 7, 34, 35
New York City, buses, 241; deferred maintenance, 102; fiscal crisis of, 116–17, 180, 194; public works needs, 2–3, 35–36; reduced demand for municipal debt, 143; transit system, 163; subway car ownership, 102
New York State, local debt service payments, 266; simplified permit process in, 54; water authority, 277
Newark, 7
North Carolina, state supervision in local bond issues, 198
North Dakota, assistance to localities, 228–30; bond banks in, 199–200; coal severance tax, 226–27; impact assessment, 212; negotiated boom towns, 218–19; project application fee in, 236

Oakland, museum lease-back, 102
Office of Management and Budget (OMB), 50, 69, 75

Oil production, subsidizes other state activities, 237
Oklahoma, panhandle, 3
Overruns, 53

Parks, admission fees for, 168; increases property value, 168–69; public pricing of, 141; special resident assessment, 168; two-tier pricing for, 149; user fees for, 168. See also State parks.
Parking, reduce subsidy for, 164
Parking lots, sales tax surcharge on, 160
Patent policy, and extra research funds, 162
Peak-load pricing, administrative costs of, 152; encourages efficient use, 149; rationale for, 149
Pedestrian malls, tax increment financing, 168
Pennsylvania, Ben Franklin partnership, 162; capital budget in, 68; loan program for water, 201
Permitting, contribution to inflated costs, 283; speed up in, 104
Personal income taxes, in boom towns, 224
Pittsburgh, 7
Planning, Programming, and Budgeting Systems (PPBS), 74–75
Plaza, tax increment financing, 168
Police and fire protection, in boom towns, 208; general revenues for, 153; local expenditure for, 123; user fees for, 152
Police protection, state and local responsibility, 136
Pollution control, debt financing of, 190; role of federal government, 117; tax-exempt issue bonds, 193
Population loss, in central cities, 116
Pork barrel projects, 7–8, 11, 193, 271
Ports, deterioration of, 2; sale to private companies, 260; taxable bond for, 276; tax-exempt debt for, 190; user fees for, 191, 167–68, 281
Preconstruction delays of public works, 43–45, 47
Preconstruction fraud, 56–57
Prepayment of taxes, to finance impact assessment, 236
Prepurchasing, as stimulus to industry, 27, 28
Pricing mechanisms, and public facilities, 158–71
Pricing, demand over time, 148–49; efficiency and consumption, 145–46; innovation reduces capital investments needed, 164; and public facilities, 158–71
Private corporations, support for R & D, 162–63
Private developers, build own streets, 137; commitment to state's economic develop-

324

325

public funds, 137; user fee for, 281

Refinancing existing asset, lease-back of public facilities, 253

Regional variations, and public works programs, 26, 28, 84

Regulation of private suppliers, alternative to ownership, 138

Regulation of state and local actions, 80

Regulatory agencies, financed through user fees, 170

Rehabilitation of property, leased to government, 248–49

Renovation of public facility, and sale lease-back, 253

Repair and replacement cost data, unavailable, 271

Replacement standards for public works, 269

Repurchase, public sector option, 265

Research, funding of, 161–63, 283; user fee for, 281

Residential mortgage debt, growth, 173; tax exempt bonds for, 193

Resource depletion, 237–38

Resource management, 133

Resource recovery facilities, service contracts for, 255–56

Retrenchment, of state and local governments, 137

Revenue bonds, increase in, 173; versus general obligation bonds, 181

Revenue sharing, 25, 80–81, 83; distributed by need and fiscal capacity, 117; intrastate, 106; versus project-specific assistance, 143

Revenue sources, earmarked, 142; responsive to inflation and economic growth rate, 157; traditional, 133

Revenues, legislative limits on, 101; state and local trends, 122–23

Road transportation, revenues for, 158–59

Roads, in boom towns, 208; cost-effective deterioration, 140; maintenance financing, 142; public pricing of, 141; taxable bond for, 276; user fee for, 281

Rural areas, public works in, 3, 33

Rural Facilities Simplification Process, 64

Safe harbor lease, 247, 249–53, 265

St. Louis, 4, 7

St. Petersburg, capital spending cut, 115; deferred maintenance, 102

Sale of public facilities, to private firms, 240, 260–65

Sale/lease-back, 253

Sales and property tax, increment financing of, 197

Sales tax, advance planning for use, 142; in boom towns, 224; earmarked, 168; increment financing of, 197; and limited obliga-

tion bonds, 237; regressive, 155; revenue for state governments, 122

San Bernardino, delays in public works construction, 47

San Francisco, investments cut, 115

Sanitation, municipal responsibility, 136

School district funds, limited, 128; in Montana, 230–31; in North Dakota, 228, 230; in Wyoming, 230

Schools, in boom towns, 208

Seattle, dispute mediation in, 53–54

Section "38" property, 246

Service charges, 122

Service contract, 240, 248, 253–60, 266

Service delivery, innovation in, 164

Service financing, indirect way of reducing costs, 270

Severance tax, 222, 223, 225–28, 237

Sewage hook-up, subsidies, 165

Sewer, debt financing of, 190; local expenditure for, 123; marginal costs of, 148; refinancing of, in New York, 266; sale/leaseback agreement, 265; state spending for, 120

Short-term debt, increase in, 181–89

Short-term financing, high interest rates cause, 173

Smithsonian Air and Space Museum, 40

Social programs, expenditures on, 116

Solid waste management, 213

Special Analysis, to accompany annual budget, 87

Special interest groups, 81

State, amendment of taxing powers, 283

State actions, reduce cost of issuing bonds, 172

State and local debt, 173–90, 191

State and local government, aid to private for-profit firms, 136; borrowing subsidies, 192; compete with federal government in securities, 194; deversify fiscal bases, 121; responsibility, history of, 136–37

State and local guidelines, 138

State and local officials, 101

State and local policy options, within federal action, 272

State and local public services, demand for, 132

State and local tax revenues, shrunk by recession, 101

State assistance, to local governments, 105–6, 280, 282–83

State assumption, of local responsibilities, 106

State bond banks, 105, 172

State bond rating, 202

State borrowing, constitutional limits on, 181, 182–83

State capital budgets, 280

328

CONTRIBUTORS

Michael Barker is Executive Director of The Gallatin Institute, an economic policy research group based in Washington, D.C., and Editor of *Politics & Markets*, a monthly newsletter. He was formerly Director of Policy Studies at The National Governors' Association's Council of State Planning Agencies, where he was responsible for advising the nation's governors on the development of alternative economic policies. From 1975 to 1978 he was an aide to Massachusetts Governor Michael Dukakis. Mr. Barker is editor of the twelve-volume *Studies in State Development Policy*, published by the National Governors' Association. He has written widely on industrial policy, financial regulation, business finance, and economic and community development. He also has been economic policy adviser to the National Urban Coalition, the Democratic National Committee, and numerous federal and state officials.

Pat Choate is a Senior Policy Analyst for Economics at TRW Inc. Prior to joining TRW he was a Visiting Federal Fellow at the Academy for Contemporary Problems. Dr. Choate has held positions in the U.S. Department of Commerce's Economic Development Administration as Director of the Office of Economic Research and as Regional Director for the Appalachian and Southern Regional Offices. He also worked as Commissioner of Economic and Community Development for the State of Tennessee and as Director of State Planning for the State of Oklahoma. Most recently he coauthored *Being Number One: Rebuilding the U.S. Economy* and is the author of *As Time Goes By: The Costs and Consequences of Delay*. Dr. Choate holds a Ph.D. in economics from the University of Oklahoma.

Roger J. Vaughan is a Senior Fellow at The Gallatin Institute in Washington, D.C., and Senior Editor of the monthly newsletter *Politics & Markets*. He has been an aide to former New York Governor Hugh Carey, an assistant vice president in Citibank's economics department, and an urban economist at the Rand Corporation. He is a frequent economy policy adviser to members of Congress and has been a consultant to the Democratic National Committee. A graduate of Oxford University, he received a Ph.D. in economics from the University of Chicago. He writes regularly on industrial policy, employment training, federal tax policy, and infrastructure finance. Under the sponsorship of The Twentieth Century Fund, Dr. Vaughan is currently completing a study of the impact of public policy on innovation and entrepreneurship in the U.S. economy.

Susan Walter is Manager for State Government Issues at the General Electric Company. Prior to joining General Electric she was the Associate Director for Executive Management of The Council of State Planning Agencies. Ms. Walter has had diverse experience in the analysis and management of public policy issues for both the legislative and executive branches of government. Before her association with The Council of State Planning Agencies, she was a Special Assistant to former Florida Governor Reubin Askew and the Executive Director of the Florida Advisory Council on Intergovernmental Relations. In addition, she has held senior staff positions for both the Florida House of Representatives and Senate in human services and appropriations. Ms. Walter received her master's degree from the Maxwell School of Syracuse University.

The Council of State Planning Agencies, formed in 1965 as an affiliate of the National Governors' Association, is a membership organization composed of the policy and planning staffs of the nation's governors. Through its Washington, D.C., office the Council provides technical assistance to governors' offices and state officials on a wide spectrum of policy issues. From time to time the Council also performs both policy and technical research on state and national affairs.